THREE APPROACHES TO COMBATING
TORTURE IN CHINA

THREE APPROACHES TO COMBATING TORTURE IN CHINA

Edited by

Chen Weidong
Taru Spronken

This Action has received EU
funding EIDHR/2008/148-024

intersentia

Cambridge – Antwerp – Portland

Intersentia Publishing Ltd.
Trinity House | Cambridge Business Park | Cowley Road
Cambridge | CB4 0WZ | United Kingdom
Tel.: +44 1223 393 753 | Email: mail@intersentia.co.uk

Distribution for the UK:
Hart Publishing Ltd.
16C Worcester Place
Oxford OX1 2JW
UK
Tel.: +44 1865 517 530
Email: mail@hartpub.co.uk

Distribution for the USA and Canada:
International Specialized Book Services
920 NE 58th Ave. Suite 300
Portland, OR 97213
USA
Tel.: +1 800 944 6190 (toll free)
Email: info@isbs.com

Distribution for Austria:
Neuer Wissenschaftlicher Verlag
Argentinierstraße 42/6
1040 Wien
Austria
Tel.: +43 1 535 61 03 24
Email: office@nwv.at

Distribution for other countries:
Intersentia Publishing nv
Groenstraat 31
2640 Mortsel
Belgium
Tel.: +32 3 680 15 50
Email: mail@intersentia.be

Three Approaches to Combating Torture in China
Chen Weidong and Taru Spronken (eds.)

© 2012   Intersentia
          Cambridge – Antwerp – Portland
          www.intersentia.com | www.intersentia.co.uk

Cover photographs taken during the training programme at Sichuan Police Training College in Luzhou (Sichuan) from 4th to 7th November 2011

ISBN 978-1-78068-088-0
NUR 828

PREFACE

This book focuses on three approaches to the prevention of torture in China. It is the culmination of over 40 months of close collaboration between Renmin University of China (RUC), The University of Maastricht (Netherlands), The Rights Practice (UK) and the Great Britain China Centre (GBCC). The collaboration took the form of a carefully-planned programme of seminars, training workshops, expert roundtable meetings, study visits, desk-based and field research. It was funded by the European Instrument for Democracy and Human Rights, the UK Foreign and Commonwealth Office, and the Foreign Ministry of the Embassy of the Kingdom of the Netherlands.

The programme[1] began in 2009 and will end in June 2012. It is, to some extent, the continuation of an earlier EU-funded Action to combat torture in China which took place from 2006-2008. During that project, researchers from RUC collaborated with the University of Essex (UK) to publish a book on the weaknesses in the Chinese domestic legislative and regulatory framework for the prevention of torture, particularly as it applies to arrest, detention and interrogation; 50 senior police officers from across China were trained on international human rights standards; and the notion of independent monitoring of detention centres was introduced by means of a six month pilot 'lay visitor scheme'. Project partners collaborated with a procuratorate in Liaoning, north east China, to devise a model to promote independent monitoring of a pre-trial detention centre. This involved 20 non officials or 'lay visitors' interviewing pre-trial suspects, assessing conditions, and filing reports which were submitted to the procuratorate.

This second EU-funded Action, Preventing Torture in the PRC, aimed to build on and further the achievements of the first Action. To this end, collaborative research has improved a number of EU experts' understanding of China's legal system, in particular the two new evidence rules and the management of detention centres. In turn, Chinese academics and legislative officials have a broader understanding of EU legal systems and in particular the Optional Protocol the UN Convention Against Torture. On the practical side, an intensive week-long police training workshop in Belgium showcased

---

[1]   The programme is called: Preventing Torture in the People's Republic of China, EIDHR/2008/148-024.

EU best practice in interview skills to senior instructors from four of China's leading police training academies. The training focussed on EU best practice, the intolerance to the use of any form of torture and ill-treatment, and the dangers of relying on confessions to solve crimes. The training was modified into a model for interviewing skills workshops. These were jointly delivered by Chinese and EU experts to over 60 Chinese police instructors and experts from 23 Chinese provinces at workshops in Gansu and Sichuan, in the west of China.

Due to government restrictions it was not possible to test the pilot lay visitor scheme in two further detention centres as originally planned. In spite of this, project partners trained a further 60 lay visitors from Zhejiang and Shaanxi provinces in the hope that those restrictions would be lifted. To some extent our hopes were realised: in October 2011, the Ministry of Public Security issued an official notice making it mandatory for 'specially invited supervisors' to monitor detention centres which we consider a very positive development. Also in 2011, as part of the project, a new pilot was launched – and is on-going – to test improved procedures for pre-trial suspects to lodge complaints at a pre-trial detention centre in Anhui province. Based on initial results from Anhui, if funding can be secured, we plan to modify and improve this pilot to test at two other detention centres in different provinces in China.

Overall, in spite of the challenges faced to meet our objectives, we are extremely encouraged by the progress that has been made, the commitments to undertake reforms and the efforts to further improve existing legal procedures to protect the rights of criminal suspects.

None of this could have happened without the hard work and help of a large number of people. It is not possible to thank everyone, but I would like to thank our friends at Renmin University whose efforts helped to open so many doors to enable the pilots, the training, and the workshops to happen, and for this, special thanks must go to Professor Chen Weidong and Dr. Cheng Lei. Not only have they written over half of this book, but under their direction a capable army of researchers from the Centre for Criminal Procedure and Reform at Renmin University of China have undertaken valuable research, written and produced informative reports. Professor Chen has also helped to facilitate relationships with various Chinese associate partners; from Chinese police training academies across China, to local and central government level officials at the Supreme People's Procuratorate and Ministry of Public Security. Their involvement and willingness to engage is a very positive sign for the future development of the rule of law in China.

I would also like to thank the numerous European practitioners without whose help and generous support many of the project activities would not have been possible. For their briefings and help during the European study visits I would like to thank the European Committee for the Prevention of Torture, the Association for the Prevention of Torture, the Danish Institute for Human Rights, Vivianne and Han Jahae Lückers; for the police training Luc Francois, Rudi Schellingen, their colleagues and all the Directors and staff at the Province of Limburg Police Training College (PLOT); for their briefings and work on complaints mechanisms and detention centre monitoring activities, I thank Nigel Newcomen, the UK Prison and Police Ombudsman and Ian Smith at the Independent Custody Visitor Association.

The translators He Jing and Stephanie Guz have worked tirelessly to communicate difficult legal concepts and terminology and deserve to be congratulated on an excellent job. Nicola Macbean and her colleagues at the Rights Practice have provided invaluable comments throughout the editing process. My gratitude also goes to Marina Jodogne and Joost Groenhuijsen from Maastricht University for editing the text of this book. Finally, I would like to thank all my friends at Maastricht University, in particular those who have co-authored, shaped and edited this book that is to say Gerard de Jonge, Miet Vanderhallen, and most of all, Taru Spronken who has been the driving force behind this book.

May 2012

Orlando Edwards
Great Britain-China Centre

CONTENTS

BIOGRAPHIES

Gerard de Jonge

Gerard de Jonge is professor emeritus Detention law at Maastricht University, the Netherlands. Preceding his academic career he acted as a defence lawyer with special interest in prisoners' rights. As an expert in this field he was invited by the Council of Europe to contribute to the drafting of the European Prison Rules which contain minimum standards for the treatment of prisoners in all Member States of this Council.

Cheng Lei

Dr. Cheng Lei is associate professor of Law and Assistant Director at the Center for Criminal Justice and Reform at School of Renmin University of China (RUC). His research interests include criminal justice and judicial reform. He has worked on a number of research projects in China relating to the prevention of torture, criminal procedure code models, and sentencing reforms. He has published over 30 articles and several books on China's criminal justice reform. In 2011, he advised the Legislative Affairs Committee of the National People's Congress on revisions to the Criminal Procedure Law which was passed in March 2012. Lei Cheng is Deputy Secretary-General for the China Society of Criminal Procedure.

Taru Spronken

Taru Spronken is Professor of Criminal Law and Criminal Procedure at Maastricht University, the Netherlands. Both as a practicing lawyer and an academic she specialises in criminal procedure and human rights and she has published extensively on these topics. Her current research focuses on the implications of EU cooperation in criminal matters for procedural rights. Her research publications in this field include: *A place of greater safety* (2003); *Procedural Rights in criminal proceedings: Existing Level of Safeguards in the European Union* (2005); *Suspects in Europe* (2007); *EU Procedural Rights in Criminal Proceedings* (2009); *Effective Criminal Defence in Europe* (2010); *An EU-Wide Letter of Rights* (2011).

Miet Vanderhallen

Miet Vanderhallen graduated in 1996 as a social worker and in 1999 as a criminologist. In 2007 she finished her doctoral thesis on 'The working alliance in police interviewing'. Currently, she is professor psychology and law at Antwerp University in Belgium and an assistant professor criminology at Maastricht University, the Netherlands. Her main research interest is investigative interviewing. Besides, she is involved in advanced interview training at the National Police Investigation Academy and at the Regional Police Academy Limburg, Belgium where she coordinates and teaches 'investigative interview skills in presence of a lawyer'. In line with this, she is involved in local interview supervision projects.

Chen Weidong

Professor Chen Weidong is the Director of the Center for Criminal Procedure and Reform at Renmin University Law School of China (RUC). His recent research interests include the management of detention centres, civil participation in criminal justice, reform of sentencing procedures, and empirical research methodology in relation to criminal justice. He has published over 200 articles and 10 books on Chinese criminal procedure and judicial reform. He is also Vice Chairman of the China Criminal Procedure Law Society and a Cheung Kong Scholar awardee. Chen Weidong is a recipient of a Chinese Governmental Stipend Expert award from the Chinese State Council, and a consultant for China's Legislative Affairs Committee which he advised on revisions to China's Criminal Procedure Law.

Chai Yufeng

Chai Yufeng is a Ph.D student at the Center for Criminal Procedure and Reform at Renmin University School of Law. His thesis is on the use of criminal evidence and the Chinese criminal procedure law. As a prominent member of Chen Weidong's research team, Chai has written articles for several Chinese journals and also worked part-time for the Legislative Affairs Committee of the National People's Congress on the revision of the Criminal Procedure Law in 2011.

ABBREVIATIONS

Art.	Article
Arts.	Articles
CAT	Convention against Torture and Other Cruel, Inhuman or Degrading Treatment and Punishment
CCP	Code of Criminal Procedure
CCPR	Center for Criminal Procedure and Reform
CoE	Council of Europe
CPL	Criminal Procedure Law
CPT	Committee for the Prevention of Torture and Inhuman or Degrading Treatment or Punishment
CRC	Convention on the Rights of the Child
DNA	Deoxyribonucleic acid
ECHR	European Convention for the Protection of Human Rights and Fundamental Freedoms
ECtHR	European Court of Human Rights
EPR	European Prison Rules
EU	European Union
HIV	Human Immunodeficiency Virus (causing AIDS)
HR	Hoge Raad (Supreme Court in the Netherlands)
ICC	International Criminal Court
ICCPR	International Covenant on Civil and Political Rights
ICTY	International Criminal Tribunal for the Former Yugoslavia
LL	Lawyers' Law
NPC	National People's Congress
OLPC	Organic Law of the People's Courts
OLPP	Organic Law of the People's Procuratorate
OPCAT	Optional Protocol to the Convention Against Torture
PACE	The Police and Criminal Evidence Act
PIP	Professionalization Investigation Programme
SMR	Standard Minimum Rules for the Treatment of Prisoners
SPT	Subcommittee on Prevention
TBC	Tuberculosis
UK	United Kingdom
UN	United Nations
UNCAT	United Nations Convention Against Torture

UNDU	UN Detention Unit
USA	United States of America

千里之行始于足下

A 1000 mile journey starts with one step...

A THREE-WAY APPROACH TO
THE FIGHT AGAINST TORTURE
PROCEDURAL SANCTIONS, PREVENTION IN PLACES
OF DETENTION, AND IMPROVEMENT OF POLICE
INTERROGATION TECHNIQUES

Chen Weidong, Cheng Lei and Taru Spronken

The EU-China programme 'Preventing Torture in the People's Republic of China'[1] is approaching completion, thanks to the joint efforts over the past three years of the Centre for Criminal Procedure and Reform at Renmin University of China, the Great Britain China Centre, The Rights Practice and Maastricht University of the Netherlands. Both the Chinese and the European taskforces have carried out successful collaborative studies on how to promote the fight against torture in China. Before presenting the academic achievements of the programme, we would first like to give a brief introduction of its content and research philosophy.

1. THE RESEARCH PERSPECTIVE

The Chinese government has long pursued the fight against torture. In addition to ratifying the United Nations Convention Against Torture (UNCAT) in 1988, it has devised laws and rules against torture in domestic legislation and reiterated its position against torture in law enforcement in practice. However, the developments in recent years indicate that torture still exists in China, albeit in more diverse forms, and the fight against torture remains a momentous task. We believe that, a three-way approach should be adopted, in order to combat torture more effectively. Simply put, the exclusionary rule as a sanction against torture should be made operational,

---

[1] Undertaken by the Great Britain-China Centre in partnership with Maastricht University, the Netherlands, the Center for Criminal Procedure and Reform (CCPR), Renmin University of China and the Rights Practice, London and Supported by a grant from the European Initiative for Democracy and Human Rights, Support to Human Rights and Democracy actions on Torture and other forms of ill-treatment EIDHR/2008/148-024.

prevention mechanisms in places of detention should be set up, and the police should be trained to master effective and lawful interrogation techniques whilst keeping its power in check. This philosophy has been entrenched in our EU-China programme – 'Preventing Torture in the People's Republic of China' that has run from 2009 to 2012.

As of 14 March 2012, China's old Criminal Procedure Law merely stated that 'the extortion of confessions by torture shall be prohibited', without prescribing the exclusion of evidence obtained through extortion of confessions by torture. As a result, police officers face no sanctions even if they resort to illegal means of evidence collection, making the prohibition an empty slogan without consequences. Furthermore, holding perpetrators of torture criminally liable does not necessarily bring remedy to defendants who have suffered torture, although, according to the Criminal Law of China, the extortion of confessions by torture is a crime. The exclusion of illegally obtained evidence, as a procedural law, offers sanctions and procedural consequences. Therefore, substantive law alone is not sufficient to curb a procedural violation such as the extortion of confessions by torture. Such an argument is the basis of our selection of the exclusion of illegally obtained evidence as our first focus of research.

International efforts to combat torture over the past half century have shown that the key to success is prevention rather than sanctions, despite the crucial importance of the latter in addition to accountability. That is why through our research, we have striven to set up two prevention mechanisms in detention centres (places of pre-trial detention), which are: a lay custody visiting scheme and a detainee complaint handling system. The pilot schemes in two cities in China, for these two mechanisms, designed to prevent torture, yielded promising results. At the same time, in order to promote the rule of law in detention centres, where all criminal suspects are held for varying lengths of time, we have, together with our European expert colleagues, jointly drafted a Draft Detention Centre Law, to serve as a reference for those officials involved in the on-going effort to legislate detention centres. This has been the second focus of our programme.

As in most countries in the world, the regulation of police power is one of the main obstacles to the push for criminal judiciary reform in China. Torture and extortion of confessions by torture are often directly linked to one investigation approach, namely the interrogation of criminal suspects. Assisting police officers to master and apply different interrogation techniques could reduce their reliance on extortion of confessions by torture and other illegal interrogation strategies. Therefore, the third focus of our programme is the training of police in interrogation techniques. Interrogation experts from Belgium and the Netherlands worked closely with experts from the Chinese police training colleges in organising two training sessions. The training provided not only detailed knowledge concerning various interrogation techniques used by European police officers, but also a platform for in depth discussion between Chinese and European colleagues on specific cases, scenarios and skills. Chinese trainers were also greatly impressed and inspired by the interactive training methodology used by their European counterparts.

2. THE IMPORTANCE OF CHINA-EU COOPERATION IN TORTURE RESEARCH

The European research work and relevant practice in combating torture is of great reference value to China and many countries across the world. The European Convention on Human Rights, the European Convention for the Prevention of Torture, and the precedents of the European Court of Human Rights have underpinned the pathway, approaches, and the principle of rule of law adopted by European countries to curb torture. Home to both civil and common law countries, Europe has seen the confluence of different rule-of-law traditions with the common goal of torture prohibition, generating an array of common systems and legal rules. The relevant institutional arrangements are, in large part, more pragmatic and rigorous in Europe. For example, a lay custody visiting scheme, an important mechanism to prevent torture, started off in the European continent, was developed and then finally written into the Optional Protocol to the UN Convention against Torture, thus becoming a mainstream weapon in the fight against torture in most countries of the world. Another good example is the exclusionary rule regarding illegally obtained evidence. Many European countries have taken a more pragmatic and cautious policy on exclusion. Their design of evidence collection procedure has meant that there has been steady and gradual progress in standardising the power of police, with a strong commitment to the balance between human rights protection and crime control. Such experience and practice has resonance for Chinese researchers and as a result, the China-EU dialogue and exchange of ideas has been even more profound and effective.

3. LATEST DEVELOPMENTS IN CHINA'S JUDICIAL REFORM AND LEGISLATION

The three-year EU-China programme has coincided with radical judicial reform and legislative changes in China. The second round of judicial reform began in 2009. Its agenda included the amendment of 15 items concerning the criminal justice system and how it works. The majority of those have been written into the Revision of the Criminal Procedure Law passed by the National People's Congress in March 2012. The revision is only the second of its kind since the birth of the Criminal Procedure Law back in 1979. It covers more than half of the existing provisions and the total number of provisions rises from 225 to 290.

Turning now to the research outcome of our programme, we are delighted to see that our efforts have coincided with the recent developments in China concerning judicial and legislative reform. The reform itself proves that our choice of a three-way approach is consistent with the direction of China's systemic transformation and reform.

(1) Establishing the Exclusionary Rule Regarding Illegally Obtained Evidence and a Relevant Procedure

The new CPL law for the first time sets forth the exclusionary rule and procedure by making clear the scope, procedures, burden of proof and the method of proof for exclusion.[2] Such rules and procedures are an important part of the institutional arrangements for preventing extortion of confessions by torture and combating torture. Other torture-related amendments include: investigators are required to immediately transfer criminal suspects to detention centres for detention after their custody and arrest;[3] interrogations can only be held inside a detention centre;[4] interrogations of suspects of serious and complex cases, in particular those eligible for life imprisonment or death penalty, must be audio/videotaped and the audio/videotaping must be entire and complete.[5] Furthermore, the new law establishes the principle of no forced self-incrimination, which leads to the rule that a confession must be based on the free will of the suspect.[6]

It is important to emphasise that not only does the exclusionary rule and the procedure how the rule should be implemented studied by our research programme provide good reference material for the legislative process, but more importantly, lawmakers in China are gradually shifting towards accepting the subtle differences between the fight against torture and the control of extortion of confessions by torture. As a result, the concept of 'combating torture' has been further strengthened. A testament to this change

---

2   See Arts. 54-58 of the new Criminal Procedure Law.
3   See Arts. 83, 91 of the new Criminal Procedure Law.
4   See Art. 116 of the new Criminal Procedure Law.
5   See Art. 121 of the new Criminal Procedure Law.
6   See Art. 50 of the new Criminal Procedure Law.

is that Chinese lawmakers attempt to use the definition of torture to expand the interpretation for 'extortion of confessions by torture', which is a term commonly used in China. The extortion of confessions by torture in the traditional sense only refers to the use of corporal punishment and corporal punishment in disguised forms to extract a confession, which is much narrower than the definition given by the UNCAT. In order to widen the sanction scope of illegal collection of evidence, the legislature interprets 'extortion of confessions by torture' as the use of corporal punishment or corporal punishment in disguised forms, which inflicts severe pain or suffering, whether physical or mental, on a person and makes him or her have no other choice but to confess. The fact that the interpretation adopts the description in the UNCAT – 'severe pain or suffering, whether physical or mental' demonstrates, to a certain extent, China's commitment to the implementation of the UNCAT.

(2) Detention Centres Play a Crucial Role in Combating Torture

The new CPL law also stresses that detention centres, places for holding non-convicts, should play a bigger role in combating torture. To this end, it requires the investigators to immediately transfer detained and arrested criminal suspects to a detention centre for detention, within a maximum period of 24 hours, and post-detention interrogations can only take place inside detention centres. The reason for such a change is that a series of studies, including our own, has found that extortion of confessions by torture rarely occurs inside a detention centre and the majority of illegal means are used to collect evidence in the period before a suspect is handed over to a detention centre. Some extortion takes place when a suspect is fetched from the detention centre where he is held in custody. Revolutionary reform measures have been carried out in China's detention centre system since 2009. Thanks to such measures, interrogation rooms within detention centres now have a physical separation between interrogators and suspects; detention centres have a strict detainee physical check-up system; the public can visit and inspect detention centres; some detention centres have set up a detainee complaint handling mechanism. Such measures have made the detention centre a 'safe haven' for detainees to avoid torture. The new law acknowledges the crucial role played by detention centres in combating torture, hence requiring immediate transfer of arrested suspects to detention centres and all post-detention interrogations to take place inside detention centres.

The purpose of this amendment is to improve on the legal system of detention centres. Frankly speaking, the laws and rules of detention centres are rather backward and far from robust. Only with a better legal system in detention centres can their legislative purpose be fulfilled.[7] We have come up with a Draft Detention Centre Law which offers solutions for the future drafting of a detention centre law based on the current practice in China. We hope that it will serve to substantially support the formulation of the upcoming detention centre law.

(3) The Transformation of Investigation Model Requires Improvement in Interrogation Techniques

Article 50 of the new Criminal Procedure Law adds the principle of no forced self-incrimination. This addition may push China closer to the ratification of the International Covenant on Civil and Political Rights and enable further transformation in terms of China's investigation model. This has long been confession-centred with limited attention being paid to other investigation methods in legislation and enforcement. Such excessive dependence on confessions is more likely to lead to extortion of confessions by torture. This amendment appears in the Chapter of Investigation in order to confirm the principle of no forced self-incrimination, to strictly standardise the interrogation procedure, and to offer alternative investigation options to investigators. These alternatives are: more places for interviewing witnesses, increased compulsory sampling, and the use of covert investigation. With the imminent transformation of China's investigation model, and particularly the effects of standardisation on future interrogation procedures by the principle of no forced self-incrimination, the interrogation techniques of investigators become increasingly important. Therefore, the improvement of the interrogation model serves to facilitate the successful transformation of the investigation model and thus helps investigators meet the new requirements of a rule-of-law society for investigative interrogation.

That is why the third focus of our programme is the development of training to improve the interrogation technique of police officers. Interrogation experts from Belgium and the Netherlands shared interrogation techniques commonly used by European police officers with Chinese police trainers through a case-based interactive training methodology. Some of the techniques shown could be used in China right away while some may not be directly applied in practice any time soon. We sincerely hope that with the gradual transformation of China's interrogation model, all these techniques will find their place in China in the foreseeable future.

---

[7] CHEN WEIDONG 2012.

4. HOW TO READ THE BOOK

The book is designed to serve as a report of the 'Prevention of Torture in the People's Republic of China' project and includes three parts. In Part I we deal with the exclusionary rule starting with a chapter setting out the context and general characteristics of criminal justice systems in China and Europe, such as the status of the courts, the implications of case precedent systems and case guidance systems and the procedural rights of suspects in relation to the collection of evidence. In the second chapter of this part an account and analysis is given of the application of the exclusionary rule in Europe, in which we focus on the Netherlands and the standards that are developed by the ECtHR case law. The third chapter analyses the developments of the exclusionary rule in China and includes a description of cases in which the exclusion of illegally obtained evidence was a central issue and in chapters 4-6 we analyse the barriers to exclusion of evidence in China and recommendations are made about how to improve the effectiveness of the application of the exclusionary rule.

Part II contains an annotated version of the draft Detention Centre Law that has been developed within this programme, preceded by an introduction describing relevant international detention standards and empirical research that has been conducted in this project, such as the evaluation of a pilot inspection system and experimental prisoners' complaint procedures. In the final Part III various interview techniques are set out that have been developed in Europe providing guidelines on interview skills that respect procedural rights of suspects. In addition a description is given of the training programmes that have been developed and piloted within this programme.

PART I

THE EXCLUSIONARY RULE
IN CHINA AND EUROPE

1. THE PREMISE OF OUR DISCUSSION: COMPARING GENERAL CHARACTERISTICS OF THE CRIMINAL JUSTICE SYSTEMS IN CHINA AND THE EU

Chen Weidong, Taru Spronken and Chai Yufeng

1. INTRODUCTION

European criminal justice systems have a complex and intertwined past. All have been affected by great imperialist ambitions and the results of the conquests by Rome and Napoleon are still to be seen in the civil law traditions of the countries of mainland Europe. It is however important to recognise that jurisdictions of the European states that are regarded as having the same legal tradition have developed in very different ways. The common law or adversarial tradition is based on the notion that the best way of determining guilt or innocence is by contest between two parties who are responsible for the investigation and gathering of evidence. The judge is not involved in the investigation and at trial plays a relatively passive role, determining questions of law whilst the jury adjudicates the facts. The trial is the focus of the adversarial model, the point where parties present their case and witnesses are heard. What the civil law criminal justice systems share is the centralised procedure deriving from the inquisitorial model, where the evidence is a product of an enquiry for which a public prosecutor or investigating judge is responsible. Therefore the inquisitorial model places greater emphasis on the pre-trial phase.[1] The trial is not the focus for the determination of issues, but for the verification and confirmation of a criminal investigation by state officials. Conforming to their own historical traditions, societal culture and legal backgrounds, many European nations have developed a modern inquisitorial procedural model with unique characteristics. All European countries have however a common commitment being members of the Council of Europe and signatories to the European

---

[1] CAPE ET AL. 2007.

Convention on Human Rights (ECHR). The ECHR was adopted after the Second World War as a reaction to the serious human rights violations that Europe had witnessed during that war. Compared to other international human rights treaties, the ECHR has a very strong enforcement mechanism as it provides for both state and individual applications and accepts the right of citizens to bring claims of a human rights violation to the European Court of Human Rights. Judgments of this court are binding and its jurisprudence has had an enormous influence on the legal systems of Europe.[2]

Although requiring criminal procedure to be in compliance with the rights of the ECHR, Europe and China share the basic assumption that crime control and the discovery of truth are fundamental goals of criminal justice. The procedural model of civil law countries has long influenced and shaped China's criminal justice procedure. Such influence can be traced back to the year of 1905, when the then Qing Dynasty sent a delegation of 'five senior officials' (headed by Zai Ze) to Japan and Europe to 'study their constitutional government'.[3] In addition, Shen Jiaben, a respected law expert who presided over the revision of the legal code during that period, translated the criminal law and codes of criminal procedure in France, Germany and Italy.[4] Following the disintegration of the traditional Chinese legal system, China turned to the civil-law system, which paved the way for the subsequent development and reform of its criminal procedure. After the birth of the People's Republic of China (PRC) in 1949, the Criminal Procedure Law (CPL) featuring the inquisitorial procedural pattern of civil law systems was put in place in 1979.[5] The revision in 1996 regulated the established procedural mode by introducing certain, what were considered 'reasonable', elements from the adversarial model. This revision marked a legislative attempt to shift from the inquisitorial model to the adversarial one. The ensuing changes and discussions persist to this day. Thanks to the development of the rule of law and progress within society, another revision to the CPL was placed firmly on the legislative agenda. After repeated deliberations, on 14th March 2012, the Standing Committee of the National People's Congress (NPC) adopted the new CPL, which comes into force on 1 January 2013. This follows three guiding principles: firstly, it is supported by the Central government, and takes on board the beneficial achievements of judicial reform; secondly, to offer practical solutions for problems encountered by the police in handling

---

[2]   HARRIS, O' BOYLE & WARBRICK 2009.
[3]   ZENG XIANYI 2000, p. 244.
[4]   ZHENG JINFAN 1982, p. 346.
[5]   CHEN WEIDONG 2004, p 31.

cases; and thirdly, to promote judicial progress.[6] By fulfilling these three goals, the new CPL is able to showcase the distinctive features of China's criminal procedure and represent a mixed procedural model. It is hard to label this revision either as a simple 'victory for the adversarial system' or as a 'compromise for the inquisitorial model'. A noteworthy phenomenon is that nations across Europe also face the problem of the convergence or transformation of their criminal procedure. The experience of Germany and the Netherlands demonstrates that even traditional civil law countries, under the influence of judgments delivered by the ECHR, are gradually taking in elements of the adversarial system.[7] In this sense the criminal justice systems in China and Europe have undergone similar transitions. This is the premise for our discussion.

Within our research project we have chosen the exclusionary rule as a main theme on the grounds that this is closely related to abandoning the use of torture to extract confessions. As a category of judicial remedy measures, the exclusionary rule with regard to illegally obtained evidence is derived from the Fourth Amendment of the United States (USA) Constitution, and specifically guards against illegal searches and seizures and is designed to prevent illegal collection of evidence by police. As such the exclusionary rule is an imported concept for both China and continental Europe. Although originating in the USA, the exclusionary rule has had great influence globally in both adversarial and inquisitorial systems especially with regard to the evaluation of evidence in relation to the rule of law. This is particularly so for China, which established the exclusionary rule, in the regulatory sense, as late as 1998. The procedure on how to exclude evidence in China only came into being in the practical sense, in 2009, when the 'Two Evidence Provisions' were promulgated.[8] The new CPL has now absorbed the essence of these provisions and has included the exclusionary rule. However, despite the new legislation, some scholars and professionals still question the future prospects of the exclusionary rule in practice.[9] We hope, through the study of the latest developments of the exclusionary rule in China and Europe, to discover the systemic 'soil' necessary for growth and development of the inquisitorial procedure model in civil law countries in accordance with human rights requirements. In addition we will analyse both successes and failures in

---

6   CHEN WEIDONG 2011.

7   TAK 2003, p. 19.

8   See for further elaboration chapter 3 and for academic discussion: CHEN GUANGZHONG 2010; FAN CHONGYI 2010; CHEN WEIDONG 2010a; CHEN WEIDONG 2010b; LONG ZONGZHI 2010; SONG YINGHUI 2010.

9   See chapter 4.

Europe's practice regarding the application of the exclusionary rule and what can be learned from these in China. In order to do this in a meaningful way we will in this chapter first compare the general characteristics of the Chinese and European criminal law systems.

2. COMPARISON OF THE BASIC ELEMENTS OF THE CRIMINAL JUSTICE SYSTEMS IN CHINA AND EUROPE

In this chapter we will focus on those aspects of criminal procedure which are closely related to the theme of the exclusionary rule. We will address judicial independence which provides the legal context for courts to apply the exclusionary rule. Another related topic is the case law system being a powerful instrument for courts to fine-tune the exclusionary rule in a dynamic way. And finally procedural rights of suspects form the premise for initiating proceedings to exclude evidence.

2.1. THE STATUS OF COURTS: INDEPENDENCE OF JUDGES

One important element of comparison of the Chinese and European criminal justice systems is the status of the courts and their independence.

In Europe, back in the 18th century, the French Enlightenment thinker Montesquieu, wrote in The Spirit of the Laws:

> 'There is no liberty, if the judiciary power be not separated from the legislature and executive. Were it joined with the legislature, the life and liberty of the subject would be exposed to arbitrary control; for the judge would be then the legislator. Were it joined to the executive power, the judge might behave with violence and oppression'.[10]

According to European doctrine that is reflected in Article 6 of the ECHR,[11] courts should be independent and impartial. By 'independent' is meant independent of the executive and also of the parties.[12] With regard to independence, the manner of appointment of the court's members, the duration of their term of office and guarantees against outside pressures are taken into account. Impartiality means lack of prejudice or bias which

---

[10]   C. de Montesquieu: The Spirit of the Laws, 1st volume from The Complete Works of C. de Montesquieu (London: T. Evans, 1777), translated by ZHANG YANSEN, published by Commercial Press in 1982, p. 156.

[11]   'In the determination of his civil rights and obligations or of any criminal charge against him, everyone is entitled to a fair and public hearing within a reasonable time by an independent and impartial tribunal established by law'.

[12]   ECtHR 16 July 1971, *Ringeisen v. Austria*, no. 2614/65.

involves either functional or personal impartiality. Functional impartiality may be questioned when the same person exercises different functions within the judicial process that may raise doubt as to the impartiality. Personal impartiality is at stake when a judge's personal conduct indicates actual bias. There is a close inter-relationship between the guarantees of an independent and impartial tribunal. A court that is not independent of the executive is likely to be in breach of the requirement of impartiality also in cases to which the executive is a party. These concepts of independence and impartiality have become internationally accepted principles of the judiciary in the Western democracies. Article 97 of the Constitution for the Federal Republic of Germany (*Grundgesetz* GG) states: 'Judges shall be independent and subject only to the law'. Article 117 of the Constitution of the Netherlands states: 'Members of the judiciary responsible for the administration of justice and the Procurator General at the Supreme Court shall be appointed for life by Royal Decree'.

In China, academics often refer to 'independent trials' when discussing judicial independence. This is because according to Article 126 of the Constitution of the PRC and Article 5 of the new CPL, the people's courts should, in accordance with the law, exercise judicial power independently and are not subject to interference from administrative organs, public organisations or individuals. Such provision emphasizes the independence of the trial procedure in court, without addressing the issues of 'independence of judges' which is considered to be a different issue. Articles 180 and 243 of the CPL have established the trial committee deliberation system and the trial supervision system,[13] whereby, if the president of a people's court at any level

---

[13] Art. 180: The collegial panel shall, after court hearing and deliberation, render a judgment. With regard to a difficult, complex or major case, if the collegial panel considers it difficult to make a decision thereon, the collegial panel shall refer the case to the president of the court to decide to submit the case to the judicial committee for discussion and decision. The collegial panel shall execute the decision made by the judicial committee. Article 243: The president of a people's court at any level who finds a definite error in a legally effective judgment or ruling made by the court in the ascertainment of facts or the application of law must submit the case to the judicial committee for handling. The Supreme People's Court which finds a definite error in a legally effective judgment or ruling made by a people's court at any lower level, or a people's court at the higher level which finds a definite error in a legally effective judgment or ruling made by a people's court at any lower level, shall have the power to bring the case up for trial by itself or order the people's court at the lower level to conduct a retrial. The Supreme People's Procuratorate which finds a definite error in a legally effective judgment or ruling of a people's court at any level, or a people's procuratorate at the higher level which finds a definite error in a legally effective judgment or ruling made by a people's court at the lower level, shall have power to lodge to the people's court at the same level a protest against the judgment or ruling pursuant to the procedure for trial supervision. With respect to a case against which a people's procuratorate
→

finds some error in a court judgment or ruling, the matter shall be referred to the trial committee. Academics and theorists in China agree therefore, that judicial independence in the Chinese context is only about independence of institutions and not about the independence of individual judges or courts.[14] It is particularly clear from a micro and practical perspective, that judges are not independent. This is a major difference between China and Europe.

Although the prosecution comes in general into the category of executive power,[15] the nature of the prosecutorial power and the independence of the procuratorate need to be discussed here as they have a unique status in the Chinese system. On the one hand, according to Article 129 of the Constitution of the PRC, Article 8 of the CPL and Article 5 of the Organic Law of the People's Procuratorate (OLPP), the people's procuratorates are state organs of legal supervision and should, in accordance with the Law, exercise legal supervision over criminal proceedings.[16] In addition, Article 34 of the Organic Law of the People's Courts (OLPC) and Article 12 of the OLPP provide that presidents of local people's courts at all levels are appointed or removed by the standing committees of local people's congresses of the corresponding level. A proposed appointment or removal of a chief procurator, at all levels, should however be reported to the chief procurators of the people's procuratorate of the next level for approval by the standing committee of the people's congress at the corresponding level. As a consequence, the legal procedure to appoint or remove a chief procurator is more rigorous and prudent than for a chief judge or chief justice, which is appropriate for the role of State organ of legal supervision. According to Article 129 of the Constitution, the people's procuratorate is the State organ of legal supervision of both the public security authorities and the court in respect of criminal procedure. However, this supervisory role has no necessary association with the actual functions of the procuratorate. 'Certain types of powers, obviously, may not necessarily be exercised by only one

---

has lodged a protest, the people's court that has accepted the protest shall form a collegial panel for trial again, or if the facts in the original judgment is unclear and the evidence therein is insufficient, it may order the people's court at the lower level to conduct a retrial.

[14] Arts. 5, 180 and 243 from the CPL referred to in this paragraph clearly illustrate this point.

[15] CHEN WEIDONG 2005a, p. 92.

[16] Apart from the Constitution and the law, the government also agreed with the view that the procuratorates are not judicial organs. See 'Wen Jiabao's speech at the Opening Ceremony of the 5th Summer Davos', <http://news.xinhuanet.com/2011-09/15/c_122034802.htm>, visited on 3 November 2011. Wen said, 'the procuratorates and the judicial organs should keep their deserved independence and should not be interfered by administrative organs, social groups and individuals. Judicial justice reflects justice and equality in society. We must stick to this direction'.

institution and certain institutions may have different types of powers'.[17] The supervision of case filing and approval of arrest by the procuratorate are in essence reviews of investigation and detention by the investigating authorities which in the eyes of the West, belong to judicial review.[18] So, the procuratorate in China do exercise judicial powers, which in the European context belong to the courts. Although Article 9 of the Public Procurators Law (amended in 2001)[19] states that procurators shall not be subjected to any interference from administrative organs, public organisations or individuals in performing prosecutorial functions and duties according to law, the procuratorate follows the principle of procuratorial integration and works within a strict hierarchy. Consequently, the procuratorate and procurators in China are subject to the influence of integration and subordination of power. They are not truly independent compared with courts and judges.

2.2. THE STATUS OF CASE LAW: THE CASE PRECEDENTS SYSTEM AND CASE GUIDANCE SYSTEM

Another issue closely related to the status of courts is the importance of the role case law plays in shaping criminal procedure rules. Unlike in common law jurisdictions, civil law countries all have a systemic and detailed criminal procedure code. Courts can only explain the law or make judgment on the applicable law. But they do not have the power to create new laws and regulations through cases. However, judgments of case precedents in fact play an important role in judicial practice in the civil law systems. For example, in Germany, 'judgments which can be referred to as case precedents only include those capable of providing guidance on cases being tried. In other words, the precedents must have a certain correlation with cases pending decision'. 'Though precedents do not have any legal status in Germany, German judges and lawyers are consciously bound by such precedents when

---

[17] ZHANG QIANFAN 2004, p. 284.
[18] See Chen Weidong: 'Solution to the Conflict in the Role of Procuratorates – Separation of Legal Supervision and Prosecution', <http://www.legaldaily.com.cn/bm/content/2011-02/23/content_2481042.htm?node=20740>, visited on 3 November 2011.
[19] Art. 9 Public procurators shall enjoy the following rights: (1) to have the power and working conditions which are essential to the performance of functions and duties of public procurators; (2) to brook no interference from administrative organs, public organizations or individuals in performing procuratorial functions and duties according to law; (3) to be not removed from the post or demoted or dismissed, and to be not given a sanction, without statutory basis and without going through statutory procedures; (4) to be remunerated for work, to enjoy insurance and welfare benefits; (5) to enjoy safety of the person, property and residence as ensured by law; (6) to receive training; (7) to lodge petitions or complaints: (8) to resign their posts.

they try cases or represent their clients'.[20] Also in the Netherlands, the Supreme Court often uses applicable precedents to restrain lower courts. Though such precedents do not have legal force and lower courts are not obliged to follow them, the lower courts generally choose to respect the precedents decided by the Supreme Court.[21] As a result, precedent decisions made by the Supreme Courts of Germany and the Netherlands have a clear influence on cases being tried in lower courts despite the fact that both countries do not recognize the principle of binding precedents. Judges often make a conscious decision to follow such precedents. In addition, the Supreme Court tends to use flexible precedents to provide guidance for lower courts in order to adapt to social changes, resolve new cases and maintain the stability and consistency of law. Collections of case precedents with case notes published online and in law journals, also offer clear guidance for judicial staff and lawyers.[22]

Unlike in common law and civil law countries, the Supreme People's Court of China does not try many cases. Instead, it guides and binds trials at lower people's courts by drafting and publishing general judicial interpretations, publishing excellent judgments delivered by lower courts in the Gazette of the Supreme People's Court, and replying to problems identified in individual cases tried by lower people's courts. China has something similar to the case precedents system of civil law countries. 'Although China denies the legal status of precedents in legislation, precedents publicized by the Supreme People's Court are, in the vast majority of circumstances, followed as legal origins',[23] which forms the 'case guidance system' in China. The Gazette of the Supreme People's Court started to publish cases with guiding significance in 1985. On 15 November 2010, the Judicial Committee of the Supreme People's Court adopted the Supreme People's Court's Regulations on Case Guidance, which provide that cases which offer guidance on trials and proceedings of courts should be decided and issued by the Supreme People's Court. But the procuratorate and public

---

[20] The Supreme Court Taskforce: 'Report on Studying Germany Precedents System', People's Judicature, 7th ed. in 2006.

[21] TAK 2003, p. 35.

[22] Take Germany as an example. Judgments delivered by the Federal Constitutional Court and the Federal Appeal Court are collected in official publications – BverfGE and BGHSt. Judgments delivered by Federal Appeal Court, State Appeal Court and lower courts are published on law journals such as NJW. See [Germany] WEIGEND THOMAS, translated by YUE LILING, WEN XIAOJIE: German Criminal Procedure, published by China University of Political Science and Law Publishing House in 2004, p. 266.

[23] CHEN WEIDONG & LI XUNHU 2004.

security organs may also issue guidance cases for procurators and the police respectively.[24]

2.3. PROCEDURAL RIGHTS OF CRIMINAL SUSPECTS AND DEFENDANTS IN RELATION TO THE COLLECTION OF EVIDENCE

As mentioned in the introduction, civil law jurisdictions across Europe have taken in elements of adversarial procedure. This development is not limited to enhancing equality of arms between prosecution and defence in the trial phase but also introduces adversarial elements in the pre-trial phase. For example, in 1999, the Criminal Procedure Code of Italy was reformed to expand the investigation power of the defence by enhancing the role of lawyers in evidence collection so as to increase defence capacity.[25] In 2000, France also amended its Criminal Procedure Law by adding more provisions increasing adversariality between prosecution and defence. Follow-up reforms further enhanced the rights of suspects during the pre-trial phase and opened up the prosecution's monopoly over evidence collection and investigation.[26]

We believe that equality of arms can only be achieved by enforcing suspects' or defendants' procedural rights relating to evidence collection. The exclusion of evidence obtained by infringing upon the suspect's personal rights is a more effective remedy to safeguard the integrity of the criminal justice system but is a post remedy solution. Therefore the law should provide criminal suspects or defendants with procedural rights that prevent such infringements taking place and put suspects in a position where they can effectively defend themselves against allegations made by the investigating authorities. Essential rights in this respect are the right to silence, the right to legal aid, the right to private communication with lawyers, the right to be informed of the crime the suspect is accused of and the defendant's right to participate actively in the process. These rights may be classified into two categories: procedural safeguards allowing the suspects or defendants to remain silent on the one hand and procedural rights to allow them to participate in the investigation and obtain evidence on behalf of the defence on the other.[27]

---

[24] See 'Hu Yunteng, Director of Supreme People's Court Research Office: Building a Precedents Guidance System for People's Courts', <http://www.legaldaily.com.cn/bm/content/2011-01/05/content_2427562.htm?node=20739>, visited on 3 November 2011.

[25] See CHEN WEIDONG, JIU JIHUA & CHENG LEI 2004a.

[26] See CHEN WEIDONG, JIU JIHUA & CHENG LEI 2004b.

[27] See CAPE ET AL. 2010, Chapter 13.

2.3.1. Right to Silence

In the Middle Ages the criminal suspect in Europe was considered the object of the investigation and often torture was used to extract confessions or information. Many countries abolished this practice after the French revolution at the end of the 18th century and by the beginning of the 20th century most codes of criminal procedure in western countries recognized the right to silence. Article 14(3) of The International Covenant on Civil and Political Rights that came into effect in 1976 states clearly that everyone charged with a criminal offence shall 'not to be compelled to testify against himself or to confess guilt'. Similar provisions were incorporated in codes of criminal procedure. For example, according to Article136 (First Examination) of the German Code of Criminal Procedure, the accused shall be advised that the law grants him the right to respond to the charges, or to not make any statement on the charges at the commencement of the first interrogation. Another example is Article 29 of the Dutch Code of Criminal Procedure, which provides that the suspect or defendant is not compelled to answer questions raised by the police, the prosecutor or the judge. When the police has reasonable doubts that someone is guilty, the person shall be informed that he is not compelled to answer questions before he is interviewed as a suspect.[28]

Theorists and practitioners have long argued whether the right to silence should be introduced to China. The debate began in 1996 when the CPL was first revised and reached a peak when China signed the International Covenant on Civil and Political Rights in 1998. Discussions are still ongoing. There are three main views in academia – recognition, denial, and trade-off.[29] The new CPL adopted the recognition view as the provision – 'no one shall be compelled to prove his guilt' was added to Article 43. But regrettably, the new CPL failed to remove Article 93, which requires that the criminal suspect 'shall answer the investigators' questions truthfully'. It merely adds that when interrogating a criminal suspect, the investigators shall inform the suspect of the rule that he may be dealt with leniently if he confesses his guilt truthfully. As the criminal suspect is still compelled to confess truthfully when being interrogated, his right to silence cannot be effectively protected. Therefore, we can merely conclude that the Draft has absorbed the spirit of the right to silence but has not established the system in the regulatory sense.

---

[28] SUN CHANGYONG 2000, p. 294.
[29] See YI YANYOU 1999.

2.3.2. Right to Legal Aid and Right to Confidential Communication with Lawyers

The criminal suspect generally has two defence approaches: self defence and defence handled by a lawyer. The former is the inherent right of any criminal suspect while the latter includes the right to hire a lawyer and to legal counselling. In particular, the criminal suspect's rights to legal aid and confidential communication with his counsel are essential to the protection of his defence right. Article 14 (3-b) of the International Covenant on Civil and Political Rights states that everyone shall be entitled 'to have adequate time and facilities for the preparation of his defence and to communicate with counsel of his own choosing'. Principle 8 of the UN Basic Principles on the Role of Lawyers states: 'All arrested, detained or imprisoned persons shall be provided with adequate opportunities, time and facilities to be visited by and to communicate and consult with a lawyer, without delay, interception or censorship and in full confidentiality. Such consultations may be within sight, but not within the hearing, of law enforcement officials'. Article 6(3-c) of the ECHR provides that any criminal suspect has the right to defend himself through legal assistance of his own choosing or, if he has not sufficient means to pay for legal assistance, to be given it free when the interests of justice so require. The extent to which the right to defence is protected varies across different European countries and depends on their inquisitorial procedural traditions. In the Netherlands, defence lawyers have the right to meet with criminal suspects in custody freely, without being monitored. The biggest constraint on effective legal assistance is that neither the law nor the case law grants that lawyers be present during interrogations.[30] According to Article 136(1) of the German Code of Criminal Procedure, the accused shall have the right, at any stage, even prior to his examination to consult with defence counsel of his choice. 'If such rules are not followed, the statement made by the criminal suspect afterwards cannot be used as evidence'.[31]

The Regulation on Legal Aid of China was promulgated in 2003. It sets the basic principle that legal aid is the government's responsibility. In the new CPL Article 34 was revised so that the criminal suspect or defendant may directly apply to legal aid institutions. In circumstances which require the defence to be designated, the people's courts, the people's procuratorate and the public security authorities shall notify legal aid institutions to designate lawyers to provide legal assistance. Article 37 of the new CPL has also notably

---

[30] TAK 2003, p. 61.
[31] BGHSt 38, 372(1992); BGHSt 42, 15(1996); WEIGEND 2004, p. 53.

added new provisions to regulate the criminal suspect or defendant's right to confidential communication with his lawyer, which provides that a defence lawyer's meeting with a criminal suspect or defendant shall not be monitored. This resolves the contradiction that existed between Article 33 of the new Lawyers' Law (LL) of 2007 providing for confidentiality and no monitoring (stating that a defence lawyer's meeting with a criminal suspect or defendant shall not be monitored) and Article 96 from the 1996 CPL, now deleted, which allowed monitoring and therefore no confidentiality (stating that when a lawyer meets a suspect already taken into custody, personnel from the investigating authorities may, in light of the circumstances and needs of the case, be assigned to be present).

2.3.3. Right to be Informed

The right to information is a crucial aspect of the overall right to defend oneself. It is also the premise for defendants and their defence lawyers to investigate and collect evidence. Three dimensions can be distinguished. Firstly, the right of anyone charged with a criminal offence to be informed of the nature and the reason for the accusations against him. Secondly, the right to information in the sense of being informed of the defence's rights and thirdly, the right to have access to the evidence on which these accusations are based.[32] According to Article 9(2) of the International Covenant on Civil and Political Rights, 'anyone who is arrested shall be informed, at the time of arrest, of the reasons for his arrest and shall be promptly informed of any charges against him'. Article 5(2) of the ECHR states: 'Everyone who is arrested shall be informed promptly, in a language which he understands, of the reasons for his arrest and the charge against him'. A similar provision can be found in Article 6(3) ECHR. International treaties merely prescribe the exercise of this right during arrest, which poses the biggest threat to a citizen's personal liberty. But in effect, the right to be informed applies to the whole criminal procedure. In Germany the law specifies notification obligations of investigators and judges during arrest, interrogation, detention and seizure, which in turn safeguards the criminal suspect's right to be informed. The arrest warrant must state the crime the suspect is accused of, the cause for the arrest and the legal basis of the arrest. In addition, the content of the arrest warrant should be read out to the person when he is being arrested. During interrogation, the judge should also inform the accused of the unfavourable circumstances and his right to make a statement about the accusation or remain silent. If the arrest decision is to be upheld,

---

[32] See SPRONKEN 2010, p. 45-67.

the accused should be informed of his right to other legal remedies. During pre-trial detention, a suspect without a defence lawyer should be informed of the right to have a lawyer designated. At the commencement of the first interrogation, the accused should be informed of the charge against him and applicable punishments.[33] Evidently, unlike the direct oral notification in common law countries, 'the civil law system favours fulfilling the right to be informed by engaging the criminal suspect in the procedure and giving his appointed lawyer the right to read the case file and its notification procedure, and the rules are very clear and complete'.[34]

Based on its inquisitorial model, China's CPL does not prescribe that the investigative authorities are obliged to notify the suspect. Nor does it say anything about the obligation of investigators to inform the arrested person of the crime that he is accused of and the reason for his arrest at the first interrogation or arrest. The criminal suspect or defendant's right to be informed is realized via his lawyer. It is only upon meeting his lawyer, that the suspect learns of the reason for his arrest. Therefore, the lawyer is the first to know by means of access to the case files. The new CPL notably contains one major improvement to the 2008 amendment of the Law on Lawyers by identifying the status of lawyers as defence counsel during the investigation phase. According to Article 35 of the new CPL, defence lawyers may provide legal assistance to criminal suspects, represent them to file complaints and charges, apply for alteration of compulsory measures and obtain information about the accused crimes and cases from the investigative authorities. It is a big step forward, because the former CPL did not contain provisions about lawyers' access to information on alleged crimes, held by the investigative authorities. There are additional provisions[35] requiring that investigators should ask suspects their personal details, background, criminal record etc. Furthermore, when interrogating suspects, the investigating personnel shall first ask them whether or not they have committed any criminal act, and allow them to state the circumstances of guilt or explain their innocence, and then proceed to questioning. However, there is no article stating that the investigator should inform the suspect of the alleged crime and case details.

---

[33] Stop re arrest see Arts. 114, 114a, 115; re interrogation see Art. 136; re detention see Art. 117; re seizure see Art. 101. Translated by LI CHANGKE: German Code of Criminal Procedure (text effective on 1 December 1994).

[34] LIU MEIXIANG 2004.

[35] Arts. 178 and 179 of 'the Procedures for Handling Criminal Cases by Public Security Organs' published by the Ministry of Public Security.

2.3.4. The Right of Criminal Suspects and Defendants to Investigate and Participate in the Proceedings

The possibilities for the defence to seek evidence, investigate facts, and interview prospective witnesses during the preliminary investigations depend highly on the nature of the criminal procedure and vary significantly within Europe. Inquisitorially based criminal justice systems often prohibit active defence at the pre-trial phase and merely allow reactive defence: only when the results of the official (pre-trial) investigation are made known to the accused is he in a position to propose further investigation. In most systems the accused lacks power and financial resources to, for instance, interview unwilling witnesses or conduct an investigation into the facts. If the suspect or accused wishes to investigate, he has to ask the police, prosecutor or investigating judge for permission and for help.[36] In China, the CPL does not grant the criminal suspect or defendant the right to investigate or make applications to the authorities to do so. The right is fulfilled through the defence lawyer's right to evidence investigation, which has just been granted in the new CPL. It is still early days and there is doubt about how this will actually work in practice. For example, the new CPL adds another provision to Chapter Four,[37] prescribing that when the defence lawyer believes during the investigation, examination and prosecution phases, that some evidence materials collected by the public security authorities and the people's procuratorates, which can prove the innocence or mitigate the guilt of the suspect or defendant are not submitted, he may apply to the people's procuratorate and the people's court to retrieve the relevant evidence. The provision can, to a certain extent, resolve the problem that it is difficult for lawyers to investigate and collect evidence. The right to investigation or application for investigation discussed here, as well as the right to be informed mentioned above, are derived from the defence right enjoyed by the criminal suspect or defendant. Therefore, they are the basic requirements

---

[36] CAPE ET AL. 2010, p. 44-48.

[37] CPL Art. 39: When the defence lawyer believes during the investigation, examination and prosecution phases, that some evidence materials collected by the public security organs and the people's procuratorate which can prove the innocence or lighter guilt of the suspect or defendant is not submitted, he may apply to the people's procuratorate and the people's court for retrieving the relevant evidence. Art. 41A defence lawyer may, with the consent of the witness or any other unit or person concerned, gather therefrom materials related to the case, he also may apply to the people's procuratorate or people's court to gather therefrom an order for evidence, or apply to the people's court to notify the witness to appear before the court to testify. A defence lawyer, with permission of the people procuratorate or the people's court and with the consent of the victim or his near relative and the consent of the witnesses provided by the victim, may gather therefrom materials related to the case.

for equality of arms between the defence and the prosecution and the premise for the person being prosecuted to be engaged in the evidence investigation procedure or to apply for exclusion in the future. However, the CPL has failed to directly regulate the above-mentioned rights. The criminal suspect or defendant can only carry out an investigation and collect evidence by having his hired or designated defence lawyer become familiar with the basic information of the case. That is why some academics have proposed the idea of granting the suspect or defendant the right to apply for evidence preservation. In doing so, the criminal suspect and the victim can apply to the people's procuratorate for evidence preservation during the pre-trial phase. The defendant, the private prosecutor, and the victim all have the right to apply to the people's court for retrieving evidence in their favour on the day of the commencement of proceedings at the people's court.[38]

3. CONCLUDING REMARKS

Although China and mainland Europe share common ground at the macro level, by both having inquisitorial features, China has a stronger inquisitorial criminal procedure that is demonstrated by the status of the courts and less developed defence rights, such as the right to silence and the other rights described in this chapter. Given the common context, we hope through further analysis and comparison in the following chapters to discover pillars supporting the operation of the exclusionary rule in China. In addition, we will explore what China can learn from developments within the European criminal justice systems to help prevent statements adduced through torture being admitted in any proceedings as evidence, except against the person accused of torture.

BIBLIOGRAPHY

CAPE ET AL. 2007
CAPE, E., HODGSON, J., PRAKKEN. T. & SPRONKEN, T., *Suspects in Europe, Procedural Rights at the Investigative Stage of the Criminal Process in the European Union*, Antwerp/Oxford/Portland: Intersentia, 2007.

CAPE ET AL. 2010
CAPE, E., NAMORADZE, Z., SMITH, R. & SPRONKEN, T., *Effective Criminal Defence in Europe*, Antwerp/Oxford/Portland: Intersentia, 2010.

---

[38] CHEN WEIDONG 2005b, p. 231-232.

CHEN GUANGZHONG 2010
CHEN GUANGZHONG, 'Discussing Several Theoretical and Practical Issues in the Reform of Criminal Evidence System – from the Angle of "the Two Evidence Provisions"', *China Legal Science*, 6th edn., 2010.

CHEN WEIDONG 2004
CHEN WEIDONG, *Criminal Procedure Law*, Beijing: Renmin University of China Publishing House, 2004.

CHEN WEIDONG 2005A
CHEN WEIDONG, *Road to Procedural Justice*, Law Press, 2005.

CHEN WEIDONG 2005B
CHEN WEIDONG, *Model Criminal Procedure Code*, Beijing: Renmin University of China Publishing House, 2005.

CHEN WEIDONG 2010A
CHEN WEIDONG, 'Progress and Drawbacks in the Two Evidence Provisions', *Evidence Science*, 5th edn., 2010.

CHEN WEIDONG 2010B
CHEN WEIDONG, 'New Developments in China's Criminal Evidence Law – Assessing the Two Evidence Provisions', *Jurists Review*, 5th edn., 2010.

CHEN WEIDONG 2011
CHEN WEIDONG, 'Guiding Thoughts on Revision of Criminal Procedure Law', *Legal Information*, 8th edn., 2011.

CHEN WEIDONG, JIU JIHUA & CHENG LEI 2004A
CHEN WEIDONG, JIU JIHU & CHENG LEI, 'Italian Criminal Justice System', *People's Procuratorial Semi-monthly*, 12th edn., 2004.

CHEN WEIDONG, JIU JIHUA & CHENG LEI 2004B
CHEN WEIDONG, LIU JIHUA & CHENG LEI, 'New Developments in Reform of French Criminal Procedure Law', *People's Procuratorial Semi-monthly*, 10th edn., 2004.

CHEN WEIDONG & LI XUNHU 2004
CHEN WEIDONG & LI XUNHU, 'Judicial Reform of Case Precedents System', *Application of Law*, 1st, 2nd edn., 2004.

FAN CHONGYI 2010
FAN CHONGYI, 'Substantive Justice Is Impossible without Procedural Justice – Studying "the Two Evidence Provisions"', *Law Science Magazine*, 6th edn., 2010.

HARRIS, O'BOYLE & WARBRICK 2009
HARRIS, D.J., O'BOYLE, M. & WARBRICK, *Harris, O'Boyle & Warbrick: Law of the European Convention on Human Rights*, Oxford: Oxford University Press, 2009.

LIU MEIXIANG 2004
LIU MEIXIANG, 'Preliminary Exploration of Criminal Suspect's Right to Be Informed', *Journal of National Prosecutors College*, 4th edn., 2004.

LONG ZONGZHI 2010
LONG ZONGZHI, 'Studying Several Issues on Regulation and Implementation of the Two Evidence Provisions', *China Legal Science*, 6th edn., 2010.

SONG YINGHUI 2010
SONG YINGHUI, 'The Exclusionary Rules of Illegally Obtained Evidence in China and Their Application', *Law Science Magazine*, 6th edn., 2010.

SPRONKEN 2010
SPRONKEN, T., *An EU-wide Letter of Rights. Towards Best Practice*, Antwerp/Oxford/Portland: Intersentia, 2010.

SUN CHANGYONG 2000
SUN CHANGYONG, *Investigation Procedure and Human Rights – Comparative Study*, Beijing: Fangzheng Publishing House, 2000.

TAK 2003
TAK, P.J.P., *The Dutch Criminal Justice System: Organization and Operation*, Den Haag: Boom Juridische uitgevers, 2003.

WEIGEND 2004
Weigend, T., translated by YUE LILING & WEN XIAOJIE: *German Criminal Procedure*, published by China University of Political Science and Law Publishing House, 2004.

YI YANYOU 1999
YI YANYOU, 'Privileges against Self-Criminalization', *Journal of Comparative Law*, 2nd edn., 1999

YUE LILING & WEN XIAOJIE 2004
[Germany] Weigend Thomas, translated by YUE LILING & WEN XIAOJIE: *German Criminal Procedure*, published by China University of Political Science and Law Publishing House, 2004.

ZENG XIANYI 2000
ZENG XIANYI, *History of the Chinese Legal System*, Beijing: Renmin University of China Publishing House, 2000.

ZHANG QIANFAN 2004
ZHANG QIANFAN, *Constitution – Theory and Application*, Law Press, 2004.

ZHENG JINFAN 1982
ZHENG JINFAN, *History of the Chinese Legal System*, Mass Press, 1982.

2. A SUMMARY OF THE APPLICATION OF THE EXCLUSIONARY RULE IN EUROPE

Taru Spronken and Chai Yufeng

1. INTRODUCTION

In this chapter the application of the exclusionary rule in the Netherlands and the ECtHR case law will be analysed. This choice is based on the fact that the Netherlands features a typical civil law system that shares basic assumptions with the Chinese system as set out in chapter 1. The ECtHR case law provides a broader insight into the application of the exclusionary rule in criminal justice systems across Europe and it is interesting to determine in what way the standards that are developed by the ECtHR in this respect take into account the differences within the legal traditions and practices in the European Member States. For example in England and Wales, a common law jurisdiction, the courts need not consider the legality of the source of evidence but must review the overall fairness of the proceedings. If a guilty confession however is obtained through oppression, which includes torture, inhuman or degrading treatment and the use or threat of violence, exclusion is compulsory because of the statutory provision of section 76 Police and Criminal Evidence Act 1984,[1] which hinges upon the European Convention

---

[1] Section 76 of the Police and Criminal Evidence Act 1984: (1) In any proceedings a confession made by an accused person may be given in evidence against him in so far as it is relevant to any matter in issue in the proceedings and is not excluded by the court in pursuance of this section. (2) If, in any proceedings where the prosecution proposes to give in evidence a confession made by an accused person, it is represented to the court that the confession was or may have been obtained –
(a) by oppression of the person who made it; or
(b) in consequence of anything said or done which was likely, in the circumstances existing at the time, to render unreliable any confession which might be made by him in consequence thereof.
The court shall not allow the confession to be given in evidence against him except in so far as the prosecution proves to the court beyond reasonable doubt that the confession (notwithstanding that it may be true) was not obtained as aforesaid.
(3) In any proceedings where the prosecution proposes to give in evidence a confession made by an accused person, the court may of its own motion require the prosecution, as a
→

of Human Rights and the judgments of the ECtHR. In Germany the exclusionary rule is court-created, automatic exclusion applies only to evidence obtained in violation of section 136a of the German Code of Criminal Procedure and the Wiretapping Law. The exclusion of evidence obtained by other illegal means and by intruding upon personal rights and human dignity is left to the discretion of the court which may balance the various interests.[2] In France the only legal source to exclude evidence is through the system of procedural nullities that is applied in the pre-trial phase and that has been initially designed to regulate the behaviour of investigating authorities. Investigative acts may fall under the penalty of nullity for instance if the formalities to respect rights of the defendant are not respected. As in all inquisitorial models, the case file in France is the basis for ascertaining the facts during the trial phase. Once an investigative act has been annulled by the investigating judge the results have to be withdrawn from the case file and cannot be used at trial.[3]

In this chapter we aim to focus more in depth on the procedures to exclude evidence that are in place in the Netherlands and on the jurisprudence of the ECtHR, on evidence that has been obtained by torture or other ways of coercion amounting to a violation of Article 3 ECHR.

2. THE EXCLUSIONARY RULE IN THE NETHERLANDS

2.1. CHARACTERISTICS OF THE DUTCH CRIMINAL JUSTICE SYSTEM

The Netherlands is a traditional civil law country which applied Napoleon's Code of Criminal Instruction (*Code d'instruction criminelle*) before 1838. In 1838, the Netherlands established its own Code of Criminal Procedure, which was in effect a revision of the Code of Criminal Instruction, featuring a strong inquisitorial flavour. The Netherlands published its current Code of Criminal Procedure (*Wetboek van Strafvordering*) in 1926. To date it has however tried to rectify the traditional inquisitorial procedure by absorbing elements of the adversarial system, under the influence of the ECHR and the case law

---

condition of allowing it to do so, to prove that the confession was not obtained as mentioned in subsection (2) above.

(8) In this section 'oppression' includes torture, inhuman or degrading treatment, and the use or threat of violence (whether or not amounting to torture).

[2] See for instance the judgments of the German Supreme Court of 22 February 1978, 27 BGHSt 355 (1978) and of 18 April 1980, 29 BGHSt 244 (1980) and the judgment of the German Federal Constitutional Court of 31 January 1973, BverfG 34, BverfG 238.

[3] THAMAN 2010, p. 346.

of the ECtHR.[4] As a typical civil law country, the Netherlands has never run a jury system due to the public belief that an ordinary citizen is not up to the job of being a juror and playing its due role given the sheer size and professionalism of modern law. According to the Dutch tradition, at the heart of ensuring trial quality are the higher independence and quality of judges. Criminal trials should therefore be left in the hands of professional judges. Thus, the Netherlands has never adopted the participation system of other civil law countries nor has it experimented with the jury system of common law countries. Furthermore, the public does not think such a choice affects the credibility of its criminal justice system.[5]

The Dutch criminal procedure is centred on dossiers. Five means of evidence are defined by the Dutch Code of Criminal Procedure:[6]

1. the court's own observations during the court hearing, e.g. photos or tapes;
2. the statement of the accused in court or out of court, provided the statement is filed;
3. the statement of a witness in court, including hearsay testimony;
4. the statement of an expert in court; and
5. written (police) materials.[7]

In particular, not only the statement of the accused out of court recorded in the dossier may be used as evidence, but the statement of a witness is not restrained by the rule of hearsay evidence. As a result, criminal trials are extremely reliant on dossiers provided by the police. In the Netherlands, the dossier keeps a thorough record of all steps of the investigation and its conduct. The trial is not a forum for oral argument but for the evaluation of the written evidence contained in the dossier.[8] Consequently, some scholars take the view that the Dutch system relies on the skill and competence of the professional judge to decide on the basis of cold files.[9] In order to make sure that this dossier-centred, truth-seeking criminal justice system does not derail due process, the Netherlands has developed two restraint mechanisms.

The first one is the restraint within the proceedings. Due to the importance attached to the dossier, the outcome of criminal investigation shapes the quality of the subsequent criminal trial. The public prosecutor, the

---

[4]   TAK 2009, p. 19.
[5]   LANG SHENG & XIONG XUANGUO 2003, p. 3.
[6]   Section 339, CCP.
[7]   TAK 2009, p. 65.
[8]   See NIJBOER 1992, p. 63. Annotated by ELLISON 1998.
[9]   See BEIJER, COBLEY & KLIP 1995, p. 299. Cited from ELLISON 1998, p. 29-43.

examining magistrate, the defence and the trial judge all play an important role in its compilation. Dutch criminal procedure ultimately relies upon cooperation and relationships of trust between these key criminal justice professionals. Institutional incentives motivate public prosecutors and examining magistrates to ensure that the dossier is a thorough statement of the evidence.[10]

The second one is the restraint outside the proceedings. The Dutch Constitution provides for fundamental rights of the people of the Netherlands, such as the right to privacy in Article 10; Article 11 on the right to inviolability of the person; the right to respect for the home and correspondence in Articles 12 and 13; and the right to liberty and habeas corpus in Article 15. It however fails to offer a provision on the right to fair trial. Moreover, the Dutch courts are not authorized to review Acts of Parliament against fundamental rights laid down in the Constitution (Article 120 of the Constitution), which ultimately restricts remedies available to a defendant during criminal proceedings.[11] On the other hand, Article 93 of the Constitution specifies the principle of direct application of international law. In addition, Article 94 establishes that statutory regulations in force within the Netherlands shall not be applicable if such application is in conflict with provisions of treaties that are binding on all persons.[12] As a consequence, a series of international human rights treaties and resolutions, including the European Convention on Human Rights, have influenced and shaped the development of criminal procedure in the Netherlands. Under the influence of the case law of the ECtHR, the adversarial principle nowadays gets more emphasis for example by summoning regularly more witnesses to testify at trial and by allowing the suspect to have access to lawyers in the phase of police interrogation.[13]

Currently, the Dutch criminal justice system has undergone a paradigm shift from mildness to stringency. The Netherlands has long been well-known for the mildness of its criminal system, which was once distinguished by very low incarceration rates in the 1970s, with merely 20,000 per 100,000 criminals being in custody. However a sharp rise in crime and the emergence of violent and organized crime imposed huge pressure on the mild traditions of its justice system. As a result, a series of adjustments were made to the Dutch criminal justice system, including the reshuffling of police officers and

---

10 ELLISON 1998, p. 29-43.
11 VAN KEMPEN 2009, p. 6-7.
12 VAN KEMPEN 2009, p. 2.
13 TAK 2009, p. 65. See: ECtHR 27 November 2008, *Salduz v. Turkey*, no. 36391/02.

prosecutors and the expansion of judiciary power, and prison capacity.[14] It is now, in the early twenty-first century, sometimes viewed as having one of Europe's most severe criminal justice systems, perhaps following that of England and Wales.[15]

2.2. THE DUTCH EXCLUSIONARY RULE

To safeguard the basic procedural rights of the people of the Netherlands, the Dutch Code of Criminal Procedure specifies that prosecutors and judges should jointly regulate illegal collection of evidence by the police. In particular, the prosecutor and the prosecution office play a pivotal role. The prosecution in the Netherlands has the investigation power and is held responsible for the final result of criminal investigation. Prosecutors do not directly conduct investigation themselves. Instead, they provide guidance for the police in conducting investigation. According to Article 148 of the Dutch Code of Criminal Procedure and Article 13 of the Dutch Police Code, the prosecutor has the power to guide criminal investigation and command the investigation conduct of police; the prosecutor shall supervise the investigation conduct of police and have the obligation to ensure that the police work by conforming to the Code of Criminal Procedure so as to protect the basic rights of the people.[16] However, except for a few very important cases, in practice police officers do not have frequent contacts with prosecutors as the prosecution is limited in capacity.[17] The lack of supervision is seen as one of the reasons investigation units resort to illegal collection of evidence by infringing upon criminal suspects' basic rights. Therefore, the courts need to carry out judicial examination of investigation to safeguard the basic rights of suspects or defendants, and this is done inter alia by excluding illegally obtained evidence.

2.3. LEGAL PROVISIONS RELATED TO THE EXCLUSION OF ILLEGALLY OBTAINED EVIDENCE

Consistent with its criminal justice system, the Dutch criminal evidence system also stresses the importance of uncovering the truth. The standard of proof in the Dutch Code of Criminal Procedure (CCP) is expressed in the requirement that a judge – notwithstanding that enough evidence is available

---

[14] TAK 2009, p. 9.
[15] TONRY & BIJLEVELD 2007, p. 1-30.
[16] TAK 2009, p. 27; VAN KEMPEN 2009, p. 10.
[17] TAK 2009, p. 27.

to convict a defendant – may not assume that the offence charged is proven if he is not convinced of it.[18] The judge may consider two reasons for excluding evidence: unreliability and illegal gathering. If evidence is considered unreliable, its exclusion is based directly on pursuit of the substantive truth. The exclusion of illegally gathered evidence has a separate legal basis: Article 359a CCP. In some cases, evidence is unreliable because certain legal rules on gathering evidence have been violated. In that case, where unreliability coincides with illegal gathering of the evidence, the evidence is already excluded on the basis of unreliability. In principle, the rule of Article 359a CCP need not be applied.[19]

Article 359a of the Dutch CCP is the legal source of the exclusionary rule.[20] It prescribes that, if evidence is gathered illegally in the investigation of a case, and the irregularity cannot be repaired, the judge may determine as follows by taking into account the seriousness of the illegal collection:

1. The prosecution is inadmissible when the judge finds that the prosecution intentionally used illegal means to gather evidence, which severely violates the defendant's legal rights and undermines judicial justice. As a result, the judge delivers a written judgment, stating that the court refuses to admit the prosecution and the prosecutor should not attempt to initiate another prosecution on the same case. In fact, the case is dismissed by the judge. The Dutch CCP does not define the circumstances in which the prosecution is inadmissible. Such circumstances are instead established by case law. For example, the use of torture or oppression by the police and unauthorized interception of telephone conversations may make the case inadmissible. Moreover, apart from serious illegal conduct during the collection of evidence, such as the prosecution deliberately providing false evidence against the defendant, or detaining the defendant illegally, other acts may also lead to inadmissibility of the prosecution.

---

[18] Section 338 CCP.

[19] BORGERS & STEVENS 2010, p. 1-21.

[20] '1. The [trial court] can, if it appears that in the preliminary investigation procedures have been disrespected that can no longer be repaired and the legal consequences thereof do not appear from the law, determine that:

a. the gravity of the sentence be mitigated in relation to the seriousness of the defect, if the disadvantage caused by the fault can be compensated in this way;

b. the results of the investigation having been obtained by the defect may not be used in evidence;

c. the prosecution is inadmissible, if owing to the defect there cannot be an examination of the case in compliance with the principles of proper proceedings.

2. In applying the first paragraph, the [trial court] takes into account the interests served by the infringed rule, the seriousness of the defect and the disadvantage caused by it'.

2. Illegally obtained evidence may be excluded. This is at the discretion of the court. If the illegally obtained evidence is the main evidence proving the guilt of the defendant, the judge may admit the case but the exclusion of the evidence may lead to the acquittal of the defendant.
3. The defendant's sentence is mitigated. This is a special rule in the Dutch criminal proceedings and derives from the case law of the Supreme Court. It mainly applies to cases in which the importance of the illegally collected evidence is negligible but nevertheless causes certain damage to the defendant. In addition, if a case drags on for too long, thus violating the principle of prompt trial as expressed in Article 6 para. 1 of the ECHR, the judge may also give a mitigated sentence.
4. There is no substantive consequence. This applies to light illegal collection of evidence. If a procedural violation does not cause any negative consequence to the defendant, nor does it affect the fair trial, the judge may not use any of the above three measures to deal with the illegally obtained evidence, except for stating the fact that there has been an irregularity in the collection of evidence.[21]

The Dutch CCP does not prescribe when the judge should adopt which measure. In practice, a judge should consider the interests served by the infringed rule, the seriousness of the defect and the disadvantage caused by it for the defence or the trial court. The court enjoys wide discretionary power to decide which measure is applicable.

2.4. EXCLUDING STATEMENTS OF A SUSPECT

A statement of a suspect that is obtained by putting unlawful pressure on him or her during the interrogation will be excluded as evidence. If the treatment violates the prohibition against torture in Article 3 of the ECHR, the prosecution shall be declared inadmissible. In case the treatment constitutes inhuman or degrading treatment in the sense of Article 3 of the ECHR, it will depend on the circumstances whether this must lead to inadmissibility of the prosecution, or only to exclusion of the statement obtained through the ill-treatment. An official who conducts such an unlawful interrogation could be disciplined internally or punished in a criminal trial.[22]

The extortion of confessions by torture is rather rare in the Netherlands. Torture is generally perceived by the public as uncivilized and unacceptable and this is mirrored in police culture. The police is trained and supervised in

---

[21] LANG SHENG & XIONG XUANGUO 2003, p. 22.
[22] VAN KEMPEN 2009, p. 29.

accordance with this view. In addition, a criminal suspect may consult a lawyer at any time when he is deprived of his liberty and have private consultations with his lawyer, who would get to know whether torture or other means of coercion had occurred. The suspect must be brought in front of the examining judge within three days of his first interrogation and the judge may see if he is injured or the suspect may directly tell the judge whether he has been mistreated. The suspect is initially held in the police station and if he is to be held in custody after seeing the examining judge, he is then transferred to an official detention centre, which means he is protected from police control. In order to prevent continuous interrogation, the interrogation records must truthfully record when the interrogation starts and ends, and the detention centre should also keep such detailed records.[23]

2.5. CASE LAW ON THE EXCLUSIONARY RULE

Article 359a was introduced into the CCP in 1996, and was further developed in the case law of the Dutch Supreme Court.[24] A very important judgment is that of 30 March 2004,[25] in which the Dutch Supreme Court gave a summary of the case law passed up to then on Article 359a:

Firstly, Article 359a pertains only to breaches of procedural rules committed during the preliminary investigation, in so far as that preliminary investigation relates to the offense with which the accused is charged and thus on which the judge has to decide. An example: in the investigation of accused A, in conflict with the rules, a telephone tap is placed. During the monitoring of the calls, incriminating material is collected on B. This material can be used in the criminal case against B, because the breach of procedural rules did not take place in the context of the investigation relating to the offense with which B is charged.[26]

Secondly, Article 359a only applies to irremediable breaches of procedural rules. An example is failure to inform the accused of the results of a DNA test, through which the accused is not given the opportunity to request a second opinion. The session judge then needs to examine whether it is still possible to obtain a second opinion. If that is the case, the accused must still be given the opportunity to obtain it. This, of course, has to be a remediable breach of procedural rules. If a search of a home has been conducted without the

---

[23] LANG SHENG & XIONG XUANGUO 2003, p. 22.
[24] The overview in this paragraph as well as the examples referred to are taken from BORGERS & STEVENS 2010.
[25] HR 30 March 2004, *NJ* 2004, 376 annotated by BURUMA. See BORGERS & STEVENS 2010, p. 3.
[26] HR 18 October 1988, *NJ* 1989, 306. See BORGERS & STEVENS 2010, p. 4.

required authorization, no remedy is possible. Such authorization must be granted prior to the search.[27]

Thirdly, the Supreme Court stated that in deciding whether a legal consequence will be attached to a breach of procedural rules, and if so, what consequence, the judge must take account of the points of view formulated in the second sub-Article of Article 359a:

i. the interest that the breached rule serves. One must see what interest the breached rule is intended to protect, and to what extent this interest relates to the accused. The rules relating to searches of homes are intended to protect the (privacy) interests of the occupant. An example is a situation in which someone uses a room in a house only as a storage place (for drugs), while not being an occupant of that house. In such a case, no consequences need be attached to a breach of the rules on searches of homes;[28]

ii. the gravity of the breach. This point of view is especially important for the choice of the sanction. In the event of very grave breaches of procedural rules, the most severe sanction – barring the Public Prosecution Service from prosecuting – is likely, while the most minor breaches are settled by some reduction of the sentence or by the mere determination of illegality. Under certain circumstances, the good faith of the investigating officers who caused the breach of procedural rules can play a part. For example: an investigating officer enters premises which he presumes to be vacant. After he enters, the premises prove to be occupied. In that case, the absence of the written authorization required to enter the premises does not have to result in exclusion of the evidence if the judge is of the opinion that this investigating officer could and was entitled to assume that the premises were unoccupied;[29]

iii. the harm caused by the breach. If a provision is breached that was written in the interest of a suspect, this is as a rule harmful to the suspect. Under certain circumstances, however, no harm is done. An example is not informing a suspect his right to remain silent. This is in itself harmful to the suspect, unless the suspect is a lawyer. The suspect then knows, after all, without being told, that he has the right to remain silent.

---

[27] Cf. HR 3 June 2001, *NJ* 2001, 536. See Borgers & Stevens 2010, p. 4.

[28] Cf. HR 26 March 2002, *NJ* 2002, 343. See Borgers & Stevens 2010, p. 4.

[29] Cf. HR 19 June 2001, *NJ* 2001, 574 annotated by Reijntjes. See Borgers & Stevens 2010, p. 4.

By considering all the above three factors, if the judge is of the opinion that a legal consequence should be attached to a breach of procedural rules, the judge may choose the following sanctions:

1. *Barring prosecution.* The Supreme Court has repeatedly ruled that barring prosecution is an option only in exceptional cases. There is room for this sanction only if investigating officers or the Public Prosecution Service has seriously breached principles of due process, through which, either on purpose or with gross disregard for the interests of the accused, his right to a fair trial has been breached to a considerable extent. This is also consistent with the spirit of Article 6 of the ECHR.

2. *Exclusion of evidence.* The Supreme Court actually sets two requirements. Firstly, a (sufficient) causal connection must exist between the breach of procedural rules and gathering of the evidence. Secondly, an important rule or legal principle must have been breached to a considerable extent. It is not usually problematic to determine a causal connection between a breach of procedural rules and evidence. An example of this is the situation in which a suspect is unlawfully arrested, while subsequently, when asked, the suspect gives permission for a search of his home. Giving such permission breaks the causal connection between the arrest and the search. Exclusion of evidence will generally follow, for instance from a breach of rules pertaining to the suspect's right to make a voluntary statement. This also holds if an illegal body search is conducted during which drugs are found in a natural cavity of the suspect's body.[30]

3. Sentence reduction. The Supreme Court formulates four conditions for the use of sentence reduction as a sanction on a breach of procedural rules: a. the suspect has actually been harmed; b. the harm was due to the breach; c. the harm is suitable for compensation by sentence reduction; and d. sentence reduction is justified in light of the importance of the breached rule and the gravity of the breach. Examples are a search during which the main, but not all legal requirements are met,[31] or systematic surveillance of a home from the public road without permission from the public prosecutor.[32]

---

[30] HR 29 May 2007, *NJ* 2008, 14 annotated by REIJNTJES. See BORGERS & STEVENS 2010, p. 6.
[31] Cf. HR 2 July 2002, *NJ* 2002, 624. See BORGERS & STEVENS 2010, p. 7.
[32] HR 21 March 2000, *LJN* AA5254. See BORGERS & STEVENS 2010, p. 7.

2.6.   FRUITS OF THE POISONOUS TREE

According to the Dutch Supreme Court, two conditions must be taken into consideration for applying the exclusionary rule: 1. whether there is a direct connection between the breach of procedural rules and the failure to consider the accused's interests; and 2. what harm is actually suffered by the accused by this breach. This means that the fruit of the poisonous tree doctrine will not easily be applied as may be illustrated by the following example: a man was arrested, and asked whether he had burglar's tools on him. The man threw his bag and jacket on the ground and yelled: 'See for yourself!' Burglar's tools were then found in the bag and jacket. It was argued in the criminal proceedings that the man had been arrested unlawfully (because there was no suspicion) and that finding the burglar's tools had to be considered fruit of the poisonous tree of that illegal arrest. The Supreme Court held that, insofar as the arrest should be considered unlawful, it could not be said that this evidence was the direct result of the arrest, as the suspect gave away the evidence voluntarily.[33] An example of the fruits of the poisonous tree doctrine being applied is a case where, in conflict with the applicable rules, a telephone conversation between the accused and a doctor was tapped. At the hearing, the accused was confronted with the phone tapping report. The Supreme Court held that the way in which the accused reacted to confrontation with the report of the tapping could not be used as evidence. The reaction could be considered a direct result of the breach of procedural rules.[34]

2.7.   SUMMARY

In conclusion, though the Dutch CCP only provides simple and broad provisions on the exclusion of illegally obtained evidence, the rule of Article 359a has been developed further in the case law of the Dutch Supreme Court. In judicial practice, as required by the Supreme Court, the judge needs to consider different standards and take into account the case law when excluding illegally obtained evidence. He should not only review whether the collection of evidence by the investigators and the prosecutors is illegal but also choose sanctions accordingly. This has in effect considerably restricted the judge's discretionary power to exclude evidence, demonstrating the basic characteristic of the inquisitorial procedure – seeking the truth.

---

[33]   Cf. HR 24 February 2004, *NJ* 2004, 226. See BORGERS & STEVENS 2010, p. 7.
[34]   See BORGERS & STEVENS 2010, p. 7.

3. CASE LAW OF THE EUROPEAN COURT OF HUMAN RIGHTS ON THE EXCLUSIONARY RULE RELATING TO ILLEGALLY OBTAINED EVIDENCE

The ECtHR is a unique body of international law at the centre of human rights protection binding virtually all democratic legal orders of Europe. More than 800 million people have direct access to the ECtHR to complain of violations of their fundamental rights as enshrined in the ECHR. The ECtHR which was set up in 1959 has delivered more than 10,000 judgments. These are binding on the countries concerned and have led governments to alter their legislation and practice in a wide range of areas of law including criminal justice. This was achieved through the exercise of the right of individual petition.[35]

When dealing with complaints in the area of criminal law, and more specifically the admission of evidence, the Court does not regard it as its function to deal with errors of fact or of law, nor does it lay down any rules on the admissibility of evidence as such, which is therefore primarily a matter for regulation under national law.[36] As a consequence it is not the role of the Court when assessing a complaint under Article 6 ECHR, to determine, as a matter of principle, whether particular types of evidence – for example, unlawfully obtained evidence – may be admissible or, indeed, whether the applicant was guilty or not. The Court sees it as its task to consider whether the proceedings as a whole, including the way in which the evidence was obtained, were fair. This means the Court does not set general rules on the exclusion of illegally obtained evidence in a criminal trial. There are however some exceptions to this general approach and one of them is when evidence is obtained in violation of Article 3 ECHR. Another exception is made, when confessions have been made during police interrogation whilst the suspect has not had access to a lawyer. Both exceptions will be addressed below. But first we will set out how the ECtHR distinguishes between the two different categories of ill-treatment listed in Article 3: torture on the one hand and inhuman treatment on the other. We will only concentrate on these two categories because they are the most relevant to situations that deal with interrogation of suspects. Therefore the application of Article 3 on conditions of detention and treatment of detainees, extradition or deportation, or inhuman punishment are left aside in this chapter.

---

35 HARRIS, O'BOYLE & WARBRICK 2009, p. 811.
36 See for instance ECtHR 12 July 1988, *Schenk v. Switzerland*, no. 10862/84 and ECtHR 12 May 2000, *Khan v. The United Kingdom*, no. 35394/97.

3.1.   DEFINITION OF TORTURE AND INHUMAN TREATMENT

Article 3 of the European Convention on Human Rights states: 'No one shall be subjected to torture or to inhuman or degrading treatment or punishment'. State parties have a positive obligation not to use torture or inhuman treatment and to prevent such practices. During criminal proceedings, a state party should not only refrain from obtaining evidence through torture or inhuman treatment, but should also be proactive in preventing illegal collection of evidence to ensure any institution or individual committing torture or inhuman treatment receives criminal sanction.

The Court has defined torture as 'deliberate inhuman treatment causing very serious and cruel suffering' and has found that torture had occurred in numerous cases, all involving physical and sometimes mental ill-treatment by state agents.[37] In the case of *Aksoy v. Turkey*, the Court found that torture had occurred when the applicant's arms were paralyzed after he had been stripped naked and suspended by his arms which were tied behind his back.[38] The accumulation of acts of physical and mental violence may also amount to torture as was the case in *Aydin v. Turkey*, where a seventeen-year-old girl was detained by security forces and raped by an unidentified person, kept blindfolded and beaten during questioning, spun in a tyre under water pressure and paraded naked.[39] The same threshold was applied in the case of *Selmouni v. France* where the applicant had been beaten in police custody, called upon to perform oral sex with a police officer, urinated upon when he refused to do so and threatened with a blow lamp and a syringe.[40]

Inhuman treatment contrary to Article 3 ECHR must according to the Court 'attain a minimum level of severity' which means that less intense suffering may amount to inhuman treatment than in the case of torture.[41] It must 'cause either actual bodily harm or intense physical or mental suffering' and another difference with torture is, that inhuman treatment needs not be *intended* to cause suffering.[42] Mental suffering by itself has been found

---

[37]   See the Overview of 50 Years of Activity, The European Court of Human Rights, Some Facts and Figures, that can be accessed on the ECHR website <www.ehrc.coe.int>, p. 15. In the period of 1959-2009 in 56 cases the prohibition of torture was violated.

[38]   ECtHR 18 December 1996, *Aksoy v. Turkey*, no. 21987/93.

[39]   ECtHR 25 September 1997, *Aydin v. Turkey*, no. 23178/94; see also ECtHR 24 January 2008, *Maslova & Nalbandov v. Russia*, no. 839/02.

[40]   ECtHR 28 July 1998, *Selmouni v. France*, no. 25803/94.

[41]   According to the Overview of 50 Years of Activity, The European Court of Human Rights, Some Facts and Figures, that can be accessed on the ECHR website <www.ehrc.coe.int>, p. 15. In the period of 1959-2009 in 607 cases of inhuman and/or degrading treatment or punishment was established.

[42]   ECtHR 18 January 1978, *Ireland v. The United Kingdom*, no. 5310/71.

sufficient in several cases.[43] One example of inhuman treatment was the case of *Jalloh v. Germany*[44] where an emetic was forcibly administered to the applicant, causing him to regurgitate a drug bubble which he had swallowed and which was consequently used as the main evidence against him in criminal proceedings for a drug dealing offence. Since the emetic was administered forcibly by a tube, which must have caused pain and anxiety, the Court held that this amounted to inhuman and degrading treatment contrary to Article 3.

3.2. THE OBLIGATION TO INVESTIGATE AND THE BURDEN OF PROOF

In its case law the ECtHR has not only defined torture and inhuman and degrading treatment, but also set procedural standards that should be applied when allegations of torture or inhuman and/or degrading treatment are made.

Firstly, Article 3 imposes a procedural obligation on the State to investigate allegations of a breach of this article and to provide an effective remedy in response to an arguable claim of ill-treatment.[45] This requires an effective official investigation that will be thorough and 'capable of leading to the identification and punishment of those responsible'.[46] The investigation must be launched *ex officio* and the person conducting the investigation must be independent of those implicated. Police officers responsible must be punished and imposition of lenient sentences may not fulfil the requirements. When the obligation to investigate has not been adequately met, this in itself constitutes a violation of Article 3 ECHR.[47]

Secondly, the burden of proof may be reversed in cases of assault during police detention. Although the applicant must first provide medical or other evidence as to the injuries claimed to have occurred, once there are proven injuries, it is for the State to show that no force was used by the police or that the force that was used was not excessive.[48] An example where this burden of

---

[43] ECtHR 18 June 2002, *Orhan v. Turkey*, no. 25656/94; ECtHR 16 November 2000, *Bilgin v. Turkey*, no. 23819/94.

[44] ECtHR 11 July 2006, *Jalloh v. Germany*, no. 54810/00, paras. 94-96.

[45] This was first identified in ECtHR 28 October 1998, *Assenov and others v. Bulgaria*, no. 24760/94.

[46] ECtHR 28 October 1998, *Assenov and others v. Bulgaria*, no. 24760/94.

[47] In the period of 1959-2009 in 190 cases a violation of Art. 3 was found because of a lack of effective investigation. See the Overview of 50 Years of Activity, The European Court of Human Rights, Some Facts and Figures, that can be accessed on the ECHR website <www.ehrc.coe.int>, p. 15.

[48] See ECtHR 4 December 1995, *Ribitsch v. Austria*, no. 18896/91. According to the applicant, the officers questioning him grossly insulted him and then assaulted him repeatedly in order

→

proof was not met by the State is in the case of *Rehbock v. Slovenia* where the applicant, suspected of drug dealing while crossing a border, suffered a broken jaw when being arrested by thirteen policemen. The Court took into account that the police had time to plan the arrest; that the applicant had not resisted arrest; that the government's claim that the injuries had occurred when the applicant fell against a car was not credible and that there had been no arguments or evidence put forward that the force used was justified.[49]

3.3. EXCLUSION OF EVIDENCE OBTAINED IN BREACH OF ARTICLE 3 ECHR – THE GÄFGEN CASE

The ECtHR takes the stand that evidence obtained by means that amount to a breach of Article 3 ECHR always raises serious issues as to the fairness of the proceedings, even if the admission of such evidence was not decisive in securing a conviction.[50] The Court has held, in several judgments, that confessions obtained as a result of torture or other forms of ill-treatment render the proceedings as a whole unfair, irrespective of the probative value of the statements.[51] The latest case handled by the Court concerning the exclusion of evidence obtained by torture or inhuman or degrading treatment was the case of *Gäfgen v. Germany*. It has spurred dissenting views in the Grand Chamber of the Court, as well as in Germany itself. One of the main questions the Court had to answer was whether evidence obtained by an act classified as inhuman and degrading treatment, but falling short of torture, always render a trial unfair or, in other words, to what extent is there an absolute obligation to exclude such evidence.

The facts of the Gäfgen case can be summarised as follows. Gäfgen, a 27 year old law student, was sentenced to life imprisonment in Germany for the

---

to wring a confession from him. He received punches to the head (*Kopfnuß*), kidneys and right arm and kicks to the upper leg and kidneys. He was pulled to the ground by the hair and his head was banged against the floor. Ninety per cent of his injuries were inflicted by blows from Police Officer Markl. When released he had bruises on his right arm and one thigh and suffered from a cervical syndrome, vomiting, diarrhoea and a violent headache.

[49] ECtHR 28 November 2000, *Rehbock v. Slovenia*, no. 29462/95; see also ECtHR 12 July 2007, *Vasilef v. Bulgaria*, no. 48130/99.

[50] See ECtHR 15 January 2004, *İçöz v. Turkey*, no. 54919/00; ECtHR 11 July 2006, *Jalloh v. Germany*, no. 54810/00, paras. 99 and 104; ECtHR 17 October 2006, *Göçmen v. Turkey*, no. 72000/01, paras. 73-74 and ECtHR 28 June 2007, *Harutyunyan v. Armenia*, no. 36549/03, para. 63.

[51] See ECtHR 15 January 2004, *İçöz v. Turkey*, no. 54919/00; ECtHR 11 July 2006, *Jalloh v. Germany*, no. 54810/00, paras. 99 and 104; ECtHR 17 October 2006, *Göçmen v. Turkey*, no. 72000/01, paras. 73-74 and ECtHR 28 June 2007, *Harutyunyan v. Armenia*, no. 36549/03, para. 63.

abduction and murder of J. a child, aged 11 and the youngest son of a well-known banking family in Frankfurt am Main. Gäfgen, who was acquainted with J.'s sister lured J. into his flat by pretending that J.'s sister had left a jacket there. He then suffocated the child. Subsequently, Gäfgen deposited a ransom demand at J.'s parents' home, requiring them to pay one million Euros to see their child again. He abandoned the child's corpse under the jetty of a pond one hour's drive away from Frankfurt. After collecting the ransom Gäfgen was placed under police surveillance and was arrested several hours later. During interrogation by the police he refused to give details of the whereabouts of J. and pretended that J. was still alive. The police officers responsible for questioning Gäfgen, on the instructions of the Deputy Chief of Frankfurt Police, warned the applicant that he would face considerable suffering if he persisted in refusing to disclose the child's whereabouts. They considered that threat necessary as they assumed J.'s life to be in great danger from lack of food and exposure to the cold. As a result of those threats, the applicant disclosed where he had hidden the child. Following that confession, the police drove to the pond together with the applicant and secured the child's body and further evidence, notably the tyre tracks of the applicant's car at the pond, and the corpse. The German courts decided that all his confessions made throughout the investigation could not be used as evidence at trial as they had been obtained under duress, in breach of Article 136a of the CCP and Article 3 of the ECHR. Despite the fact that Gäfgen had been informed at the beginning of the trial of his right to remain silent and that all his earlier statements could not be used as evidence against him, he nevertheless again confessed at trial that he had kidnapped and killed J. The court's findings of facts concerning the crime were essentially based on that confession. However, the courts did, in addition, allow the use in the criminal proceedings of the material evidence obtained as a result of the statements extracted from the applicant under duress, namely the autopsy report and the tyre tracks at the pond.

Gäfgen complained to the ECtHR that he had been subjected to torture when questioned by the police, in violation of Article 3. Relying on Article 6, he further submitted that his right to a fair trial had been violated in particular by the use of evidence secured as a result of his confession obtained under duress. The case was referred to the Grand Chamber of the ECtHR. First the Court held that Gäfgen was threatened with torture in order to make him disclose J.'s whereabouts and that this method of interrogation constituted inhuman treatment as prohibited by Article 3. In its general observations the Court repeats its earlier case law that 'incriminating real evidence obtained as a result of acts of violence, at least if those acts had to be characterised as torture, should never be relied on as proof of the victim's guilt, irrespective of its probative value. Any other conclusion would only serve to legitimise, indirectly, the sort of morally reprehensible conduct which the authors of Article 3 of the Convention sought to proscribe or, in other words, to "afford brutality the cloak of law"'.[52] The Court also repeated that 'both the use in criminal proceedings of statements obtained as a result of a person's treatment in breach of Article 3 – irrespective of the classification of that treatment as torture or inhuman or degrading treatment – and the use of real evidence obtained as a direct result of acts of torture make the proceedings as a whole automatically unfair, in breach of Article 6'. The Court also stressed that because of the fact that Article 3 enshrines an absolute right, there can be no weighing of other interests against it, such as the seriousness of the offence or the public interest in effective criminal prosecution, or the stressful situation the police officers were in, in the Gäfgen case, attempting to safe a child's life. Nevertheless the Court held by eleven votes to six that there had been no violation of Article 6(1) and (3) of the Convention on the grounds that the German courts had excluded the guilty confession extracted by threats. As the main basis for Gäfgens conviction was his voluntary guilty confession made during the trial proceedings, the Court considered the real evidence that was found as a result of the confession made under threats (the autopsy report and the tyre tracks at the pond) to not have a bearing on Gäfgens conviction and sentence.[53]

The Court's decision in the Gäfgen case is clearly a compromise in order to strike a balance between the interests at stake. The Court notices that there is no clear consensus among the Contracting States about the exact scope of application of the exclusionary rule, especially if evidence is more remote from the breach of Article 3 than evidence extracted immediately as a consequence of a violation of this provision. The Court mentions in particular whether it would have to weigh a situation where the impugned evidence would in any event have been found at a later stage, independently of the prohibited acts of the police officers. Six out of 17 judges of the Grand Chamber dissented with the opinion of the majority and stated that the admission into criminal proceedings of any evidence obtained in violation of Article 3 raises fundamental questions of principle. They regret that the Court has not 'answered that question categorically by asserting, in an unequivocal manner that irrespective of the conduct of an accused, fairness, for the purpose of Article 6, presupposes respect for the rule of law and requires, as a self-evident proposition, the exclusion of any evidence that has been obtained in violation of Article 3. A criminal trial which admits and relies, to any

---

[52] Para. 167.
[53] ECtHR 1 June 2010, *Gäfgen v. Germany*, no. 22978/05.

extent, upon evidence obtained as a result of breaching such an absolute provision of the Convention cannot a fortiori be a fair one. The Court's reluctance to cross that final frontier and to establish a clear or "bright-line" rule in this core area of fundamental human rights is regrettable'.

Nevertheless the Court takes a firm position that investigators in State parties in the frame of Article 3 are absolutely prohibited to collect and secure evidence by torture or other ill-treatment. With regard to evidence obtained by inhuman or degrading treatment, that is assessed in the context of Article 6 ECHR's fair trial, the court allows the States to consider the procedure of evidence collection in a comprehensive way, as well as the other evidence, to weigh the degree of oppression the defendant was subjected to and the voluntariness of his confession. If the evidence obtained by a breach of Article 3 has a bearing on the outcome, according to the threshold the Court has set in the Gäfgen case, the procedure would be deemed unfair and the evidence should be excluded. The question however remains, how evidence secured in breach of Article 3 and thereafter admitted into trial, can be regarded as having no bearing upon the outcome of the proceedings.

3.4. THE EXCLUSION OF EVIDENCE OBTAINED IN VIOLATION OF ARTICLE 6 OF THE ECHR

Article 6 of the ECHR is designed to safeguard a person's right to fair trial. It offers a list of basic procedural rights (including presumption of innocence) to which everyone is entitled in criminal proceedings.[54] As this provision covers

---

[54] Art. 6:

1. In the determination of his civil rights and obligations or of any criminal charge against him, everyone is entitled to a fair and public hearing within a reasonable time by an independent and impartial tribunal established by law. Judgment shall be pronounced publicly by the press and the public may be excluded from all or part of the trial in the interest of morals, public order or national security in a democratic society, where the interests of juveniles or the protection of the private life of the parties so require, or the extent strictly necessary in the opinion of the court in special circumstances where publicity would prejudice the interests of justice.

2. Everyone charged with a criminal offence shall be presumed innocent until proved guilty according to law.

3. Everyone charged with a criminal offence has the following minimum rights:

(a) to be informed promptly, in a language which he understands and in detail, of the nature and cause of the accusation against him;

(b) to have adequate time and the facilities for the preparation of his defence;

(c) to defend himself in person or through legal assistance of his own choosing or, if he has not sufficient means to pay for legal assistance, to be given it free when the interests of justice so require;

→

a wide range of rights, defendants subjected to illegal collection of evidence often claim their right to fair trial has been violated on the grounds that the guilty verdict was based on illegally obtained evidence and thus demand for exclusion of such evidence. However in *Bykov v. Russia*,[55] the Court emphasized in its decision that its obligation is merely to ensure that State parties comply with the Convention and that it is not the Court's responsibility to deal with wrong application of law by the domestic court, unless such defect may violate the basic rights and liberties safeguarded in the Convention. Article 6 provides for the right to fair trial without addressing the admissibility of evidence and it is established case law of the Court that the admissibility of evidence should be regulated by domestic laws.[56] It is therefore not the role of the Court to determine, as a matter of principle, whether particular types of evidence – for example, evidence obtained unlawfully in terms of domestic law – may be admissible or, indeed, whether the applicant was guilty or not. The question which must be answered is whether the proceedings as a whole, including the way in which the evidence was obtained, were fair. This involves an examination of the 'unlawfulness' in question and, where a violation of another Convention right is concerned, the nature of the violation found. In determining whether the proceedings as a whole were fair, regard must also be had to whether the rights of the defence were respected.[57] In particular, whether or not the applicant was given the opportunity of challenging the authenticity of the evidence and of opposing its use must be examined. In addition, the quality of the evidence must be taken into consideration, including whether the circumstances in which it was obtained cast doubt on its reliability or accuracy.

In practice, cases in which the appellant's procedural rights prescribed in Article 6 are violated and the evidence obtained as such is excluded are diverse and complex. For example, evidence may be excluded due to the

---

(d) to examine or have examined witnesses against him and to obtain the attendance and examination of witnesses on his behalf under the same conditions as witnesses against him;

(e) to have the free assistance of an interpreter if he cannot understand or speak the language used in court.

[55] ECtHR 10 March 2009, *Bykov v. Russia*, no. 4378/02.

[56] ECtHR 12 July 1988, *Schenk v. Switzerland*, no. 10862/84, para. 45; ECtHR 9 June 1998, *Teixeira de Castro*, no.25829/94, para. 34 and ECtHR 11 July 2006, *Jalloh v. Germany*, no. 54810/00, paras. 94-96.

[57] ECtHR 25 September 2001, *P.G. and J.H. v. the United Kingdom*, no. 44787/98, para. 76; ECtHR 1 March 2007, *Heglas v. The Czech Republic*, no. 5935/02, paras. 89-92 and ECtHR 5 November 2002, *Allan v. The United Kingdom*, no. 48539/99, para. 42.

illegal use of covert investigation by the investigation units.[58] In *Allan v. the United Kingdom*, the police officers conducted covert investigation in the detention centre while the Court took the view that the suspect was extremely vulnerable and the covert investigation was oppressive. As a result, it ruled that all evidence should be excluded.

A recent development dealing with exclusion of evidence can be found in the Court's case law regarding the access of a suspect to a lawyer before and during interrogation by the police. In a landmark case *Salduz v. Turkey*,[59] the ECtHR established that in order for the Article 6 right to a fair trial to remain sufficiently 'practical and effective', Article 6(1) must be interpreted as requiring that access to a lawyer should as a rule be provided as from the first interrogation of a suspect by the police, unless it is demonstrated in the light of the particular circumstances of the case that there are compelling reasons to restrict this right. Even where compelling reasons may exceptionally justify denial of access to a lawyer, such restriction – whatever its justification – must not unduly prejudice the rights of the accused under Article 6.

Furthermore the judgment implicitly contains an exclusionary rule because the Court has held that the lack of legal assistance during a suspect's interrogation would constitute a restriction of his defence rights and that these rights will in principle be irretrievably prejudiced when incriminating statements, made during police interrogation without access to a lawyer, are used for a conviction.

The Salduz principle has been reaffirmed in subsequent cases.[60] In the case of *Sebalj v. Croatia* the Court confirmed that the right to legal assistance does include the right to have a defence lawyer present during the police interview.[61] Moreover, in the case of *Dayanan v. Turkey* the Court ruled that the right to legal assistance at the pre-trial stage does not refer only to police interrogation, but 'the whole range of services specifically associated with legal assistance', including, among other things, the defence lawyer's unrestricted ability to: prepare the accused's defence; support an accused in distress, and check the conditions of the accused's detention.

Until now more than 100 judgments have confirmed the so called Salduz doctrine: It comprises the following elements: 1. the right to consult a lawyer

---

[58]   ECtHR 5 February 2008, *Ramanauskas v. Lithuenia*, no. 74420/01; ECtHR 26 October 2006, *Khudobin v. Russia*, no. 59696/00 and ECtHR 5 November 2002, *Allan v. The United Kingdom*, no. 48539/99.

[59]   ECtHR 27 November 2008, *Salduz v. Turkey*, no. 36391/02.

[60]   ECtHR 11 December 2008, *Panovits v. Cyprus*, no. 4268/04; ECtHR 24 September 2009, *Pishchalnikov v. Russia*, no. 7025/04; ECtHR 13 October 2009, *Dayanan v. Turkey*, 7377/03 and ECtHR 5 January 2010, *Diallo v. Sweden*, no. 13205/07.

[61]   ECtHR 28 June 2011, *Sebalj v. Croatia*, no. 4429/09.

before the first police interrogation; 2. the right to have a lawyer present during police interrogation; 3.exclusion of statements (confessions) made by the suspect when the rights under 1 and 2 are violated with application of the fruits of the poisonous tree; 4. the right to be informed of these rights. A waiver is possible but must be absolutely voluntary and based on the suspect being well-informed of the consequences, and a waiver is not possible in case of a juvenile or vulnerable suspect (for example low IQ) without having consulted a lawyer. The Salduz-doctrine has lead to amendments of the French, Scottish, Belgian and Dutch codes of criminal procedure and practice that did not allow access to legal assistance in the phase of police interrogation before the Salduz judgment, demonstrating the tremendous impact of the ECtHR and the ECHR on domestic criminal proceedings in Europe.[62]

4. CONCLUSION

We have examined how the exclusionary rule is applied in the Netherlands and the jurisprudence of the ECtHR. Under the influence of the case law of the ECtHR it can be said that European countries share a common philosophy and value proposition of human rights protection whatever procedural model – inquisitorial or adversarial – they are built upon. In terms of applying the exclusionary rule, it is hard to identify any distinctive difference between the various criminal law systems in the scope and the decision-making pattern, which may be explained by a common support system, which fits well with the objective of seeking truth.

The exclusionary rule across Europe is generally defined by procedural codes and case law that allow for absolute exclusion of evidence when fundamental human rights are violated, such as the prohibition of torture and inhuman or degrading treatment and a discretionary exclusion model if the investigation upon a citizen's procedural rights such as the right to fair trial in Article 6 of the ECHR. In addition, we have seen from the example of the Netherlands that there are many ways to deal with illegally obtained

---

[62] See for France: LOI n° 2011-392 du 14 avril 2011 relative à la garde à vue, JORF n°0089 du 15 avril 2011; Scotland: UKSC 2010 43, 20 October 2010, *Cadder v. Her Majesty's Advocate* and the Criminal Procedure (Legal Assistance, Detention and Appeals) (Scotland) Bill (SP Bill 60) as introduced in the Scottish Parliament on 26 October 2010; Belgium: Loi modifiant le Code d'instruction criminelle et la loi du 20 juillet 1990 relative à la détention préventive afin de conférer des droits, don celui de consulter un avocat et d'être assistée par lui et à toute personne privé de liberté, *Moniteur Belge* 5 septembre 2011, no. 56347. In the Netherlands a legislative proposal to amend the Dutch Criminal Procedure in accordance with the Salduz Judgment has been forwarded for consultation.

evidence, other than exclusion, such as sentence reduction and dismissal of prosecution. These characteristics demonstrate a combination of principles and flexibility by attaining both procedural justice and procedural efficiency.

It would however have been impossible for European countries to deal with the exclusionary rule in a robust manner without external and internal mechanisms within the criminal proceedings providing support and safeguards. At the heart of such a structure is the common pursuit of the rule of law. The following conditions must be met in order to make the exclusionary rule work properly and effectively:

1. The law must provide detailed and pragmatic substantive and procedural rules on the exclusion of illegally obtained evidence. 'Detailed' means that a country's procedure code and case law should be explicit about the scope, the method and the consequence of exclusion. 'Pragmatic' means that the exclusionary rule should be consistent with the country's criminal justice system. The exclusion stage, procedure and relevant procedural requirements set forth in the procedure code must be implementable.
2. The exclusionary rule is very complex and technical. The implementation requires the full protection of the rights of the defence including the suspect's right to legal assistance and admitting the lawyer to defend his client effectively at all stages of criminal proceedings.
3. The exclusionary rule must be endorsed by judicial practitioners. In particular where tension exists between the task of investigation and prosecution and the exclusion of evidence by the court, the success of the exclusionary rule boils down to whether the police officer and the prosecutor respect the judge's decision and whether they can refrain from resorting to measures outside the procedural system to interfere with a judicial trial and exert pressure on the judge.

BIBLIOGRAPHY

BEIJER, COBLEY & KLIP 1995
BEIJER, A., COBLEY, C. & KLIP, A., 'Witness Evidence, Article 6 of the European Convention on Human Rights and the Principle of Open Justice', in: C. HARDING, P. FENNELL, N. JÖRG & B. SWART (eds.), *Criminal Justice in Europe: A Comparative Study*, Oxford: Clarendon Press, 1995, p. 283-300.

BORGERS & STEVENS 2010
BORGERS, M.J. & STEVENS, L., 'The Use of Illegally Gathered Evidence in the Dutch Criminal Trial', *Electronic Journal of Comparative Law*, 2010, p. 1-21.

ELLISON 1998
ELLISON, L., 'The Protection of Vulnerable Witnesses in Court: An Anglo-Dutch Comparison', *Journal of Evidence and Proof*, 1998, p. 29-43.

HARRIS, O'BOYLE & WARBRICK 2009
HARRIS, D.J., O'BOYLE, M. & WARBRICK, C., *Law of the European Convention on Human Rights*, Oxford: Oxford University Press, 2009.

KEMPEN VAN 2009
KEMPEN, P.H.P.H.M.C., VAN, 'The Protection of Human Rights in Criminal Law Procedure in the Netherlands', *Electronic Journal of Comparative Law*, 2009, p. 1-37.

LANG SHENG & XIONG XUANGUO 2003
LANG SHENG & XIONG XUANGUO, *Initial Observation and Comparison of Dutch Judicial Institutions*, China Law Press, 2003.

NIJBOER 1992
NIJBOER, J.F., 'The Law of Evidence in Criminal Cases (The Netherlands)', in: J.F. NIJBOER, C.R. CALLEN & N. KWAK (eds.), *Forensic Expertise and the Law of Evidence*, Amsterdam: Elsevier, 1992, p. 63-66.

TAK 2009
TAK, P.J.P., *The Dutch Criminal Justice System: Organization and Operation*, Nijmegen: Wolf Legal Publishers, 2009.

THAMAN 2010
THAMAN, S.C., '"Fruits of the Poisonous Tree" in Comparative Law', *Southwestern Journal of International Law*, 2010, p. 333-384.

TONRY & BIJLEVELD 2007
TONRY, M. & BIJLEVELD, C., 'Crime, Criminal Justice and Criminology in the Netherlands', *Crime and Justice*, 2007, p. 1-30.

3. A SUMMARY OF THE EXCLUSIONARY RULE OF ILLEGALLY OBTAINED EVIDENCE IN CHINA

Chen Weidong and Chai Yufeng

1. LEGAL SOURCES FOR THE EXCLUSIONARY RULE IN CHINA

Lawmakers around the world seek to strike a balance between the punishment of criminals and the protection of human rights when designing and drafting criminal procedure regulations. China is no exception. Article 1 of the Criminal Procedure Law (CPL) states: 'This Law is enacted in accordance with the Constitution and for the purpose of ensuring correct enforcement of the Criminal Law, punishing crimes, protecting the people, safeguarding State and public security and maintaining socialist public order'. Article 2 adds that 'the aim of the CPL of the PRC is to ensure accurate and timely ascertainment of facts about crimes, correct application of law, punishment of criminals, and protection of the innocent against being investigated for criminal responsibility'. Balance signifies a form of unity between opposites. Therefore, in order to strike a balance between the punishment of criminals and the protection of human rights, efforts must be made to manage their opposing but unified relationship. The reason is two-fold. At one end, penalizing criminals means that investigators should uncover facts about crimes in a timely and accurate manner and fully collect and secure criminal evidence by following procedures specified by the CPL. But in practice, due to the complexity of cases and the time pressure in solving them, investigators often use the least costly but most efficient ways of investigation, which tend to infringe upon the basic rights of criminal suspects such as resorting to the extortion of confessions by torture during interrogations. At the other end, the protection of human rights requires public institutions to offer the maximum respect for and protection of the fundamental rights of citizens. In particular, they should refrain from treating suspects as objects under investigation. They should not collect evidence and obtain clues by violating personal rights, human dignity, privacy and property rights of suspects or defendants. The overlap of the two areas in criminal justice is the area of evidence, that is, the issue of whether evidence obtained by investigators through unlawful means is admissible in court. In order to address this issue, different countries have developed rules on the exclusion of evidence, with their own characteristics, summarised as 'The Exclusionary Rule'.

Both theorists and practitioners in China take this issue very seriously. Relevant discussions have been closely tied to the amendment of the CPL. Thanks to continuous efforts, from identifying whether there is a need to define illegally obtained evidence and to establish an exclusionary rule at the outset, to holding detailed discussions on particulars such as scope, approach and procedure, the launch of the 'Two Evidence Rules' (Two Rules) and the revision of the CPL, a framework for the exclusionary rule has taken shape in China. The strict exclusion of oral evidence and discretionary exclusion of physical evidence obtained as a result of using unlawful means of interrogation or investigation are the main features of the new approach. Admittedly, this framework looks rudimentary when compared with the Western common law and civil law countries. That said, given that it is rooted in China's criminal justice practice, and based on a consensus drawn from academic research findings, it will make its mark on the global development of the exclusionary rule. Furthermore, it highlights the progress China has made in criminal justice and the protection of human rights. Therefore, before getting down to the study, it is necessary to first introduce and describe the background and basic framework of China's exclusionary rule.

1.1. SOURCES OF INTERNATIONAL LAW

Owing to its special function in striking a balance between the punishment of criminals and the protection of human rights in criminal proceedings, the exclusionary rule is not only widely accepted around the world, but also reflected in the United Nations conventions on criminal procedure. It has in fact become a common currency of the international criminal justice system. However, the Constitution of China is not clear about the applicability of international law to domestic law. In reality, there are different practices; some international treaties are applied directly, some are implemented in parallel with domestic ones whilst others are converted into domestic law. In general, international treaties prevail when they conflict with domestic provisions in the field of civil and commercial law; otherwise, the applicability is based on the specific situation.

Simply put, criminal courts in China cannot exclude evidence by directly invoking provisions from international treaties. Nevertheless the provisions in relevant international declarations and conventions provide valuable guidance for China's criminal legislation, judicial practice and theoretical study.

Adopted by the General Assembly of the United Nations on 10 December 1948, the Universal Declaration of Human Rights is the first pledge made by the UN to protect human rights and civil liberty worldwide. It is not an international treaty, nor does it have the legal effect of international law. But, as a permanent member of the UN Security Council, it is natural for China to observe the Declaration. For example, Articles 3 to 12 of the Declaration, concerning the right to life, liberty, privacy and fair trial, provide macro-level guidance for the exclusionary rule in China.

The Convention against Torture and Other Cruel, Inhuman or Degrading Treatment or Punishment was adopted by the General Assembly of the United Nations in December 1984. China signed the Convention on 12 December 1986 while stating its reservations to Article 28 and Article 31(1). It ratified the Convention on 4 October 1988. The Convention came into effect in China on 3 November of the same year. Article 1 of the Convention defines the concept of torture.[1] Article 15 states: 'Each State Party shall ensure that any statement which is established to have been made as a result of torture shall not be invoked as evidence in any proceedings, except against a person accused of torture as evidence that the statement was made'. This article is directly relevant to the treatment of oral evidence in the exclusion of illegally obtained evidence.

The International Covenant on Civil and Political Rights was adopted by the General Assembly of the United Nations in 1966. China signed it on 5 October 1998 but it has still not come into effect. The Covenant also addresses many fundamental civil rights in criminal procedure. For example, Article 7 reaffirms the basic spirit of the Convention against Torture and

---

[1] 'Torture' means any act by which severe pain or suffering, whether physical or mental, is intentionally inflicted on a person for such purposes as obtaining from him or a third person information or a confession, punishing him for an act he or a third person has committed or is suspected of having committed, or intimidating or coercing him or a third person, or for any reason based on discrimination of any kind, when such pain or suffering is inflicted by or at the instigation of or with the consent or acquiescence of a public official or other person acting in an official capacity. It does not include pain or suffering arising only from, inherent in or incidental to lawful sanctions.

Other Cruel, Inhuman or Degrading Treatment or Punishment.[2] Article 17 emphasizes the protection of the universal right to privacy.[3] Paragraph 3 of Article 14 is particularly relevant to the exclusion of illegally-obtained oral evidence, stating that, 'in the determination of any criminal charge against him', no one must 'be compelled to testify against himself or to confess guilt'.

All these international conventions and treaties have affected the legislative process in China. For example, Article 50 in the new CPL complies with Article 14 of the ICCPR and states that no person may be forced to prove his or her own guilt. Also, in the interpretation of the new CPL published by the National People's Congress (NPC), the understanding of 'extort confessions by torture' in Article 54 follows The Convention against Torture and Other Cruel, Inhuman or Degrading Treatment or Punishment.[4]

1.2. SOURCES OF DOMESTIC LAW

The Constitution, criminal procedure law and actual cases generally are the sources for the exclusionary rule in both common law and civil law countries, where the Constitution provides a list of fundamental rights of citizens, against which the act of illegal collection of evidence is a direct violation. Criminal procedure law should, in addition to having provisions for the admissibility and assessment of evidence, also serve as the 'security net' of the Constitution as these two are intimately related. Furthermore, representative cases ruled by courts concerning exclusion help shape a country's exclusionary rule to make it fit its criminal justice system. Such cases help to achieve a balance between penalizing criminals and protecting human rights in a dynamic manner.

In China however, the exclusionary rule mainly originates from the CPL, judicial interpretations issued by the Supreme People's Court and the Supreme People's Procuratorate, and the Two Rules issued by five judicial agencies in 2010. Although the Constitution provides for the fundamental rights enjoyed by all Chinese citizens only the NPC and its Standing Committee have the power to interpret the Constitution. A judge can neither interpret the Constitution and the law nor cite the Constitution as the basis

---

[2]   No one shall be subjected to torture or to cruel, inhuman or degrading treatment or punishment. In particular, no one shall be subjected without his free consent to medical or scientific experimentation.

[3]   No one shall be subjected to arbitrary or unlawful interference into his privacy, family, home or correspondence, nor to unlawful attacks on his honour and reputation. Everyone has the right to the protection of the law against such interference or attacks.

[4]   LANG SHENG 2011, p. 124.

for assessing evidence, determining guilt and sentencing in a criminal trial.[5] Furthermore, as China does not have a case law system, the Supreme People's Court is dependent on judicial interpretations to interpret the exclusionary rule in an abstract manner.

1.3. FUNDAMENTAL CIVIL RIGHTS PROTECTED BY THE CONSTITUTION

Though the Constitution cannot be directly invoked in criminal trials, it provides the basic rights enjoyed by criminal suspects in criminal procedure as it sets the boundaries of fundamental civil rights. For example, Article 37 of the Constitution states that any citizen's personal freedom is inviolable;[6] Article 38 specifies that the personal dignity of citizens is inviolable;[7] Article 39 says that the home of citizens is inviolable;[8] Article 40 specifies that the freedom and privacy of correspondence of citizens are protected by law.[9] In addition, the amendments to the Constitution showcase the progress China has made in the protection of human rights. For example, the 1999 Amendment added the clause – 'the PRC exercises the rule of law and builds a socialist country governed according to law' to the Constitution. In the 2004 Amendment, 'the State respects and guarantees human rights' was included in the Constitution. However, there is no provision in the Constitution specifically addressing criminal law or criminal procedure law.

---

[5]   See 'the Supreme People's Court's Reply regarding Inappropriate Citation of the Constitution as Basis for Determining Guilt and Sentencing' (30 July 1955).

[6]   Art. 37: 'The personal freedom of citizens of the PRC is inviolable. No citizen may be arrested except with the approval or by decision of a people's procuratorate or by decision of a people's court, and arrests must be made by the public security authorities. Unlawful deprivation or restriction of citizens' personal freedom by detention or other means is prohibited; and unlawful personal searches of citizens is prohibited'.

[7]   Art. 38: 'The personal dignity of citizens of the PRC is inviolable. Insult, libel, false charge or framing directed against citizens by any means is prohibited'.

[8]   Art. 39: 'The home of citizens of the PRC is inviolable. Unlawful search of, or intrusion into, a citizen's home is prohibited'.

[9]   Art. 40: 'The freedom and privacy of correspondence of citizens of the PRC are protected by law. No organization or individual may, on any grounds, infringe upon the freedom and privacy of correspondence of citizens except in cases where, to meet the needs of state security or of investigation into criminal offences, public security or procuratorial bodies are permitted to censor correspondence in accordance with procedures prescribed by law'.

1.4. EVOLUTION OF THE LAW AND RELEVANT JUDICIAL INTERPRETATIONS

Article 43[10] of the 1996 CPL, regarding the collection of evidence, shows no progress or revision compared with the equivalent Article 32[11] in the 1979 law. There is simply a declaration that judges, procurators and investigators must not use unlawful means to collect evidence, but it ignores the questions of what constitutes illegal evidence and how it should be excluded.

To further improve the exclusionary rule, Article 61 of the Interpretations of the Supreme People's Court on Some Issues Concerning the Implementation of the Criminal Procedure Law of the PRC issued in 1998 states clearly that 'it shall be strictly forbidden to collect evidence by unlawful means. Witness testimony, victim statements and defendants' confessions, which are established to have been extorted by torture or collected by threats, enticement, deceit or other unlawful means, cannot be used as the basis for deciding cases.' Article 265 of the 1999 Criminal Litigation Rules for People's Procuratorates issued by the Supreme People's Procuratorate states: 'It shall be strictly forbidden to collect evidence by unlawful means. Testimonies by witnesses, statements from victims and confessions by defendants which are extorted by torture or collected by threats, enticement, deceit or other unlawful means cannot be used as the evidence for filing charges.' These two articles underscored that evidence obtained illegally could not be used as the basis for deciding cases and as evidence for filing charges and thus began to shape the exclusionary rule in China.

1.5. THE TWO EVIDENCE RULES (TWO RULES)

1.5.1. Basic Content and Significance

The Two Rules comprise two sets of provisions, namely, the Provisions on Several Issues Concerning the Examination and Judgment of Evidence in

---

[10]   Art. 43 of the 1997 CPL states: 'Judges, procurators and investigators must, in accordance with the legally prescribed process, collect various kinds of evidence that can prove the guilt or innocence of criminal suspects or defendants and the gravity of the crime. It shall be strictly forbidden to extort confessions by torture and to collect evidence by threats, enticement, deceit or other unlawful means'.

[11]   Art. 32 of the 1979 CPL states: 'Judges, procurators and investigators must, in accordance with the legally prescribed process, collect various kinds of evidence that can prove the guilt or innocence of criminal suspects or defendants and the gravity of the crime. It shall be strictly forbidden to extort confessions by torture and to collect evidence by threats, enticement, deceit or other unlawful means'.

Death Penalty Cases (hereafter 'Provisions on Evidence in Death Penalty Cases') and the Provisions on Several Issues Concerning the Exclusion of Illegal Evidence in Criminal Cases (hereafter 'Provisions on the Exclusion of Illegal Evidence') jointly issued in 2010 by five judicial agencies (the Supreme People's Court, the Supreme People's Procuratorate, the Ministry of Public Security, the Ministry of State Security and the Ministry of Justice). In the history of the development of the criminal procedure system in China, these two documents are the first attempt to establish the exclusionary rule and to identify the scope and procedure for exclusion in the form of a judicial interpretation. They were intended to be implemented in practice and laid a foundation for the revision of the CPL. They therefore represented a big step forward in China's criminal justice system and also reaffirmed the Chinese government's commitment to the elimination of torture in line with the United Nations Convention against Torture.

The Two Rules consist of 56 clauses altogether – the Provisions on Evidence in Death Penalty Cases have 41 while the Provisions on the Exclusion of Illegal Evidence have 15, ten of which are related to the exclusion of illegally obtained evidence.[12] The significance of the Two Rules is twofold.

Firstly, they form the basic rules for criminal evidence in China. In just eight articles Chapter Five of the 1996 CPL describes basic principles such as types of evidence and how the evidence shall be applied, but there are no provisions concerning proof, nor are there any general principles regarding criminal evidence.[13] The Two Rules filled the gap. For example, Article 2 of the Provisions on Evidence in Death Penalty Cases expressly establishes for the first time the principle that judgments must be based on evidence.[14] Articles 3 and 4 establish procedural principles for the verification of evidence and the examination of evidence in court.[15] Such basic principles of criminal evidence are essential to the transformation of the substantive evidence philosophy of the three agencies – police, procuratorate and courts, all of which have, in the customary saying, 'favoured substance over procedure and objective facts over legal facts'. Given China's lack of criminal evidence law and of basic principles relating to evidence within the 1996 CPL, the Two Rules were a crucial development in applying the exclusionary

---

[12] Two Rules: Arts. 3, 12, 14, 18, 19, 22, 27, 28, 34 and 38.

[13] CPL Arts. 42-49.

[14] Art. 2: 'The ascertainment of facts about cases shall be based on evidence'.

[15] Art. 3: 'Judges, procurators and investigators must, in accordance with the legally prescribed process, collect, examine, verify and ascertain evidence in a holistic and objective manner.' Art. 4: 'Only evidence which is established to be true by being presented, identified and questioned in court can be used as the basis for conviction and sentencing'.

rule, particularly as they relate to collection of evidence by the investigating authorities.

Secondly, the Two Rules form the basis for the exclusionary rule in China. Although at the legislative level, their status is inferior to the Criminal Procedure Law, the Rules still apply to all courts, procuratorate and public security authorities. The Two Rules address the need to define which illegal evidence must be excluded. The word 'illegal' does not refer to the inherent attributes of the evidence itself, but to the procedures used by investigators to obtain the evidence; in other words, evidence that has been produced unlawfully is illegal evidence.[16] Illegal evidence may be broadly defined as flawed evidence created by infringing upon the constitutional rights and the general procedural rights of criminal suspects, or by illegal parties, approaches and procedures. Whilst the definition of illegally obtained evidence is commonly accepted internationally, decisions regarding which types of illegal evidence should be excluded depend on the unique circumstances of each country as reflected through regulations and case law.

According to Articles 1, 2 and 15 of the Provisions on the Exclusion of Illegal Evidence,[17] illegal oral evidence obtained by unlawful means such as the extortion of confessions by torture shall be categorically excluded. The exclusion of physical evidence obtained by unlawful means is subject to the judges' discretion. However, when it comes to flawed evidence obtained by minor violations of legal procedure, exclusion is not an option. Instead, investigators are required to rectify the error or provide a reasonable explanation (see Article 7 and 9 of the Provisions on Evidence in Death Penalty Cases).[18] 'Evidence in an illegal "form" (*xingshi*) may lack certain

---

[16] CHEN WEIDONG 2010a.

[17] Art. 1: 'The category of illegal verbal evidence includes statements by criminal suspects or defendants obtained through illegal means such as coerced confession as well as witness testimony or victim statements obtained through illegal means such as use of violence or threats'. Art. 2: 'Verbal evidence that has been determined to be illegal in accordance with the law shall be excluded and may not serve as the basis for conviction'. Art. 15: 'If material or documentary evidence is obtained in a manner that clearly violates the law and may have an impact on the fairness of an adjudication, redress or some reasonable explanation should be made, otherwise that material or documentary evidence may not serve as a basis for conviction'.

[18] Art. 7: 'If traces and objects such as bloodstains, fingerprints, footmarks, handwriting, hair, bodily fluid, and tissue identified in an inquest, examination or search, which may be relevant to the facts of a case, are not collected and tested as they should be, leading to doubts about the facts of the case, the people's court shall explain the situation to the people's procuratorate. The people's procuratorate may, in accordance with law, collect additional evidence, retrieve evidence, and present reasonable explanation, or return it to the investigators for further investigation and retrieval of relevant evidence'. Art. 9: 'Physical evidence and written evidence which is extracted and seized in an inquest, examination or
→

criteria and fail to meet legal requirements, but the collection of such evidence has not violated the subject's rights. Illegally obtained evidence should be treated under the exclusionary rule whereas evidence in an illegal form should be subject to a decision regarding its admissibility'.[19]

Articles 4, 5 and 8 of the Two Rules establish the procedure for excluding illegally obtained evidence at trial. These have now been partly included in the new CPL, as the 1996 CPL lacked any provision for such procedures. Articles 4 and 5 were intended to specifically address the issue of extortion of confessions by torture. Article 4 of the Provisions on the Exclusion of Illegal Evidence states: 'If, between the time that a copy of the indictment has been delivered and the time the trial commences, a defendant alleges that his or her pre-trial confession was obtained illegally, he or she should submit a written motion to the people's court. If the defendant has real difficulties with writing, he or she may make the accusation orally to be recorded by a people's court employee or the defendant's defence counsel, a copy of which the defendant shall sign or affix with his or her thumbprint. The people's court shall deliver the defendant's written motion or record of accusation to the people's procuratorate prior to the commencement of the trial.' Article 5 states: 'If, prior to commencement of the trial or during the trial, a defendant or his or her defence counsel alleges that the defendant's pre-trial confession was obtained illegally, the court should conduct an investigation in court immediately following the prosecutor's recitation of the indictment. If prior to the conclusion of courtroom debate, the defendant or his or her defence counsel alleges that the defendant's pre-trial confession was obtained

---

search and which is without inquest or examination records, search records, extraction records, seizure list, or any proof of its origin, shall not be the basis for conviction. If the procedure and the approach to collect evidence has any of the following flaws, the evidence may be admitted when the relevant investigator makes redress or reasonable explanation: (1) the inquest or examination records, the search records, the extraction records and the seizure list of the collected or retrieved physical evidence and written evidence do not include signatures of the investigator, the owner of the object and the witness, or are not clear about the physical properties, the quantity, the quality and the name of the object; (2) the photo, the video or the copy of the collected and retrieved physical evidence, and the copy or duplicate of the written evidence does not have the note that it is the same as the original, the time of the copy, and the signature (seal) of the person (unit) subject to the collection or retrieval; (3) the photo, the video or the copy of the physical evidence, or the copy or duplicate of the written evidence does not have the producer's illustration about the procedure and whereabouts of the original object or document, or the illustration does not bear the signature; (4) if the procedure or the approach to collect the physical and written evidence has other flaws, or there is suspicion in the origin and collection of such evidence and no reasonable explanation is provided, the evidence cannot be used as the basis for conviction'.

19 YANG YUGUAN 2010.

illegally, the court shall also conduct an investigation'. However, there are no stipulations regarding the conduct of such investigations.

The question of the burden of proof is dealt with in Article 7 which states that, 'If, upon investigation, the court has questions about the legality of the way the defendant's pre-trial confession was obtained, the prosecutor shall provide interrogation transcripts, original audio or video recordings of the interrogation or other evidence and request that the court notify other individuals present at the interrogation or other witnesses to provide testimony before the court. If it is still not possible to eliminate suspicion of coerced confession, the procuratorate shall request that the court notify the interrogator(s) to provide testimony before the court and confirm that the confession was obtained legally. If the prosecutor cannot provide evidence at the time of the hearing, he or she may recommend that the court postpone the trial proceedings in accordance with Article 165 of the CPL. Interrogators or other persons shall testify before the court upon legal notification. If the prosecutor submits an officially sealed [written] explanation that has not been signed or sealed by the interrogator(s) concerned, the document may not serve as evidence that the evidence was obtained legally. Prosecution and defence may cross-examine evidence and carry out debate with regard to the question of whether the defendant's pre-trial confession was obtained legally'.

According to Article 8, 'if the court has questions about the evidence submitted by either the prosecution or defence, it may adjourn the proceedings and conduct investigation and verification of the evidence. If necessary, the court may notify the procurator or defence counsel to be present'. In addition, Article 38 of the Provisions on Evidence in Death Penalty Cases states: 'If the court has questions about the evidence, it may call on the appointed procurator, the defendant or his defence counsel to produce additional evidence or provide an explanation. If it is necessary to conduct verification, [the court] may call a recess in order to investigate and verify evidence. If the court conducts an external investigation outside the courthouse, it may, if necessary, call on the appointed procurator and defense counsel to be present. If either the appointed procurator or the defense counsel or both parties are not present, the court's record shall become part of the case file. The court may solicit opinions from the appointed procurator and defense counsel regarding evidence supplemented by the people's procuratorate or defense counsel or obtained through the court's external investigation and verification. If the two sides are not in agreement and one side requests that the court hold a hearing to investigate, the court shall hold a hearing.

Under the Two Rules, the defendant may allege that his or her confession was obtained illegally at any time from when the copy of the indictment was delivered at least ten days before the trial (Article 151 of 1996 CPL) to prior to the conclusion of the courtroom debate. The 'investigation' called for under the Two Rules is intended to determine whether the defendant's pre-trial confession was made lawfully and is considered an evidence assessment procedure independent of the trial proceedings. Finally, only when the court conducts an investigation into the evidence can the proceedings be adjourned.

1.5.2. Textual Flaws and Deficiencies in the Two Rules

Whilst acknowledging their significance in terms of progress, a close study of the text reveals that the prospects for the Two Rules to be applied in China's complex criminal justice system are not very promising.[20] There are five main reasons.

Firstly, with regard to the exclusion of oral evidence, the Provisions on the Exclusion of Illegal Evidence merely provide that evidence obtained through 'extortion of confessions by torture and other illegal means' shall be excluded, a list much shorter than the one prescribed in Article 43 of the 1996 CPL where there is also mention of 'threats, enticement, deceit', three illegal means other than torture. This will definitely result in confusion in enforcement. Admittedly, defining 'threats, enticement, and deceit' is no easy task. But evading the question will not help resolve the practical problems of dealing with the three illegal means of evidence collection of Article 43 of the 1996 CPL.

Secondly, interpretations in practice may diverge when dealing with extortion of confessions by torture – the most apparent and serious illegal means for gathering evidence. Neither set of provisions provide guidance on what constitutes torture. Generally speaking, torture in China is understood to be limited to extorting evidence by violence and the use of physical force. But, it is widely known that illegal methods used to extort confessions have of late shifted from brazen violence to non-violent 'soft coercion' or 'covert coercion', such as continuous interrogation, forcing detainees to stand out in the cold or the scorching sunshine, or to squat for a long time, and to be deprived of food. It is beyond doubt that such acts, which leave no physical trace, can be interpreted as extortion of confessions by torture. Therefore, torture related provisions in both documents will demand further

---

[20] See however paragraph 3.3 below where is described how the provisions in the new CPL relate to the Two Rules.

interpretation in practice, as they fail to cover all the different practices that may amount to torture.

Thirdly, there are problems regarding the validity and the rationale of the methods that can be used by the procurator to prove the legality of evidence collection. According to Article 7 of the Provisions on the Exclusion of Illegal Evidence,[21] the procurator can use four tools to demonstrate the lawfulness of the interrogation: interrogation transcripts, original audio or video recordings, testimony provided by other individuals present or other witnesses, testimony provided by the interrogator(s), or case explanation. All these four options are problematic, to varying degrees. Interrogation transcripts are prepared by interrogators who could try to minimize procedural lapses and therefore whether or not they can prove the legality of interrogation is questionable. If audio/videotaping the whole process of interrogation is not possible at present, how can audio and video recordings validate the interrogation? Furthermore, any system is run by individuals. We need to focus on how to prevent the situation in which, it is generally alleged, 'people responsible for audio/videotaping choose not to tape when torture takes place and interrogators choose not to torture when tapes are running.' What is the value of the testimony of 'other individuals present at the interrogation or other witnesses' since in normal conditions no one other than investigators are allowed to be present at interrogations? In addition, asking the police officer who is accused of using torture to testify in court whether or not he or she has done so is like fishing in the air – a futile act with questionable validity and meaning. The most questionable tool is the so-called case explanation, which is not a document that conforms to statutory forms of evidence. Academics have long claimed that it is neither fish nor fowl and should not be counted as legal evidence, yet it has now been dressed

---

[21] Art. 7: 'If, upon investigation, the court has questions about the legality of the way the defendant's pre-trial confession was obtained, the prosecutor shall provide interrogation transcripts, original audio or video recordings of the interrogation or other evidence and request that the court notify other individuals present at the interrogation or other witnesses to provide testimony before the court. If it is still not possible to eliminate suspicion of coerced confession, the procuratorate shall request that the court notify the interrogator(s) to provide testimony before the court and confirm that the confession was obtained legally. If the prosecutor cannot provide evidence at the time of the hearing, he or she may recommend that the court postpone the trial proceedings in accordance with Article 165 of the CPL. Interrogators or other persons shall testify before the court upon legal notification. If the prosecutor submits an officially sealed [written] explanation that has not been signed or sealed by the interrogator(s) concerned, the document may not serve as evidence that the evidence was obtained legally. Prosecution and defence may cross-examine evidence and carry out debate with regard to the question of whether the defendant's pre-trial confession was obtained legally'.

up to look like a means of proof. All in all, such provisions are hardly convincing.

Fourthly, the current exclusion procedure requires the defence to provide clues or evidence strong enough to make the judge question the legitimacy of evidence gathered when he or she applies for the exclusion. It is unclear whether the requirement to provide clues is part of the burden of proof, but what is the theoretical basis for the defence to assume a partial burden of proof? Without resolving these issues, the Rules lack a solid foundation and will be hard to implement in practice.

Fifthly, with regard to the exclusion procedure, the Rules demand that special hearings must be held to reach the decision as to whether evidence should be excluded. However, the Rules fail to specify whether such a hearing is part of the trial procedure, the nature of the decision to be taken and whether the decision can be appealed. Without clarification, the procedure is insufficient to ensure comprehensive and accurate implementation of the provisions.[22]

2. JUDICIAL PRACTICE OF THE EXCLUSIONARY RULE IN CHINA

The first part of this chapter gives a brief introduction to the legal framework for the exclusionary rule in China. It is fair to say that the Two Rules issued in 2010 established the basic principles of a modern criminal evidence system at the legislative level. They have also spelled out specific provisions on the exclusion of illegally obtained evidence and put in place a relatively independent procedure. Even with the Two Rules, however, there have been very few cases of successful exclusion in judicial practice, and scholars therefore remain sceptical of the prospects and the vitality of the exclusionary rule. Take for example the scenario where a defendant retracts his confession in court due to illegal collection of evidence. A study suggests: 'most of the 69 surveyed defendants claimed that they confessed because the evidence was obtained illegally, such as extortion of confessions by torture, enticement, deceit or false promise of release. It was also a major reason for the defendants to retract their confessions. Altogether 31 defendants (44.93%) retracted confessions or defended themselves using such allegations of which only those made by 4 defendants in 2 cases were accepted by the courts'.[23]

---

[22] CHEN WEIDONG 2010b.
[23] The study analyzed 42 cases tried by some courts in Gansu (mainly from the second level Railways and Transport Courts in Lanzhou) during 1997 and 2004. These cases are representative as they involve defendants retracting confessions and confirmation of

→

It is therefore understandable that the academic world is rather sceptical. The above data only shows a small sample of cases from the criminal justice system in China. When we take a closer look at real cases in judicial practice, much of the theoretical analysis pales in comparison with the true feel of the gap between criminal legislation and criminal justice. That is why we have decided to devote the following section to several typical cases of exclusion in China some of which were successful and others not. We are confident that with such information readers will develop a more intuitive perception about the current situation concerning the application of the exclusionary rule in China.

2.1. CASES IN WHICH THE EXCLUSION OF ILLEGALLY OBTAINED EVIDENCE FAILED

Case 1: the Case of She Xianglin in Hubei[24]

She Xianglin, a villager in Hechang village, Jingshan county in Hubei province, was arrested by the local police in April 1994. The Public Security Bureau (PSB) suspected him of killing his wife, Zhang Zaiyu who had disappeared four months earlier. Villagers said she suffered intermittent mental psychosis. In the early morning of April 11, a female corpse, decomposed beyond recognition, was found in a pond in a nearby village and the police believed it to be that of Zhang Zaiyu. On 13 October 1994, She was sentenced to death. The Hubei High Court remanded the case for retrial. On 15 June 1998, She was sentenced to 15 years in prison by the Jingshan County People's Court. On 22 September of the same year, the Jingmen Intermediate People's Court rejected his appeal and upheld the original verdict, which was final.

Zhang Zaiyu, who was believed to have been 'killed' by She Xianglin 11 years earlier, suddenly reappeared on 28 March 2005. She's family

---

evidence. Among the 42 cases, 36 were for first trial and 6 were for second trial. 69 defendants retracted their confessions. There were 76 cases of confession retraction. They peaked in 2002 and 2003, 14 in each. The data highlighted that the issue of defendants retracting their confession is getting increasingly serious after the establishment of the prosecution and defense system in criminal trials. These cases involve crimes of robbery, rape, arson, murder, intentional injury, transporting drugs, transporting counterfeit money, theft, corruption, accepting bribes, embezzling public funds, obstructing workers of state organs, sabotaging production and business operation, covering up, and transferring and purchasing booty. See ZHENG GAOJIAN 2009.

[24] See 'The Case of She Xianglin in Hubei – A Miscarriage of Justice and Twists of Fate of A Group of People' <http://www.southcn.com/news/community/fzzh/200504050186.html> accessed 4 August 2011.

immediately reported this to the local police and notified the media. On 13 April 2005, the Jingshan County Court declared She Xianglin not guilty and released him. On 25 May 2005, Pan Yujun, main investigator and deputy head of the 110 Patrol Police Team of Jingshan County PSB, committed suicide. In October 2005, She Xianglin was awarded over 700,000 Rmb in compensation but the officers who carried out the torture were not held criminally responsible.

In his 30-page-long appeal, She Xianglin said, 'I suffered brutal beatings, corporal punishment, torture and enticement continuously for 10 days and nights'. 'After breaking my nose repeatedly, they brutally forced my head into a bathtub, making me choke and almost faint. They asked me to sit in a squatting position and kicked my feet with their leather shoes. The police took turns to interrogate me in groups. They did not let me sleep. My head felt so heavy that I started to see double'. Obviously, the evidence obtained illegally in this case was not excluded.

This is a typical controversial case in which the investigation was overly dependent on a confession and there was clearly extortion by torture. The court finally dealt with the case by making a compromise in sentencing, but refrained from finding the defendant not guilty.[25]

Case 2: the Case of Li Jiuming in Hebei[26]

Early in the morning of 12 July 2002, a masked person broke into a private house and committed murder in addition to inflicting serious injuries on two others in Nanbao Development District in Tangshan City, Hebei province. The Nanbao Branch PSB investigated the case and arrested Li Jiuming, director of the Political Office of No. 2 Team of Jidong Prison, as prime suspect.

From 14 to 24 July 2002, Wang Jianjun, director of the Nanbao Branch, Yang Ce, deputy director of the Nanbao Branch PSB, and their colleagues took Li Jiuming, who was in custody, to the No. 1 Criminal Police Team of Tangshan PSB for interrogation. Ten police officers tied Li's fingers and toes with electrical wires and took turns to repeatedly give him electric shocks through a hand-operated telephone over a long period of time. They forced Li to fabricate a 'murder' story, which he subsequently retracted. Wang Jianjun and Yang Ce then took him from the detention centre to the Yutian County PSB, where they interrogated him continuously for seven days and nights.

---

[25] ZHANG JUN 2010, p. 363.

[26] See 'Three Cases of Severe Infringement on Human Rights Issued by the Supreme Procuratorate', *People's Daily*, 27 July 2005, <http://news.163.com/05/0727/06/-1PL7JK0H0001124S.htm>, accessed 4 August 2011.

They tortured him until he confessed to the murder. In November 2002, Li Jiuming was sentenced with a two year suspended death penalty. But on 8 June 2004, Cai Mingxin, a convict on death row detained in Wenzhou PSB, confessed to the killing in Nanbao in 2002. The Hebei High People's Court remanded the case for retrial in August 2004. It was later confirmed that the real culprit was Cai Mingxin and Li was consequently acquitted and released in November 2004.

In December 2004, the Hejian Municipal People's Procuratorate established cases against Wang Jianjun and 11 other criminal suspects and charges were filed in January 2005. The court found Wang Jianjun and Yang Ce guilty of using torture to extort confessions and sentenced them to two years imprisonment. The other police officers who took part were also punished.

Case 3: the Case of Du Peiwu in Yunnan[27]

On 17 December 1998, the Kunming Intermediate People's Court opened the 'Du Peiwu intentional murder case'. Shortly after the opening of the trial, Du Peiwu showed the court the scars of the injuries he said had been inflicted by the investigators on his wrists, knees and feet. He alleged that he had been subjected to torture and requested the prosecutor to present photos of his injuries which were taken by the detention centre procurator on 29 July 1998. The allegations were however ignored by the court and the request denied.

When the trial reopened on 15 January 1999, Du Peiwu secretly hid a piece of torn clothing under his overcoat from when he had been tortured, with the intention of showing it to the judge. Shortly after the opening of the session, Du raised the issue of torture again and requested that the prosecutor show the photos of his injuries. He finally took out the torn piece of clothing before the judge, the prosecutors, the lawyer and the audience to prove that he had been subjected to torture and that his confession had been extorted by coercion and was therefore invalid according to the Law. The court turned a blind eye to his allegations.

'When handling Du Peiwu's case, the investigators suspended his handcuffed hands from an iron gate, in the shape of the Chinese character for the word big i.e. with outstretched legs and arms. After hanging him for some time, a stool was put under his feet. Whenever Du insisted he was innocent, the stool would be forcefully removed which meant that his body was

---

[27] See 'Seven Culprits of Yang Tianyong Case in Kunming Captured, Du Peiwu Case Redressed' <http://news.sina.com.cn/c/147037.html>, accessed 4 August 2011.

suspended in the air repeatedly. The investigators applied high-voltage batons to Du's toenails and fingers to give him electric shocks and did not allow him to sleep for 20 days. His wrists and ankles rotted and festered. The back of his hands turned dark and became swollen. Du Peiwu was forced to confess to murder'.[28]

Case 4: the Case of Zhao Zuohai in Henan[29]

On 8 May 1999, a man's torso was discovered by some villagers digging a well. They thought it was the body of Zhao Zhenshang who had been missing for some time. The case was brought to the local PSB and Zhao Zuohai, the prime suspect was kept in custody in the detention centre. On 11 November, 2002, the Sangqiu Municipal Procuratorate indicted Zhao, stating that: on the night of 30 October 1997, the defendant Zhao Zuohai was with Ms Du, a woman in the village with whom he was having an affair. They were seen by Zhao Zhenshang, a local villager who had also had an affair with Ms Du. Zhao Zhenshang stabbed the defendant who ran back to Zhao's home and allegedly waited for the victim behind the door with a knife in his hands. When the victim arrived home, the defendant allegedly stabbed him to death, and then dismembered the body before disposing of it. In December 2002, the Sangqiu Intermediate People's Court sentenced Zhao Zuohai to death with a two-year suspended sentence for the murder and deprived him of political rights for life. The Henan High People's Court reviewed the case and upheld the above verdict on 13 February 2003. Zhao did not appeal and was rewarded with sentence reduction twice, in prison. As a result, his sentence was first reduced to life imprisonment and then to 20 years.

On 9 May 2010, the 'victim' Zhao Zhenshang suddenly reappeared at his home. Zhao Zuohai was then acquitted and released. 'In this case, four or five investigators beat Zhao Zuohai daily, feeding him only half a steamed bun and not letting him sleep. They handcuffed Zhao to a bench, kicked him and hit his head with a rolling pin. They even put fireworks above his head to frighten him and pointed a pistol to his head. The investigators threatened him saying that if he did not confess they would kick him out of a car and shoot to kill, making it look like he was trying to make a get away'. He was finally forced to confess.[30]

---

[28]   ZHANG JIANWEI 2010.
[29]   See 'Obvious Doubts in Zhao Zuohai's Case, Negligence of Duty by Police, Procuratorate and Court' <http://news.qq.com/a/20100511/000033.html>, accessed 4 August 2011.
[30]   Same as above.

Case 5: Sichuan Yuechi County People's Procuratorate – Indictment of Chen for Robbery and Possession of Counterfeit Money[31]

In December 2010, Sichuan Yuechi County Procuratorate handled the first criminal case in the county applying the new exclusion provisions. The suspect Chen was accused of robbery and possession of counterfeit banknotes. On the day the case was transferred for review and prosecution, the Yuechi County Detention Centre submitted a report to the Procuratorate, stating that Chen had once tried to kill himself and had been on hunger strike for over 20 days. It asked the Procuratorate to expedite the handling of the case to avoid further risk to Chen's life. The procurator in charge then discovered that Chen had refused to answer questions or to sign the interrogation transcript as he alleged that his confession had been extorted by torture. In line with the Rules on Several Issues Concerning the Exclusion of Illegal Evidence in Criminal Cases (Two Rules) and in order to verify whether unlawful means such as extortion of confessions by torture had been used in collecting evidence the procurator in the case collected Chen's physical check-up record upon arrival in custody as well as other materials. He also asked the investigating officers to describe whether torture had been used during the investigation and to testify in court. During the trial, Chen argued that the investigators had tortured him to make a confession and the investigation procedure based on the Two Rules was duly initiated. In court, the prosecutor presented the statement provided by the investigators who claimed that no torture had been used, and other evidence such as the physical check-up report completed when the defendant arrived at the detention centre. He also applied for the investigators to testify in court. After its investigation, the court found that there had been no extortion of confessions by torture and that the pre-trial confession was obtained by legal means. Chen was found guilty of robbery and possession of counterfeit banknotes, and was awarded a combined sentence of three and a half years plus a fine of 13,000 Rmb.

Case 6: Zhang Guo's Corruption Case in Baiyin City, Gansu Province[32]

56-year-old Zhang Guo, former director of a grain management agency in Huining county, Gansu province. In March 2004, Zhang forged two employee signatures to fraudulently claim overtime payments for 2002 and 2003, totalling 121,100 Rmb, which he withdrew from the teller with the help of

---

[31] See <http://news.jcrb.com/jxsw/201012/t20101201_473674.html>, accessed 4 August 2011.

[32] See 'Gansu Baiyin Applying The Exclusionary Rule to Lodge a Protest' <http://www.legaldaily.com.cn/legal_case/content/2010-09/15/content_2288624.htm?node=-21138>, accessed 11 August 2011.

the cashier. On 6 September of the same year, Zhang Guo was transferred to another post.

The corruption came to light from an audit during the restructuring of the grain management system in 2007. On 25 April 2008, based on employees' reports, Huining Procuratorate filed a corruption case against Zhang Guo for which he was prosecuted at Huining County Court on 2 July 2008 and subsequently found guilty and given a ten year prison sentence. The defendant appealed and the Intermediate Court of Baiyin returned the case for retrial. In light of the court's request for supplementary evidence, the local procuratorate conducted an additional investigation and appointed Gansu Provincial Procuratorate to carry out a judicial evaluation of the relevant accounts. The evidence was strengthened but before the retrial, the defendant alleged that his guilty confession was extorted by torture and the court then found him innocent on 16 April 2010.

On 22 April 2010, the procuratorate of Huining County protested, in accordance with the law, against the 'not guilty' verdict. The Baiyin Procuratorate reviewed the case files and the two verdicts delivered by the courts and after verifying testimonies made by the main witnesses, it concluded that the pre-trial confession of the defendant was obtained legally and therefore accepted the protest.

On 30 July, the Baiyin Intermediate Court organized a collegial panel to try the case. During the trial, in light of the defendant's claim before the start of the retrial at Huining County Court that his confessions were obtained illegally and in accordance with the provisions in the Two Rules the prosecutors with Baiyin Municipal Procuratorate presented to the court all the defendant's pre-trial confessions and applied for relevant witnesses and interrogators to testify in court in order to prove the legitimacy of Zhang Guo's guilty confession. The court decided to admit the defendant's pre-trial confessions. The Baiyin Intermediate Court found that the criminal facts were clear and that the evidence of corruption was sufficient. Zhang Guo's pre-trial confessions were proven to have been obtained legally through the court investigation and he was found guilty of corruption and sentenced to ten years.

Case 7: Sichuan Ziyang Municipal People's Procuratorate – Indictment of Song Liguang for Bribery[33]

On 6 February 2010, Ziyang Municipal Procuratorate approved the arrest of Song Liguang, ex-director of the Bureau of Communications, on bribery

---

[33]   See CAO XIAOLE 2010, quoted from LONG ZONGZHI 2010.

charges. The procuratorate accused him of accepting six bribes totalling 755,000 Rmb while serving as the director of the Bureau of Communications. In the interrogation transcripts presented by the prosecution, Song Ligong admitted to the accusations but he later told his lawyer in their second meeting that all the confessions were fabricated. Song Ligong alleged that the police used his attachment to his family to force him to confess. They kept him in the cold for a long time, threatened to infect him with a contagious disease, hit him with an electrical baton and interrogated him continuously for five days and nights. In the lawyer's records, Song Liguang claimed that the investigators threatened that if he did not confess to the crime, his wife, brothers, father and other family members would be put in custody. When he was moved to the Liangshan Meigu County Detention Centre, he was not provided with warm clothes and bedcovers despite the freezing temperatures and was transferred to different cells four times. He admitted to a crime which he did not commit because of being subjected to huge psychological and physical pressure.

The trial began at 9:30 am, 18 August 2010 when the prosecutor first read out the indictment letter. Then the judge asked Song Liguang whether he had any objection to the charges. Song restated that he did not admit to the charges and the crimes he was accused of. According to standard criminal trial procedure, the judge asked the prosecutor to question Song about the facts of the case. Song's lawyer raised his hand to cut the prosecutor short and told the judge that in accordance with the Provisions on the Exclusion of Illegal Evidence released by relevant authorities, when a defendant alleges that his pre-trial confession was obtained illegally, the court shall start investigation in the courtroom after the reading of the indictment letter by the prosecutor. The presiding judge consulted with the other two judges and accepted the application made by the defence counsel. He then announced that the court would conduct an investigation to verify whether Song's pre-trial confessions were obtained illegally.

Firstly, the defence lawyer presented the investigation transcript in which Song claimed that he had been tortured, the letter prepared by the law firm stating they were not allowed to meet with their client normally, and the receipt from the family showing that they had asked the investigators to forward some money to Song to cover living expenses. The lawyer said that the letter proved that the investigators had not allowed normal meetings between the lawyer and the defendant, possibly to enable them to torture him; the decision made by the investigators to not forward the money proved that they planned to coerce the defendant by subjecting him to extreme living conditions. After reviewing these three pieces of evidence, the judge commented that the letter from the law firm was an issue concerning investigation and therefore not relevant to the trial. He concluded that the evidence should be immediately excluded. With regard to the receipt for the money, the prosecutor argued that it could only prove that the family had given the defendant money not that the defendant had never received the money.

The prosecutor then presented the explanation submitted by the three investigators, all of whom claimed that they had never tortured Song Liguang. In response, Song said that two out of the three had indeed not used torture but that the third had threatened him verbally. In addition, he claimed that nine other investigators had tortured him in various ways. Song listed their names and work units and all information was recorded by the court. Song Liguang claimed that an investigator named Zhang had repeatedly tortured him and had even used an electrical baton to beat him. The prosecutor responded that this investigator was on a business trip and could not respond to the charge. Song Liguang added that he had frequently been moved to detention centres in other areas, to which the prosecutor argued that this was in order to prevent collusion between suspects, and not against the law. Song further added that he had been interrogated continuously for five days and nights when he was detained in the Meigu County Detention Centre. After reviewing the files, the prosecutor said that the records did show interrogations were carried out on those five days but that the interrogation had ended each day, as the records stated that Song was sent back to his cell every evening.

Lastly, in response to Song's allegation, the prosecutor argued that during the exchange of evidence, the interrogation videotapes played in the courtroom proved that Song had confessed without any coercion and that his allegation was not true. The defence lawyer argued that altogether there were over 20 interrogation transcripts whilst the investigation unit only provided the videotapes of five, which were insufficient to prove that no torture had been used against Song to extort a confession. After spending two hours investigating the evidence, the court adjourned the proceedings as the above issues were highly controversial. When the proceedings resumed, the judge said that in accordance with the Rules on the Exclusion of Illegal Evidence, the defendant should provide evidence and clues to support his allegation of illegal collection of evidence, but the defence had only offered conceptual materials as evidence, without any specific clues. So the court decided to conduct an investigation outside the court and in addition, believed that the defence had the right to conduct its own investigation and obtain evidence. Only if the defence met obstacles, should it apply to obtain evidence through the court. The court ruled that the trial would reopen at a later date dependent on the progress of the investigation.

Case 8: Yancheng People's Procuratorate – Indictment of Wang Zhilin, Chen Chen and Yu Guangliang for Drug Trafficking, and of Zhang Linrong for Harbouring Drug Addicts[34]

According to the prosecution, the defendant Wang Zhilin sold altogether 18 grams of heroin to Zuo on four occasions and 2.75 grams of methamphetamine to Zang on 11 occasions from August 2006 to August 2009. From December 2008 to July 2009, the defendant Chen Chen sold a total of 2.75 grams of methamphetamine to Wang and others on nine occasions. The defendant Yu Guangliang sold 1.60 grams of methamphetamine to Xu and others on four occasions. These sales all took place in Binhai county apart from the latter which was in Funing county. At the trial, the defendant Wang Zhilin denied all the accusations and claimed that the confession he made during investigation was extorted by torture. His defence lawyer told the court that his client had been subjected to numerous arbitrary interrogations at the detention centre and requested the court to investigate the evidence as the defendant had suffered torture. In response, Yancheng Intermediate People's Court started the procedure for exclusion and held a hearing to review the torture allegation made by the defendant: 1. All four investigators who testified in court denied the defendant's allegation that they had broken his nose. Wang said that another detainee Zhu could verify his allegation but Zhu claimed he had not seen Wang's injuries. Both Wang and his defence lawyer failed to provide other evidence to prove the allegation and therefore, the court did not accept their argument. 2. Wang Zhilin alleged that he had swallowed a golden ring as he could no longer stand the beatings by the investigators, several days after being taken into criminal custody. On 10 August 2009, the day the Binhai County PSB put him in custody, Wang was transferred to the Binhai Detention Centre where the duty officer and the doctor asked that Wang be taken to hospital for treatment because he said he had swallowed a ring. According to the investigators' testimony, the X-ray inspection payment records and the X-ray images retrieved by the court as per the defence lawyer's request, there was indeed a piece of metal inside Wang's body when he was twice taken to Binhai People's Hospital for X-rays on 11 and 16 August 2009 respectively, but the metal object had disappeared when the defendant was taken for a third X-ray on 20 August 2009. This proved that Wang had swallowed the ring on the actual day of being put in custody or the preceding day, but not

---

[34] The case was quoted from the Report of The Exclusionary Rule Pilot Program, <http://www.legaldaily.com.cn/zbzk/content/2011-03/03/content_2495638.htm?node=-25500>, accessed 4 August 2011.

several days later as a result of being unable to stand the beatings by the investigators, as he had claimed. Therefore, the court did not accept this argument. The Yangcheng Intermediate People's Court delivered its first instance verdict on 13 September 2010 and this verdict came into effect as there was no appeal by the defendant.

2.2. CASES IN WHICH THE ILLEGALLY OBTAINED EVIDENCE WAS EXCLUDED

Case 9: Nantong Chongchuan District People's Procuratorate – Indictment of Wang Yuliang for Possession of Drugs[35]

The police claimed that they had discovered crystal methadone during a special operation but the procuratorate found the operation illegal as there had been no search warrant. This was the first case of exclusion in Jiangsu after the publication of the Rules on Several Issues Concerning the Exclusion of Illegal Evidence in Criminal Cases on 1 July 2010.

On the night of 17 January 2010, Xiao Wei and Xiao Liang bought 30 grams of crystal methadone in Changzhou and sold it to Wang Yuliang and others. Wang Yuliang hid the crystal methadone in a hotel room and went out with the defendants, Zhang Jian and Pan Gui. The police found their behaviour suspicious, followed them and stopped them on the street. They were taken to the local police station and were interrogated by police where a plastic bag with small amounts of white powder was found in Wang Yuliang's pocket. At 22:00 pm, police officers took Wang Yuliang to the hotel and searched the rooms where they seized 29.13 grams of crystal methadone hidden inside the air-conditioning unit.

The PSB then transferred the case to the Procuratorate of Chongchuan District in Nantong for review and prosecution. The procurator who handled the case found something suspicious in the recorded sequence of events. Police records showed that the first interrogation of Wang Yuliang took place at midday on 18 January 2010. The interrogation manuscript stated that the drugs were seized and that Wang Yuliang confessed to drug trafficking. However, the time shown on the search warrant and the search records was 8:00 pm, 18 January 2010.

The fact that drugs were seized meant that the search procedure was completed but the time of search should have been the same or at least earlier than the first interrogation. However, the records showed that the search had taken place 8 hours after the interrogation, which did not make sense. The

---

[35] See <http://jsfzb.xhby.net/html/2010-07/21/content_257856.htm>, accessed 4 August 2011.

procurator immediately interrogated Wang who told him that the police officers had asked him to sign the search warrant and the search records at 8:00 pm, 18 January 2010. In fact, the investigators were afraid of missing the opportunity to solve the case and therefore decided to bypass the necessary formalities. Both the search warrant and the search records were obtained later.

The procurator concluded that the police had failed to follow due procedure and that their act broke relevant laws. A Notice of Correction of Illegal Behaviour was immediately sent out and the search records and search warrant were excluded. All the police's efforts were not in vain however as the items discovered during the search were objective and relevant to the case and could prove the other evidence and reflect truthful facts. As such, they could therefore be admitted as physical evidence.

Case 10: Ningbo Yinzhou District People's Procuratorate – Indictment of Zhang Guoxi for Accepting Bribes[36]

The suspect, Zhang Guoxi, college graduate and former office director, and assistant to the bureau head of Ningbo Dongqianhu Tourist Resort Construction Management Bureau was arrested on 5 August 2010. The Ningbo Yinzhou District People's Procuratorate accused Zhang Guoxi of taking advantage of his position as a government worker during 2005 and 2009 by repeatedly accepting bribes totalling 76,000 Rmb, which constituted a crime. The Procuratorate indicted him at Ningbo Yinzhou District People's Court on 25 March 2011. The case was tried four times, on 11 April, 11 May, 20 June, and 20 July 2011 respectively. After reviewing the procedure and the substance of the case, Ningbo Yinzhou District People's Court found the following:-1. In terms of procedure, the court found that the early investigation was flawed as the prosecution could not provide the records of Dongqianhu Discipline Inspection Commission's conversation with Zhang Guoxi and other supporting evidence. The prosecution failed to provide all interrogation audiotapes as evidence to be questioned in court. Though the defence repeatedly requested the appearance of the investigators, the prosecution failed to arrange for them to testify in court. In accordance with Article 11 of the Provisions on the Exclusion of Illegal Evidence, if the prosecutor does not provide evidence to confirm the legality of the defendant's pre-trial confession or the evidence provided is not reliable or sufficient, that confession may not serve as a basis for conviction. The court therefore ruled that the pre-trial confession of Zhang Guoxi could not serve

---

[36]   See <http://jiangjiangao.fyfz.cn/art/1037921.htm#1327202>, accessed 4 August 2011.

as a basis for conviction. 2. The Indictment Letter said that the defendant had accepted 10,000 Rmb in cash from Zhou Liang; 2,000 Rmb from Cai Zhenwu and Zhao Xinpu from bank cards; and 20,000 Rmb in cash from Shi Jiandang. However, the prosecution only provided testimonies from those engaged in bribery. These testimonies were inconsistent and had no corroborating evidence and therefore, were not admitted. With regard to the 36,000 Rmb paid to Zhang Guoxi as compensation for 'lending' his Supervision Engineer Certificate, it was not a 'money for power' deal and therefore did not constitute the crime of accepting bribes. With regard to the 6,000 Rmb (in retail or bank cards) admitted by Zhang Guoxi, the court found him eligible for exemption from criminal punishment based on the fact that the amount of money involved had just crossed the threshold constituting criminal activity, and the fact that he had turned himself in, as well as the facts, nature, circumstances of the case and the level of damage to society caused. The verdict was delivered as follows: 1. The defendant was found guilty of accepting bribes and was exempted from criminal punishment. 2. The defendant was ordered to repay his illegal gains of 6,000 Rmb, to the state treasury. In this case, the Ningbo Yinzhou District People's Court initiated the exclusion procedure after the defence's allegation of extortion of confessions by torture and illegal collection of evidence. The defence had also provided proof materials such as the Detention Centre Diary which recorded the time, location, names of those involved, and methods of illegal collection of evidence, in accordance with the Two Rules. The defence counsel repeatedly asked for the display of audio/videotapes of the interrogation, the retrieval of Zhang Guoxi's physical check-up records from the detention centre, and applied for the investigators to testify in court. Accordingly, the court demanded that the prosecution comply with such requests but they failed to do so. The presiding judge of the Ningbo Yinzhou District People's Court ended up going to the detention centre to get the physical check-up records. The court finally ruled that the confession alleged to have been extorted by torture should be reasonably excluded. This is the first decision of its kind in Zhejiang and in China as a whole. Its value should not be understated as a representative case for a judicial system with scarce trial experience in the application of the exclusionary rule.

Case 11: Jiangsu Binhai County People's Procuratorate – Indictment of Li Zigao for Sabotaging Production and Business Operations[37]

According to the prosecution, the defendant Li Zigao went to an aquaculture store in Siming town, Sheyang county in March and April 2009. He bought 14 bottles of pond-cleaning agent and kept them in his home. On the night of 12 July of the same year, he poured the contents of all the 14 bottles into Liu Huaping's fish pond and as a result large numbers of fish raised in the 40-mu pond died on 13 and 14 July. The Binhai County Commodity Price Bureau placed the value of the dead fish at 46,180 Rmb. In court, the defendant denied all the facts stated in the indictment letter and argued that he had neither bought any pond-cleaning agent nor had he tried to put poison in Liu Huaping's fish pond. His confession was coerced by the investigators through violence and threats. His defence lawyer claimed that Li's confession was obtained illegally and therefore should be excluded. The exclusion procedure was initiated. It was revealed that the defendant had made five confessions during the investigations, and two claims of not guilty. Two out of the five confessions were obtained at the workplace of the investigators between 20:10-22:00 on 18 July and between 14:00-15:00 on 19 July respectively. The defendant rejected his previous confessions in the two trials, which pointed to the inconsistencies in his statements. The court found that the two interrogations, which were carried out in the workplace of the investigators, violated Article 145 of the Regulations for Procedures of Criminal Cases by Public Security Authorities, which states that 'criminal suspects and defendants who are detained and arrested should be immediately sent to the detention centre'. This was therefore a procedural breach and as such, these two confessions should not be admitted as evidence. The inconsistency in his statements, as well as the contradiction between his guilty confession and the other evidence, proved that the evidence of the former was flawed. It was then ruled that the evidence was insufficient to prove the defendant guilty of sabotaging production and business operations. In addition, the procedure for collecting physical evidence was flawed, which meant that it could not be used. On 18 October 2010, the Binhai People's Court delivered its verdict that the defendant was not guilty of sabotaging production and business operations. The prosecution lodged an appeal, which was turned down by the Yancheng Intermediate People's Court on 16 December 2010 and the original verdict was upheld.

---

[37] The case was quoted from the Report of The Exclusionary Rule Pilot Program, see: <http://www.legaldaily.com.cn/zbzk/content/2011-03/03/content_2495638.htm?node=-25500>, accessed 4 August 2011.

Case 12: Foshan Nanhai District People's Procuratorate – Indictment of Cheng Zhenjie for Appropriating Company Property[38]

On 28 April 2010, the Nanhai District People's Court received an indictment from the Foshan Nanhai District People's Procuratorate, charging Cheng Zhenjie with fraudulent appropriation of company property. The prosecution prepared the indictment letter which stated that Cheng Zhenjie had joined Taiwan Feijiang Company in 1994 and was sent to Nanhai in Foshan city to develop its business there. Taiwan Feijiang Company funded the establishment of four companies in mainland China, namely Pingzhou Feijiang Shoe Material Factory, Quanda, Hexin and Guangzhou Dongda Commerce. Feijiang controlled the finances and the operations whilst Cheng Zhenjie was appointed by Feijiang to be General Manager of Feijiang's mainland business. As a result, Cheng had the authority to trade and manage these companies. In August 2004, due to a conflict with Taiwan Feijiang, Zheng took advantage of his position to break Feijiang's control over the above four companies and embezzled all their assets valued at 20 million Rmb.

The evidence presented by the procuratorate included an important confession, in which Cheng Zhenjie admitted his guilt, during the investigation stage. Furthermore, he confessed that he was an employee of Taiwan Feijiang and that he had been posted in mainland China in 1994. The four mainland companies mentioned in the indictment letter were all funded and built by Feijiang. Cheng also acknowledged that he had appropriated the property of Feijiang. The confession showed that Cheng was explicit about his intention to return the remaining assets and those seized by the public security authorities to Taiwan Feijiang. He was also willing to use the 5 million Rmb's worth of shoe materials, which he had bought and kept in a warehouse, to provide compensation for illicit proceeds. The procuratorate submitted to the court the Statement for Returning Illicit Proceeds and the Letter of Repentance written by Cheng Zhenjie. In the Letter of Repentance, Cheng said that 'I have realized my mistake and I feel very sorry'; 'my actions have caused huge losses to Taiwan Feijiang. I apologize to Li Chunzhong, General Manager of Taiwan Feijiang and I hope he can forgive me'. He even said he was ready to return all appropriated property to Taiwan Feijiang in exchange for leniency by the court.

---

[38] 'The First Case of "No Conviction on Illegally Obtained Evidence": Not Guilty by Proving the Extortion of Confession by Torture', <http://legal.people.com.cn/GB/15894905.html>, accessed 10 January 2012.

However, when the trial first opened, Cheng Zhenjie retracted his prior guilty confession in the courtroom, claiming that the police had extorted his confession by torture and that the so-called Statement for Returning Illicit Proceeds and Letter of Repentance were in fact prepared by the investigators and copied out by him afterwards. The procuratorate showed some clips of the interrogation video and the explanation written by the investigators, denying the use of torture. However, Cheng Zhenjie gave detailed information about where and how he was tortured. He showed the court his injured toe, the nail of which had been smashed when he was tortured and which remained discoloured after it recovered. As a result, Tian Wenchang, Cheng's defence lawyer, asked the court to review the legitimacy of the defendant's pre-trial confession in accordance with the newly-issued evidence provisions, and to evaluate Cheng's injury. The judicial evaluation report suggested that the foot injury was genuine.

After several trials, the Foshan Nanhai District People's Court found Cheng Zhenjie not guilty at first instance. After evaluation, the court decided to exclude the confession made by Cheng during the investigation stage. The court believed that although the defendant admitted his guilt during the investigation stage, he subsequently claimed during the trial that he had been subjected to the extortion of confessions by torture and had presented specific evidence supporting his claim. The forensic report suggested that his left big toe had suffered tissue injury although admittedly it could not confirm the exact time of the injury and whether it had been caused by torture. In addition, the record of the physical check-up upon reception presented by the detention centre and the interrogation videos seemed to indicate that no torture had been used to extort a confession. However, the possibility that the defendant's pre-trial confession was obtained illegally could not be completely ruled out and the court thus decided to apply the exclusion rule. Furthermore, the focal point of the debate between defence and prosecution was whether Cheng Zhenjie was actually an employee of Taiwan Feijiang, as well as the relationship between the four mainland companies and Taiwan Feijiang. The court believed that the procuratorate failed to produce any direct evidence to prove that Cheng had signed a Labour Contract or any other type of employment contract with Taiwan Feijiang. The indirect evidence was only from one party – Taiwan Feijiang, and was therefore insufficient to prove that Cheng was in effect a Feijiang employee. The company could also not provide any direct evidence supporting the claim that it had funded the establishment of four companies, whose registration documents showed no connection with Taiwan Feijiang. Considering all the above factors, the court delivered the verdict that the evidence was not sufficient to prove Taiwan Feijiang had invested in the establishment of the four mainland companies and that Cheng Zhenjie had appropriated the property of these companies.

The Nanhai District People's Procuratorate protested against the decision on 30 January 2010. With regard to the admissibility of Cheng's confession during the investigation stage, the criminal protest letter argued that the guilty confession made by Cheng during the investigation stage was consistent and coherent about the facts that he was a Feijiang employee and had appropriated the property of the companies established by Feijiang in mainland China. But in the courtroom, Cheng claimed that he had been subjected to torture, provided relevant clues and argued that both his confessions and the Letter of Repentance were false. The prosecution retrieved the record of his physical check-up upon reception by the Nanhai District Detention Centre, which indicated that there was no apparent external injury when he arrived there on 14 May 2009. As per the request of the defendant, the court appointed Foshan No. 1 People's Hospital to conduct a forensic examination of the defendant, which concluded that his left big toe had suffered tissue injury. But the forensic evaluation was not conclusive and could not pinpoint the exact time of such injury, nor could it prove that the injury was inflicted by torture. It was therefore possible that the injury might have been caused by other factors. In addition, the investigative authorities provided the defendant's interrogation video clips, which showed no extortion of confessions by torture. All in all, the prosecution claimed that the possibility that Cheng had been subjected to torture during the investigation stage could be excluded and that the court should admit his pre-trial confession.

On 18 August 2010, the Foshan Intermediate People's Court held an open trial on the case and delivered a second-instance verdict to reject the protest and uphold the original verdict.

It is obvious from the successful cases mentioned above that thanks to the Two Rules, judges are beginning to apply the exclusionary rule in a proactive manner, despite the obstacles they face. For example, in Case 10, the judge excluded the suspect's guilty confession on the grounds that the location of the interrogation was not legal. In accordance with the Provisions on the Exclusion of Illegal Evidence, the procuratorates have adopted many measures to prove the legality of the evidence. These attempts have been lacklustre, however as in Cases 9 and 13. The explanation presented by the procuratorate and the testimony made by the investigators actually drew suspicion away from the defence. The procuratorates have failed to pro-actively exclude evidence obtained illegally in the arrest approval stage.

3. THE NEW EXCLUSIONARY RULE INTRODUCED BY THE 2012 REVISIONS TO THE CRIMINAL PROCEDURE LAW

3.1. THE DIRECTION OF REFORM OF THE EXCLUSIONARY RULE IDENTIFIED BY THE REVISED CPL

In March 2012, in the fifth session of the 11th NPC the CPL Revision was passed. The new CPL provides additions and changes to the rules concerning evidence principles in the current CPL, which include the perfection of the exclusion system. In addition to Article 43 of the 1996 CPL (which prohibits the extortion of confessions by torture and the use of other illegal means to collect evidence), the revision inserts a rule that no one shall be forced to incriminate himself, in order to further curb extortion of confessions by torture and the use of other illegal means to collect evidence in a systemic manner and to safeguard judicial justice and the legitimate rights of all participants in criminal proceedings. It further provides that confessions of suspects or defendants extorted by torture and other illegal means, as well as witness testimonies, victim statements collected by the use of force, threats and other illegal means shall be excluded; material and documentary evidence collected in violation of the provisions of the law that severely affect judicial justice shall also be excluded. According to the new provisions the people's courts, the people's procuratorate and the public security authorities have a responsibility to exclude illegal evidence and investigation procedures shall be put in place in a court hearing for doing so. Furthermore considering that in judicial practice, acts of extorting confessions by torture mostly occur prior to the handover of a criminal suspect to the detention centre, it is clearly stated that: upon detention or arrest, a detained or arrested person shall be promptly delivered into a detention centre for custody, where investigators interrogate a criminal suspect after he or she has been handed over to a detention centre for custody, the investigators shall implement such interrogation within the detention centre and a system for audio/videotaping interrogations shall be put in place.

There are some similarities and differences in the way the revised CPL and the Two Rules treat the exclusion of illegally obtained evidence. The revised CPL is based on the Two Rules and has drawn on the experience and lessons learned from implementing the Two Rules. The revision also shares the same legislative purpose and similar procedures. Both measures have provided for the discretionary exclusion of material and documentary evidence and both have put in place similar exclusionary procedures for the trial hearing with the complainant responsible for providing clues and evidence. In terms of legislative purpose, both aim to combat the extortion of confessions by torture in judicial practice and to ensure the efficiency of investigations and the discovery of true facts. Even though the new CPL has now been adopted, the Two Rules will continue to play a role. Where contradictory clauses exist those in the Two Rules will no longer apply, otherwise the two sets of provisions may be used jointly. The main difference between the Revision and the Two Rules is the status of the CPL. The Draft Revision was deliberated and published by the Standing Committee of the NPC and the new CPL has been enacted as law following its deliberation and approval at the 5th Plenary Session of the 11th NPC in March 2012 whereas the Two Rules were drafted by the Supreme People's Court. The higher legal status of the CPL will help ensure that the articles concerning exclusion will have an impact on the entire criminal procedure framework. The Two Rules only specify how judges should deal with exclusion of evidence at trial and the courts cannot conduct a judicial review of the investigation activities. In other words, the Two Rules only provide a mechanism for dealing with allegations after the event and cannot offer a mechanism to effectively curb and prevent the extortion of confessions by torture. The new CPL is better able to address this. In the revision the exclusionary rules are no longer a system in isolation, but can be seen as part of a larger effort to control investigative powers and improve the handling of evidence. Finally, although the new CPL has adopted many of the positive elements of the Two Rules it has not simply transplanted the 2010 provisions, but has drawn on the views of academics and practitioners to improve the exclusionary rules.

3.2. CHANGES TO THE SUBSTANTIVE RULES OF THE EXCLUSIONARY RULE IN THE REVISED CPL

In judicial practice, the illegal collection of evidence including extortion of confessions by torture, searches without a search warrant or witness, the search, seizure and freezing of personal property and family property unrelated to the crime, prolonged detention and covert detention are common occurrences. The reasons for this problem are: 'firstly, the power of the investigative authorities is too strong. In criminal procedure, the investigation power virtually includes all the powers to deprive citizens of their personal rights and property rights, whilst citizens lack effective remedy channels. As a result, the power of investigation units is too broad. Secondly, the relationship between the police and the procuratorate is far from ideal. In reality, police officers tend to be preoccupied with solving crimes, without acting from a higher perspective such as whether the case is indictable for the procuratorate and whether the court can deliver a verdict. Thirdly, issues such as extortion of confessions by torture and high detention rates abound in criminal investigations. Fourthly, defence is rarely available during investigation'.[39]

In light of the problems in practice, Article 43 of the 1996 CPL reads: 'Judges, procurators or investigators, as the case may be, must, pursuant to statutory procedures, collect all forms of evidence that prove the guilt or innocence of a suspect or a defendant as well as mitigating and aggravating evidence. The extortion of confessions by torture and the use of threats, enticement, deceit and other illegal means to collect evidence shall be strictly prohibited'. Article 50 of the new CPL amended this article to read: 'Judges, procurators or investigators, as the case may be, must, pursuant to statutory procedures, collect all forms of evidence that prove the guilt or innocence of a suspect or a defendant as well as mitigating and aggravating evidence. The extortion of confessions by torture and the use of threats, enticement, deceit and other illegal means to collect evidence shall be strictly prohibited; no person may be forced to prove his or her own guilt'. The amendment not only retains the CPL's fundamental spirit in prohibiting judges, procurators and investigators from using illegal means to collect evidence, but also includes a new provision against forced self-incrimination specifically to prevent the extortion of confessions by torture.

Articles 50, 54 and 172 of the new CPL define the concept and the scope of illegally obtained oral and material evidence. They stipulate that illegally obtained oral evidence shall be categorically excluded whilst the decision to exclude illegally obtained material evidence shall be discretionary. According to Article 54, regarding illegal evidence, confessions extorted by torture and other illegal means, as well as witness testimony and victim statements, collected by the use of force, threats and other illegal means shall be excluded. Unlawfully obtained physical evidence, however, that will severely affect judicial justice, should be corrected or justified. Otherwise such evidence shall be excluded. Where evidence that should be excluded is found during an investigation, review for prosecution or trial, such evidence shall be excluded in accordance with the law and shall not be used as a basis for opinions or decisions on prosecution and decisions of courts. In other words, illegally obtained oral evidence must be absolutely excluded whilst illegally obtained physical evidence can be treated with more discretion. The new CPL and the Two Rules support this approach to the exclusion of evidence, reflecting agreement between the public security authorities, the procuratorate and the courts.

---

[39] CHEN WEIDONG 2008.

3.3.   THE PROCEDURAL RULES TO EXCLUDE EVIDENCE IN THE REVISED CPL

In China, according to the traditional evidence theory only the probative value is of importance and the ways in which evidence is obtained does not play a significant role in itself.[40] That is why trials and arguments between the defence and the prosecution often centre on the probative value of evidence and rarely is attention paid to the qualification of evidence. Because procedural provisions concerning how to exclude evidence were lacking, judges have tended to ignore any argument made by the defence regarding the illegality of evidence. Illegal evidence has been excluded in only few cases in practice and defendants and defence lawyers often find it hard to initiate the exclusion procedure. Therefore academics argue that one of the key reasons for the difficulty in exclusion is that there were no provisions in the law that established the exclusion procedure. Even if a judge intends to exclude certain evidence, it may not actually happen as there are no detailed methods available on how it should be done

Regrettably, even since the birth of the Two Rules in 2009, few judges have initiated an exclusion procedure and the number of cases where evidence was successfully excluded is negligible. There has been no significant change in practice, where the exclusionary rule is not being applied out of fear.

Why has the exclusion procedure long advocated and promoted by academics remained an empty promise? The most important issue is that there was no detailed procedure in place.

In academia there are generally two views about the implementation of the exclusion procedure introduced by the Two Rules. One is that the procedure should be positioned as a 'trial within a trial', meaning that the exclusion procedure should deal with assessing the alleged illegality of evidence and exclude illegally obtained evidence, independent of the trial procedure. If this view prevails, the exclusion procedure itself should have the basic structure of a due process. Not only may the prosecution and defence actively produce evidence and argue about it, but the judge may also deliver a decision on the exclusion at the end of the procedure, against which either party may file a protest or appeal. The other view argues that defining the procedure as a 'trial within a trial' and allowing the parties to file an appeal undermines the normal trial proceedings. According to this view the exclusion procedure should be a part of the trial procedure. When during a trial hearing serious allegations are made that evidence has been obtained

---

[40]   CHEN YIYUN 1991, p. 140.

illegally, the judge has the right to initiate the procedure to investigate such evidence and the parties have the right to present evidence and argue their cases. The judge may explain in the verdict the reasons for his or her decision to exclude evidence at the end of the trial and the parties may then file a protest or appeal. In addition, a system of pre-trial meetings should be set up.

In response to these debates on what procedure should be adopted to exclude evidence the revision in the new CPL is rather cautious and has not completely adopted the system design and text from the Two Rules. Instead, it provides ambiguously that if, in a court hearing, a judge is of the opinion evidence has been obtained illegally, a court investigation shall be performed to establish the legality of such evidence. It does not require the judge to decide on the exclusion in the courtroom nor does it give the procuratorate and the defendant the right to submit an appeal or objection against the court's decision. It keeps the original trial model basically intact. For example, according to Article 242 of the new CPL, when a party or his or her legal representative, or close relative file a complaint that the litigation procedure has violated the law and may affect the fairness of the trial, the people's court shall conduct a retrial. Therefore, procedural violation can be a reason to appeal, protest or make an accusation, but the judge is not required to make a ruling during the trial.

In addition to this, article 182 adds a pre-trial preparation procedure, which specifies that prior to the hearing, the judge may convene the public prosecutor, the parties, the defender and their advocates to make them aware of the issues related to the trial, such as witness lists and exclusion of evidence, and to hear their views.

The new CPL has also responded to the issue of burden of proof by stipulating that a party and their legal representatives shall have the right to apply to the people's court to exclude evidence obtained illegally in accordance with the law and that according to Article 57(1) the prosecution bears the burden of proof that evidence has been obtained legally.

3.4. SUPERVISION BY THE PEOPLE'S PROCURATORATES OVER THE USE OF ILLEGAL MEANS TO OBTAIN EVIDENCE

The CPL revision has also enhanced the procuratorates' supervision over investigation activities. For example, the new Article 115 stipulates for the first time that a party, or their legal representatives, or an interested person have the right to submit a complaint or an accusation to the authority or the procuratorate, where they believe an investigator to have violated his or her legitimate rights and interests. Thereby the procuratorate's power of legal supervision is expanded, which may contribute to effectively combating extortion of confessions by torture, in addition to exclusion of evidence by judges.

The revisions have added Articles 55 and 115 to the CPL, which enhance the complaints procedure for participants in criminal procedures during the investigation stage. According to Article 55, where a people's procuratorate receives a case report, an accusation or information that the investigator has collected evidence illegally, it shall investigate and verify the allegation. According to Article 115, a party, or his legal representatives, or interested person has the right to submit a complaint or accusation to a judicial authority where he or she believes the judicial authority or the personnel to have engaged in illegal investigation. The authority admitting the complaint or accusation shall handle such issues promptly. Where the complaint or accusation is rejected, an appeal may be submitted to a people's procuratorate at the same or level or one level higher.

According to Article 55 of the new CPL, a procuratorate may deal with an investigator's illegal act of evidence collection by means of the following measures. 1) The procuratorate shall first investigate and verify clues it has discovered or that have been provided by participants in proceedings. 2) If, after investigation and verification, it confirms that evidence has been collected through illegal means, it shall recommend how to correct the situation and, when necessary, advise the investigating unit to substitute the person dealing with the case. The so-called 'correction opinion' refers to an opinion put forward by the procuratorate. 3) If, after investigation and verification, the procuratorate discovers that illegal collection of evidence constitutes a crime, it shall initiate criminal proceedings to determine criminal liability in accordance with the law. In light of the rules in the new CPL concerning the jurisdiction of case filing, a procuratorate may prosecute the investigator for offences of illegal detention, illegal search, extortion of confessions by torture, collecting evidence by use of force and subjecting detainees to abuse.

4. CONCLUSION

In conclusion it can be said that the provisions on the exclusion of illegal evidence in the new CPL have – although cautiously – for the first time, put in place a procedure in China, according to which evidence can be excluded before and during trial. Furthermore, a judge may follow concrete steps to guide the prosecution and the defence to argue for exclusion during the trial and the procuratorate's supervision powers are enhanced considerably. Both theorists and practitioners hope that the newly established exclusionary procedure will activate substantive exclusionary rules and will provide relevant judicial interpretations, thus providing judges and procurators with practical tools and will pave the way for the successful development of the exclusionary rule.

However, because most of the new articles in the revised CPL originate in the Two Rules, the application of the exclusionary rule will remain problematic due to intrinsic flaws, poorly-defined concepts and the vague scope of the regulations. Most of the problems concern the application of the exclusionary rule in practice, which we will go into in more detail in the next chapter.

BIBLIOGRAPHY

CAO XIAOLE 2010
CAO XIAOLE, 'Ex-Communication Director Subject to Torture? The Court Initiated Investigation Procedure for the First Time', *Chengdu Business Daily*, 10th edn., 2010.

CHEN WEIDONG 2008
CHEN WEIDONG, 'Problems in the Reform of Investigation Procedure and their Solutions', *People's Procuratorial Monthly*, 24th edn., 2008.

CHEN WEIDONG 2010A
CHEN WEIDONG, 'Pros and Cons of the Two Evidence Provisions', *Evidence Science*, 5th edn., 2010.

CHEN WEIDONG 2010B
CHEN WEIDONG, 'The Exclusionary Rule: Mixed News', *Legal Daily*, 11th edn., 11 August 2010.

CHEN YIYUN 1991
CHEN YIYUN, *Evidence Science*, Beijing: Renmin University of China Publishing House, 1991.

LANG SHENG 2011
LANG SHENG, *The Modification and Application of the Criminal Procedure Law in China*, XinHua Press, 2011.

LONG ZONGZHI 2010
LONG ZONGZHI, 'Studying Several Issues Concerning Standardization and Implementation of the Two Evidence Provision', *China Legal Science*, 6th edn., 2010.

YANG YUGUAN 2010

YANG YUGUAN, 'Two Issues which Need Clarification in the Implementation of the Provisions on the Exclusion of Illegal Evidence', *Procuratorate Daily*, 3rd edn., 11 August 2010.

ZHANG JIANWEI 2010

ZHANG JIANWEI, 'Law in Paper and Law in Action – Some Thoughts on the Exclusionary Rule', *Western Law Review*, 5th edn., 2010.

ZHANG JUN 2010

ZHANG JUN, *Understanding and Application of Criminal Evidence Rules*, China Law Press, 2010.

ZHENG GAOJIAN 2009

ZHENG GAOJIAN, 'Investigation and Consideration of Evidence Ascertainment in Cases of Defendants Retracting Confessions', *Journal of Gansu Political Science and Law Institute*, 3rd edn., 2009.

4. AN ANALYSIS OF THE ISSUES CONCERNING THE DEVELOPMENT OF CHINA'S EXCLUSIONARY RULE

Chen Weidong and Chai Yufeng

Why is China's exclusionary rule so toothless? Analysis done by scholars from various angles has shown that 'the prosecuted becomes an object during the pre-trial procedure; the defendant lacks sufficient assistance from counsel during the trial; the judgment powers vested in the courts lack fundamental neutrality; and, criminal courts generally do not show the necessary respect for the value of fair trial'.[1] However, with the publication of the 'Two Evidence Provisions' (Two Rules), there has been some change in practice as evidenced by the cases we have seen in which exclusion was attempted, and was even successful. The new reality demands that we look at this issue from a fresh perspective. In the introductory chapter of Part I, we compared the criminal justice systems of China and Europe on a macro level, in three areas: the status of courts, the status of case law, and the rights of criminal suspects or defendants relating to the collection of evidence. In this chapter, we will further explain and elaborate our thoughts by drawing on several real cases and the author's first-hand experience in interviews.

The complex reasons which make it difficult to implement the exclusionary rule in practice can be categorised into two main groups: firstly, there are ordinary straightforward criminal cases where the judge does not bother to exclude illegal evidence because there is enough other evidence on which to convict. Secondly, there are serious complex criminal cases without sufficient other evidence and where the judge does not dare to exclude illegally obtained evidence. It is true that a number of cases (see 4 cases referred to in chapter 3) boasting successful exclusion have emerged following the publication of the Two Rules,[2] the majority of which are promoted as model cases by local judicial authorities. In many cases, even though the illegally obtained evidence was excluded, the defendants were not

---

[1]   LI FENFEI 2006.
[2]   For example Cases 9, 10, 11 and 12 in Chapter 3.

acquitted.[3] As a result, the demonstration effect of such cases is more significant than their practical impact.[4] On further exploration, we find that the judges are often left with a dilemma. If a judge chooses pro-actively to review and exclude illegally obtained evidence there is an increased workload during the litigation proceedings, as well as objection from the parties, the victims and their close relatives; conversely, if the judge chooses to ignore illegally obtained evidence, there is the defendant's appeal to deal with. On balance, the judge obviously feels more work pressure if exclusion is implemented. Consequently, judges tend to actively avoid exclusion in ordinary criminal cases while feeling that they have no choice but to admit illegally obtained evidence in complicated criminal cases. This creates the situation in which 'a judge does not care to exclude, does not dare to exclude, or is incapable of excluding evidence' in practice.

Why is this? On the one hand, the exclusionary rule in China is a long way from being complete, neither is it sufficiently detailed or systemic. A concept is the simple abstraction of objects, which form the building block of rules and systems. The exclusionary rule is no exception as it also needs substantive law to define the scope of basic concepts like illegally obtained evidence, extortion of confessions by torture, threats, enticement and deceit. Compared to complex cases in the real world, definitions of these concepts proposed by the new CPL and the Two Rules are far too abstract. The resulting exclusionary rule is merely a simple system framework, which means a judge enjoys almost unlimited discretionary power when deciding on exclusion in a criminal case. On the other hand, the application of the exclusionary rule is constrained by the country's criminal justice system and traditions. Flexible application of the exclusionary rule by judges is certainly useful as it not only strikes a balance between punishing criminals using criminal procedure and safeguarding human rights, but also gradually shapes the public's acceptance of legal concepts. Although judges in China do enjoy huge discretionary power as regards exclusion, given the current criminal justice system and procedural structure, we need to discuss whether they have the courage and ability to actively assume this responsibility and in doing so lead the public to respect rights and procedures. There is currently the paradoxical situation of a lack of independence of judges on the one hand,

---

[3]   Up to now, only Cases 12 and 13 reported by the media saw successful exclusion of illegally obtained evidence and not-guilty verdicts.

[4]   Media reports of the above-mentioned cases are all labelled as 'first' cases of exclusion 'in the city or even across China.' They also touch on the positive significance of such cases, like changing the enforcement philosophy of the local judicial authority, implementing the basic requirements of the 'Two Evidence Provisions' and promoting local judicial trial and evidence system reform. This all smacks of propaganda.

and insufficient rules for judges to follow as regards accepting applications to exclude illegal evidence from defendants and their lawyers, on the other.

The Sub-Committee of Legislative Affairs of the Standing Committee of the National People's Congress (NPC), responsible for the amendment to the CPL, has not only extensively listened to opinions of state authorities, experts, scholars and the public, but also drawn on the latest legislation developments in other countries in their efforts to consolidate legislative and judicial experience[5] to create a substantially revised exclusionary rule. It has enriched and developed substantive and procedural rules in evidence exclusion, and customized changes in response to various problems following the implementation of the Two Rules. Only time will tell whether new provisions will have an impact on the status quo in which 'a judge does not want to exclude, does not dare to exclude, or is incapable of excluding evidence'. We still need to explore the potential difficulties and barriers China's exclusionary rule is likely to face in the future, from the perspective of judicial practice.

1. JUDICIAL TRADITIONS AND BARRIERS TO EXCLUSION

China's judicial tradition of 'big on substance, small on procedure' determines the basic structure of its criminal procedure, whilst shaping judicial workers' enforcement philosophy and value choices. Not only does this tradition wield a deeply ingrained influence on investigators, procurators and judges as the core guiding principle in China's criminal justice system, but even the general public takes trial outcomes far more seriously than trial processes. Chinese society currently lacks the nurturing soil needed to develop the exclusionary rule. The lack of conceptual understanding on the part of judicial officers and the public is the root cause for the rupture between legislation and judiciary, system and practice, rather than the problem of an incomplete system.

---

[5]   The Law Committee of the NPC Standing Committee researched and prepared for the draft revision of the CPL. After listening to the opinions of NPC deputies and other organizations and research by the central political and law authority and other organizations, the draft revision of the CPL was formed. In August 2011, at the 22th meeting of the 11th NPC standing committee the draft revision of the CPL was first read and then distributed to relevant departments of the central authority, various regions and related organizations for consultation. The CPL was modified in March 2012 based on the opinions of the NPC standing committee and other organizations, See the explanation of the draft revision of the CPL by WANG ZHAOGUO, <http://www.china.com.cn/zhibo/zhuanti/2012lianghui/2012-03/08/content_24826572.htm?show=t>, accessed on 2 April 2012.

1.1. THE DEFENDANT, THE VICTIM, OR CLOSE RELATIVES, AND THE EXCLUSIONARY RULE

Criminal trials in China need to consider whether the facts to be decided or ruled upon are clear and whether the law is correctly applied, as well as whether the parties approve of the outcome, i.e., the social response to the decision. Due to the sensitivity of exclusion, a judge's decision to exclude or admit certain evidence during a trial may trigger different responses from different parties. For the defendant, the victim or their relatives, if the judge communicates and explains his ideas beforehand to make sound preparations, the exclusion procedure will proceed smoothly. If the judge fails to psychologically prepare all parties at the outset, by clearly explaining the possibility of exclusion and its rationale, either the defendant or the victim will question the motive of the judge's decision to admit or exclude certain evidence and may react with irrational behaviour to show his or her discontent towards the judge or the entire judicial system. For example in cases where there has been a death or serious injury, the victim or close relatives will react very badly if the judge acquits the defendant on the basis of illegally obtained evidence.

Given the general lack of concern or understanding from the parties over procedural matters, including exclusion, defendants or victims can react in extreme ways to protect their rights when judgments are not in their favour or there is a suspicion of a miscarriage of justice. This might be submitting written petitions, or even having a dispute with the person handling the case. Petitioning is a convenient and useful external remedy but it has also imposed immense pressure on the overall judiciary system. It is a non-legal factor which a judge has to consider, in addition to the facts and the law.

1.2. THE PUBLIC AND THE EXCLUSIONARY RULE

The media is an important source of information about cases for the general public. If serious and complicated cases involve exclusion, public comment and opinion often exert a certain sway on the decisions of the court.

Take the case of Liu Yong as an example. Liu Yong formed a mafia-style group in late 1995 and in the four and a half years to his capture by the Shenyang police in July 2000, he had either directly committed or instigated others to commit 27 crimes, clearly causing hugely negative effects on society. Tieling Intermediate People's Court of Liaoning Province found him guilty of intentional injury and sentenced him to death at the first trial in April 2002. He was also found guilty of organizing and leading mafia-style groups, illegal business operations, intentional destruction of property, bribery, disruption of public services, and illegal possession of firearms. Delivering a combined sentence, the court decided to award the death penalty, deprive him of political rights for life, and fine him Rmb 15m. At the second trial on 11 August 2003, Liu Yong's defence lawyer raised the issue that the police had used torture to extort a confession during the investigation and therefore, according to the CPL should not be put to death, Consequently Liaoning Higher People's Court commuted the penalty for his conviction of intentional injury to suspension of execution of the death penalty[6] and deprivation of political rights for life. The combined sentence for his other convicted crimes in the first instance was upheld. This verdict drew wide public attention. The public felt that as Liu was such a vicious criminal the use of torture should not affect the death penalty decision. Public anger would clearly not fade without the death sentence being passed. Conversely legal experts thought that the public should respect the valid decision of the court, as well as procedural justice, and the legitimate rights of the suspect.

This case subsequently attracted close attention from the Supreme People's Court, which tried the case in December 2003 and concluded that the guilty judgment delivered by the second trial was correct. It confirmed that the crimes Liu Yong was accused of were extremely serious and that he should be sentenced to death. But the reasons that were invoked for commuting the sentence to suspension of execution of the death penalty, namely, that 'the possibility of police officers having extorted confessions by torture during the investigation could not be excluded' and 'in view of the facts, nature and circumstances of the crime and damage to society and the actual situation of the case', were according to the Supreme People's Court not consistent with the facts identified by the court through cross-examination. The judgment of the second trial was corrected because Liu Yong committed serious crimes and the consequent damage to society was huge. His case did not fit the statutory or discretionary circumstances for not awarding the death penalty. Therefore, it was judged that Liu Yong should be

---

[6]   According to the Art. 48 the Criminal Law in China, the death penalty shall only be applied to criminals who have committed the most dreadful crimes. If the immediate execution of a crime punishable by death is not deemed necessary, a two-year suspension of execution may be pronounced simultaneously with the imposition of the death sentence. All death sentences except for those that according to law should be decided by the Supreme People's Court, shall be submitted to the Supreme People's Court for approval. Death sentences with a suspension of execution may be decided or approved by a higher people's court. Art. 51: The term of suspension of execution of a death penalty shall be counted from the date the judgment becomes final. The term of a fixed-term imprisonment that is commuted from a death penalty with suspension of execution shall be counted from the date of expiration of the term of suspension of execution of a death.

sentenced to death for immediate execution and on 22 December 2003, Liu Yong was awarded the death penalty by the Supreme People's Court.[7]

Following the retrial by the Supreme People's Court, CCTV News had special coverage of the case due to its high-profile nature. After the execution was carried out, ordinary citizens of Tianling went out on to the streets and celebrated the news with fireworks. From this case we can get a first-hand feel for the simple values held by ordinary Chinese citizens, namely that 'those who kill will repay with their life, those who owe money will repay with money'. Since Liu Yong was an infamous mafia leader, it was impossible to commute or even exempt him from his punishment simply because he was tortured into confessing during investigation. This philosophy of 'big on substance, small on procedure' means that the exclusionary rule is still destined to have limited application space in China.

2. PROCEDURE STRUCTURE AND BARRIERS TO EXCLUSION

'Determined by the procedural objective, the structure of criminal procedure is mainly about the respective legal status and relationship between prosecution, defence and the judge as reflected in the fundamental procedural approaches in the main procedures and the evidentiary rules'.[8] We have discussed the structural differences between China and Europe in safeguarding judicial independence and the right of defence. Beyond that, the tri-lateral relationship between prosecution, defence and the judge has some characteristics unique to China. The criminal procedure model which results from this tri-lateral relationship attaches more importance to the uncovering of substantive truth, and consequently the application space of the exclusionary rule is to a certain extent limited in China.

2.1. RELATIONS BETWEEN THE PEOPLE'S COURTS, THE PUBLIC SECURITY AUTHORITIES, AND THE PEOPLE'S PROCURATORATES

Article 7 of the CPL remains unchanged and states: 'In conducting criminal proceedings, the people's courts, the people's procuratorates and the public security authorities shall divide responsibilities, coordinate their efforts and check each other to ensure the correct and effective enforcement of law'. Accordingly, the three institutions should, pursuant to the provisions of the

---

[7] See 'Shenyang Liu Yong Case', <http://news.sina.com.cn/z/liuyongsy/>, accessed 12 August 2011.

[8] LI XINJIAN 1997, p. 7.

Law, perform their respective duties, fulfil their respective responsibilities, and work together in unity. Furthermore, they should conduct criminal procedures by strictly following the division of work. There should be no mutual representation or overstepping by the respective authorities. They should also correct any of the other party's mistakes in order to correctly enforce the relevant provisions of the CPL, ensure the quality of cases, and realise the common goal of punishing criminals and protecting the people.

There is no denying that the work pattern of the three institutions – division of duties and responsibilities, mutual collaboration and mutual restriction is the result of years of historical development. It fits the procedural traditions and the basic situation of China. Interpreting the article from the legislative point of view, the people's courts, though not in a dominant position, are not subordinated to the public security authorities or to the people's procuratorates. In judicial practice, the people's court must work with the other two bodies and deliver guilty judgments as soon as possible despite doubtful or even illegal evidence, whilst it has no judicial power to review investigation activities. Nor can it review and screen prosecutions it receives from the people's procuratorates through intermediary trial procedures, (a preliminary hearing procedure which plays a significant role connecting the prosecution and the trial, as in Germany). In essence, the court is rather weak. 'The executive not only dispenses the honours, but holds the sword of the community; the legislature not only commands the purse, but prescribes the rules by which the duties and rights of every citizen are to be regulated; the judiciary, on the contrary, has no influence over either the sword or the purse; no direction either of the strength or of the wealth of the society; and can take no active resolution whatever. It may truly be said to have neither Force nor Will, but merely judgment; and must ultimately depend upon the aid of the executive arm even for the efficacy of its judgments'.[9] The de facto weakness of the people's courts and their lack of independence suggests that judges often fail to transcend the pressures from the outside world and decide on the exclusion of illegally obtained evidence in a fair manner during trials.

2.2. THE RELATIONSHIP BETWEEN THE PEOPLE'S PROCURATORATES AND THE PUBLIC SECURITY AUTHORITIES

According to the Constitution and the CPL, the procuratorate is the state institution for legal supervision. Understandably, the nature of procuratorial power has long been a source of contention among academics in the field of

---

[9]   HAMILTON, JAY & MADISON 2001, p. 402.

criminal procedure, as demonstrated by the different views coming out of research discussions in 1999. They included the executive power theory, the judicial power theory, the dual-nature theory (executive and judicial powers), and the legal supervision power theory. The essence of the contention lies in how to accurately define the relations between the procuratorial, legal supervision and prosecution powers. Generally speaking, experts of procuratorial theories agree that the procuratorial power is equal to the legal supervision power. Some scholars argue that the procuratorial power is an executive power. Conflict is inevitable since the procuratorates boast both powers (prosecution and legal supervision). Irrespective of the theoretical contention, the legal supervision function of the procuratorate comes from the Constitution, the CPL and the Organic Law of the People's Procuratorates of the People's Republic of China. The Constitution and the laws have given the procuratorate the power of legal supervision due to China's unique historical experience. The establishment of its procuratorial system is centred upon Lenin's philosophy of legal supervision as well as drawing upon the ancient censor system from China's feudal past. As a result, the procuratorial power is dual-natured, combining legal supervision and prosecution. In effect, the role of the procuratorate is consistent with China's political system, which features the NPC – one government and two houses (namely the State Council, the Supreme People's Court and the Supreme People's Procuratorate).

Inherent in the legal supervision power, the people's procuratorate's supervision over investigation units and procedure matches the basic procedural principles in which the procuratorates guide investigation and investigation serves the prosecution. However, within the current legal framework, the investigation units are led by the drive to solve cases and given the lack of outside intervention, the hope that the investigation units will proactively curb illegal collection of evidence is very unrealistic. Therefore, the people's procuratorates need to start to use the exclusionary rule to supervise investigation activities in order to achieve effective prevention of illegal collection of evidence.

On the one hand, Article 54 of the new CPL stipulates that where evidence that should be excluded is found during an investigation, review for prosecution or trial, such evidence shall be excluded in accordance with the law and shall not be used as a basis for opinions or decisions on prosecution and decisions of courts. Therefore, as the party responsible for exclusion, the people's procuratorates have an obligation to review and exclude illegally obtained evidence during their review of arrest approval and prosecution. On the other hand, apart from proactively excluding evidence, the people's procuratorates are also required to review and supervise investigation activities performed by investigation units, in order to prevent illegal collection of evidence at the root. The procurator-police relationship in China is different from that in civil law countries.[10] The procuratorates neither have the power to investigate ordinary criminal cases,[11] nor can they directly guide and lead the activities of investigation units. They can only review investigation activities through their review of arrest approval, which is too simplistic, narrow, and far from effective. Therefore, in view of the procuratorates' legal supervision function, researchers of procuratorial theories have attempted to transplant the normal role of the procuratorate – guiding and controlling investigation activities, which is commonly established by the criminal procedure of civil law countries, into the legal supervision function unique to the procuratorate of China. In essence, this marks a shift from the procedural function to the legal supervision function of the procuratorate. For example, the issuance of the Several Provisions on Intensifying the Legal Supervision of Judicial Functionaries' Dereliction of Duty in Litigation Activities (for Trial Implementation) and the Provisions on the Relevant Issues on the Supervision of Filing of Criminal Cases (for Trial Implementation) signifies the trend in the procuratorates to further enhance their legal supervision function with particular emphasis on supervision of investigations. This trend actually shows the procuratorate's hope to provide substantive control and guidance over investigation activities, so that investigation serves prosecution and that the balance between combating crime and protecting human rights is attained.

The first published draft revision to the CPL contained a provision stating that the people's procuratorates may present comments and advice on serious cases such as murder, filed and investigated by public security authorities. However, it was deleted after consultation, largely due to the fact that procuratorate-guided investigation contradicts the work pattern of the three institutions – division of duties and responsibilities, mutual collaboration and

---

[10] See Chapter 1, para. 2.1.

[11] Art. 18 of the new CPL: 'Investigation in criminal cases shall be conducted by the public security units, except as otherwise provided by law. Crimes of embezzlement and bribery, crimes of dereliction of duty committed by State functionaries, and crimes involving violations of a citizen's personal rights such as illegal detention, extortion of confessions by torture, retaliation, being framed, and illegal searches and crimes involving infringement of a citizen's democratic rights – committed by State functionaries by taking advantage of their functions and powers – shall be placed on file for investigation by the people's procuratorates. If cases involving other grave crimes committed by State functionaries by taking advantage of their functions and powers need to be handled directly by the people's procuratorates, they may be placed on file for investigation by the people's procuratorates upon the decision by the people's procuratorates at or above the provincial level. Cases of private prosecution shall be handled directly by the people's courts.

mutual restriction. The basic principles of the CPL indicate that investigation is the premise for prosecution and prosecution is the end result of investigation. The two are inseparable. China should rebuild a procurator-police relationship which features the 'integration of investigation and procuratorates' and 'procuratorate-guided investigation'. This will enhance the transparency of the investigation procedure and achieve the objective of investigation serving prosecution, thereby tackling the root of the problem of illegal collection of evidence.[12]

3. ENFORCEMENT PRACTICE AND BARRIERS TO EXCLUSION

The provisions of the CPL are divided into 'substantive' and 'implementation' provisions. The former is equivalent to the legal principles in the world of jurisprudence, which stipulate what shall be done, under which conditions and the legal consequence of failing to do so'. The latter 'prescribes how to materialize the substantive provisions, including the procedure initiator, the applied and his or her rights, the adjudicator who receives the application, deadline of action, action method, burden of proof, standard of proof, method of proof, judgment, and remedy for rejecting judgment'.[13] The objective of exclusion directly determines the design and structure of substantive and procedural provisions. It also affects how investigators, prosecutors and judges view and understand the exclusionary rule. In civil law countries exclusion aims to deter the police from illegal collection of evidence by investigation units and to protect procedural justice and safeguard the right to privacy. In China, public debates about the objective of exclusion have been ongoing ever since the publication of the Two Rules. Some overseas scholars have even suggested that the exclusionary rule set forth by the Two Rules has certain political implications.[14]

The publication of the Two Rules by the Supreme People's Court has, undeniably, demonstrated commitment to combating torture, but it has also had a positive impact on procedure and on society. Legal reform in relation to evidentiary issues is subject, on the one hand, to the influence of internal factors such as the structure of judicial institutions and the design and purpose of legal procedure, as well as external factors including the political and cultural backdrop. The launch of the Two Rules has, to a large extent, been subject to external influences. 'The extortion of confessions by torture

---

[12]   CHEN WEIDONG 2002.
[13]   SUO ZHENGJIE 2002, p. 33–46.
[14]   LEWIS 2011, p. 667.

has long plagued the criminal justice system in China. Almost all miscarriage of justice cases that have come to light so far involve this problem, which is testament to the importance of the exclusionary rule to China's criminal judicial reform'.[15] A spate of wrongful convictions caused by the extortion of confessions by torture, as evident in the case of Zhao Zuohai, have drawn wide public and media attention, and in turn triggered the formulation of the Two Rules. It was further explained by the Supreme People's Court that 'the exclusionary rule has such wide scope that it is unrealistic and unworkable for us to stipulate everything, given the current legal framework. That is why the Two Rules stress three points: one, the exclusion of illegal evidence in ordinary criminal cases; two, the exclusion of illegal oral evidence; three, the exclusion of oral evidence extracted by the extortion of confessions by torture and other illegal means'.[16] Therefore, the purpose of having the Two Rules is to combat the extortion of confessions by torture in investigation, particularly the exclusion of oral evidence extorted by torture and other illegal means. A consensus has been reached on this purpose.

On the other hand, the Two Rules have not only determined the future direction of evidentiary legislation in the amendment to the CPL but also reaffirmed the Chinese government's commitment to eradicating torture and implementing the UN Convention against Torture. In addition, the theoretical world has been active in offering detailed interpretation on the basic content, the legal background and the social significance of the Two Rules.[17] The majority of the terms in the Two Rules on exclusion are about procedural arrangements. They provide further specifics for the principles set out in the CPL and relevant judicial interpretations. They should be seen as an integral part of the 'implementation rules'. Therefore, it goes without saying that the Two Rules have had a positive impact on the legislation principles and the design of clauses by legislative authorities, as well as the enforcement philosophy and the work methodology of judicial authorities. Thanks to all the preparatory work, the exclusionary rule has been absorbed by the revision of the CPL as a mature system. It is not only a part of the basic content of the revision, but also one of its highlights. When the Standing Committee of the NPC published the draft to invite suggestions from the public, the inclusion of this system in the new law was not merely advocated by the NPC delegates, members of the Standing Committee, the public, the media, scholars and lawyers, but the public security authorities, the people's

---

[15] CHEN WEIDONG 2010.

[16] LI GUANGLUN 2010.

[17] For example, CHEN GUANGZHONG 2010; FAN CHONGYI 2010; CHEN WEIDONG 2010; CHEN WEIDONG 2010b; LONG ZONGZHI 2010; SONG YINGHUI 2010.

procuratorate and the people's courts were also united in their attitude towards this issue. Although the three institutions may have had different comments on the specifics, they did ultimately agree on establishing the exclusionary rule in the revised CPL.

BIBLIOGRAPHY

CHEN GUANGZHONG 2010
CHEN GUANGZHONG, 'Discussing Several Theoretical and Practical Issues in the Reform of Criminal Evidence System – from the Angle of "the Two Evidence Provisions"', *China Legal Science*, 6th edn., 2010.

CHEN WEIDONG 2002
CHEN WEIDONG, 'Integration of Investigation and Prosecution and Restructuring of Pre-trial Procedure', *Journal of National Prosecutors College*, 1st edn., 2002.

CHEN WEIDONG 2010
CHEN WEIDONG, 'Pros and Cons of the Two Evidence Provisions', *Evidence Science*, 5th edn., 2010.

CHEN WEIDONG 2010B
CHEN WEIDONG, 'New Developments in China's Criminal Evidence Law – Assessing the Two Evidence Provisions', *Jurists Review*, 5th edn., 2010.

FAN CHONGYI 2010
FAN CHONGYI, 'Substantive Justice is Impossible without Procedural Justice – Studying "the Two Evidence Provisions"', *Law Science Magazine*, 6th edn., 2010.

HAMILTON, JAY & MADISON 2001
HAMILTON, A., JAY, J. & MADISON, J., *The Federalist*, Indianapolis: Liberty Fund Inc., 2001.

LEWIS 2011
LEWIS, M.K., 'Controlling Abuse to Maintain Control: The Exclusionary Rule in China', *New York University Journal of International Law and Politics*, 2011, p. 629-697.

LI FENFEI 2006

LI FENFEI, 'Analysing Reasons for the "Toothless". "Provisions on the Exclusion of Illegal Evidence"', *Journal of National Procurators College*, 1st edn., 2006.

LI XINJIAN 1997

LI XINJIAN, *Criminal Procedure Structure Theory*, Beijing: Publishing House of China University of Political Science and Law, 1997.

LONG ZONGZHI 2010

LONG ZONGZHI, 'Studying Several Issues on Regulation and Implementation of the Two Evidence Provisions', *China Legal Science*, 6th edn., 2010.

LI GUANGLUN 2010

LI GUANGLUN, 'Understanding and Application of the Provisions on the Exclusion of Illegal Evidence', *People's Procuratorial Monthly*, 16th edn., 2010.

SONG YINGHUI 2010

SONG YINGHUI, 'The Exclusionary Rules of Illegally Obtained Evidence in China and Their Application', *Law Science Magazine*, 6th edn., 2010.

SUO ZHENGJIE 2002

SUO ZHENGJIE, *Legal Philosophy of Criminal Procedures*, Beijing: Publishing House of the Chinese People's Public Security University, 2002.

5. IMPROVEMENT OF THE EXCLUSIONARY RULE IN CHINA

Chen Weidong and Chai Yufeng

Since its inception in 1979, China's Criminal Procedure Law (CPL) has only ever had two major amendments, one in 1996 and one in 2012. This small number and the fact that the two amendments were over ten years apart reflects the prudence of lawmakers. Given the fact that the legislative and judicial authorities as well as the public need time to observe, accept and adapt to the revised CPL, it is therefore unlikely that the National People's Congress (NPC) will put the CPL on its legislation agenda in the foreseeable future. The starting point for the perfection of the exclusionary rule in China should be the creation of a judicial environment conducive to its implementation. The 'environment' includes both internal elements, such as judicial independence, protection of the right of defence, system of precedents, as well as external elements, such as seeking recognition by judicial administrative workers and the public of excluding and combating illegally obtained evidence.

1. PERFECTING SUPPORT SYSTEMS FOR THE EXCLUSIONARY RULE

1.1. CRIMINAL VERDICT REASONING SYSTEM

According to the 'Two Evidence Provisions' (Two Rules) and the new CPL, illegally obtained evidence cannot be used as the basis for conviction. In other words, even though a piece of illegally obtained evidence cannot act as the basis for conviction and sentencing in a criminal verdict, it may appear in the trial and affect the judge's free evaluation of evidence. Furthermore, in China, the procedure for excluding illegally obtained evidence is attached to the criminal litigation procedure. A judge can only decide to admit or exclude certain evidence as part of the written judgment. As a result, the judgment must explain and elaborate on procedural matters relating to the exclusion of illegally obtained evidence, in addition to convicting and sentencing the defendant. In China, a criminal verdict is a legal judicial document prepared by the court handling a criminal case in accordance with its mandate and criminal litigation procedure.[1] For a long time, judges have had a tendency to focus on stating facts without explaining the reasoning which lay behind the judgment. With inadequate reasoning, the judgment ends up being a simple list of the facts of the case, arguments made by the prosecution and the defence, the reason for the decision, and the decision itself. The implementation of the exclusionary rule presents a great opportunity for China to reform and improve its criminal verdict reasoning system. Take Case 15 in chapter 3 as an example, where the court of the first trial emphasized the following in its verdict:

> 'The defendant did make a guilty confession in the investigation stage. But during the trial, he claimed that he was tortured into confessing and offered detailed clues to support his claim. The result of forensic evaluation suggested the defendant's left big toe had suffered soft tissue injury. It failed to show the time of the injury and whether it was caused by a confession extorted by torture, as well as failing to show any use of torture by the police officers in the video clips of the interrogations and in the physical check-up record on arrival. Nevertheless, the possibility that the pre-trial confession made by the defendant might have been obtained illegally cannot be excluded and the court thus decides not to admit the defendant's confession in the investigation stage'.

In this verdict, the judge had to make a statement concerning the illegal method the investigators had used to obtain evidence and the illegal evidence thereby created. He also responded to each of the clues and reasons put forward by the defence and the evidence materials presented by the prosecution in order to prove the evidence was collected legally, and then ultimately made the decision based on the standard of proof for exclusion of illegally obtained evidence. Admittedly, the reasoning for evidence exclusion is relatively simple compared with that of conviction and sentencing. It is still the best response to the focal issues of arguments between the prosecution and the defence in the exclusion procedure. It is also the approach required for applying the exclusionary rule in judicial practice.

1.2. CASE GUIDANCE SYSTEM

In European countries, cases ruled by the constitutional and supreme courts and the European Human Rights Court constitute major points of reference. Such a precedent system is not the same as the narrowly-defined case law

---

[1]   CHEN WEIDONG, *Judicial Documents Writing*, Beijing: Publishing House of the Renmin University of China, 2002, p. 1.

system in common law countries. But with its broad and extensive scope, it plays an extremely important role in helping judges understand and apply the exclusionary rule. For example, by referring to precedents, a judge can grasp the standard for 'torture' and 'pressure' in different cases in a flexible manner. Publicising precedents also serves to provide positive guidance for investigators on the collection of evidence.

China does not acknowledge the status of precedents as a legal source, but has recently begun to promote a publicly available case guidance system. The Supreme People's Court issued the Provisions on Case Guidance on 26 November 2010. According to the Provisions, only cases which meet the requirements set out in the Provisions and selected by the case guidance office of the Supreme People's Court can be referred to as guiding cases. Furthermore, the key elements of judgment identified by such guiding cases offer guidance to the people's courts when they handle and deliver verdicts on similar cases and may be invoked and used as the reasoning basis in the judgments.[2] The Supreme People's Court published four 'guiding cases' on 20 December 2011, including two criminal cases. Recently, the Supreme People's Court began to devise a plan for building a national uniform judgment documents website. In doing so, the Court hopes to realise higher courts' supervision and guidance on judgment documents and to make it easy for the parties, the public and scholars to search for such documents by consolidating available internet and database resources. As a result, the online publication of judgment documents will act as a database and bring comprehensive benefits.[3]

The exclusion of illegally obtained evidence is a matter for the public security authorities, the procuratorate and the courts, but whether evidence can be successfully excluded will depend on whether these three agencies can reach a shared view With the system of guiding cases, the Supreme People's Court can, firstly, unify standards for exclusion so that similar decisions are reached in similar cases. Furthermore, it can effectively avoid the many problems experienced after the implementation of the Two Rules at the people's courts. For example, the Supreme People's Court can identify which acts of evidence collection amount to extortion of confessions by torture or other illegal means and which 'severely affect judicial justice', to help judges

---

[2]   'Head of The Supreme People's Court Research Office Takes Journalists' Questions', <http://www.court.gov.cn/xwzx/jdjd/sdjd/201112/t20111220_168539.htm>, accessed 1 February 2011.

[3]   'The Supreme People's Court Plans to Build a National Uniform Judgment Documents Website', <http://www.legaldaily.com.cn/index_article/content/2012-01/31/content_-3327390.htm>, accessed 1 February 2011.

understand and apply the exclusionary rule. Secondly, guiding cases can provide clear guidance on the process involved in applying the exclusion procedure. It is true that the four published guiding cases to date do not raise any procedural matters in criminal trials, but this does not rule out the possibility that, in future, the Supreme People's Court will select guiding cases to clarify how a judge should use the exclusion procedure and address disputes between the prosecution and defense. Finally, reference to guiding cases by the judge can help to convince the prosecution and defense and explain the reasons underlying a verdict. This will help the judge to avoid challenges by government agencies, the parties concerned and the public and direct pressure towards the Supreme People's Court.

2. EFFECTIVELY COMBATING THE EXTORTION OF CONFESSIONS BY TORTURE AND THE USE OF OTHER ILLEGAL MEANS TO OBTAIN EVIDENCE

The most common and serious act of illegal collection of evidence in China is the extortion of confessions by torture. To effectively curb this problem requires a systematic project. The exclusion of illegally obtained evidence is only a part of a larger system. We should not pin all our hopes of eradicating the problem of extortion of confessions by torture on the application of the exclusionary rule by judges, as the creation of such evidence also concerns judicial investigations, internal control of the investigative authorities and many other factors. Here we would like to discuss two other effective methods: audio/videotaping of interviews and the presence of lawyers in interrogations. The first method is commonly used by the procuratorate to prove the legal collection of evidence and the second is seen as a key issue for reform of the investigative interrogation process.

2.1.   AUDIO/VIDEOTAPING OF THE ENTIRE INTERROGATION PROCESS

'In China's judicial practice, it is quite common to see investigators in developed areas recording interrogations by the public security authorities. But such audio/videotapes tend to record one confession made by a defendant, instead of all the interrogations a defendant is subjected to'.[4] As a result, the audio/videotaping system has not only created a situation in which

---

[4]   CHEN WEIDONG, *Model Criminal Procedure Codes*, Beijing: Publishing House of Renmin University of China, 2011, p. 280.

'people charged with audio/videotaping choose not to tape when torture takes place and interrogators choose not to torture when tapes are running', but has also become one of the measures used by the prosecution to prove the legality of evidence collection. In order to prevent investigators from using audio/videotaping to secure the last guilty confession and hide the fact that they extort confessions by torture, we should promote the system of audio/videotaping the entire interrogation process.

According to Article 121 of the new CPL, an investigator may, during the interrogation of a criminal suspect, record the interrogation process electronically; where a suspect may be sentenced to life imprisonment or death, the investigator shall audio/videotape the interrogation process. Audio/videotaping shall be used during the entire process of interrogation for the purpose of completeness. This scope is, however, slightly too narrow. Given that the prevention of illegal collection of evidence needs mutual collaboration between different systems, some scholars have proposed that the entire process of interrogation for cases without the presence of a lawyer be audio/videotaped. In addition, taking into account the different development stages across different regions in China, as well as the differences in interrogation time and venue, the promotion of this system requires special grants from the judicial authorities to guarantee its successful operation.

2.2. THE PRESENCE OF LAWYERS DURING INTERROGATIONS

China's criminal justice system has been striving to protect the right of defence of criminal suspects, or defendants, and their defence lawyers. The 2007 amendment to the Lawyer's Law has perfected all the rights necessary for lawyers to participate in criminal litigation – the right to meet with the client, the right to investigate and collect evidence, and the right to review case files. But the amendment is not explicit about whether the lawyer has the right to be present during the interrogation of a criminal suspect. With regard to the issue of the system of defence, during the revision of the CPL some lawyers called for the establishment of a system allowing the presence of lawyers. However, given that there has been limited research and practical testing on the issue, the revised CPL does not include such provision.

Establishing such a system, and particularly guaranteeing the presence of a lawyer at the first interrogation, allows the suspect on-site access to legal advice and recommendations as well as support, be it emotional or otherwise.[5] It is also effective in preventing the extortion of confessions by torture and the use of other illegal means to collect evidence. In addition, the defence lawyer can lodge a prompt complaint against illegal collection of evidence and testify in court as a witness. Such a system is well established in the UK, France and Russia.[6] Some local procuratorates in China have started to experiment with this. The Xiaguan District Procuratorate of Nanjing for example was the first to promote the presence of lawyers during interrogations of criminal suspects back in 2007.[7] In 2008, the Haimen District Procuratorate of Jiangsu, Haimen Municipal Judicial Bureau, and the Lawyer's Association jointly drafted and implemented the Provisional Measures on Lawyer's Presence during Interrogation of Minor Criminal Suspects during Review for Prosecution.[8] In 2010, the No. 2 Branch of the Beijing Municipal Procuratorate issued the Rules on Defence Lawyers Attending Interrogations (Trial Operation), which provide that a criminal suspect may ask his or her defence lawyer to attend his or her interrogation, provided the suspect is on bail.[9] According to media coverage, since 2006, Xuzhou, Tianjin, Suzhou, Nanjing, Taixing, Zhuzhou, Jinhua and Beijing (altogether 8 cities in 5 provinces) have either conducted pilot programs or actually put in place such a system.[10] The above pilot programmes are carried out in the review for prosecution stage. There is no precedent in China for allowing the presence of lawyers during the investigation stage but, it is inevitable that this system will come one day in the future. In addition, in order to fully achieve a system allowing the presence of lawyers requires the collaboration of duty lawyers so that criminal suspects or defendants can have access to counsel at any time, and thus obtain the legal consultation and advice they require.

---

[5]   The Salduz-doctrine allowed the suspect to have access to lawyers in the phase of police interrogation. See ECtHR 27 November 2008, *Salduz v. Turkey*, no. 36391/02.

[6]   Art. 2 of the Criminal Law Act 1977 of the UK; Arts. 114 and 116 of the Criminal Procedure Code of France; Art. 53 of the Russian Federation Code of Criminal Procedure – CHEN WEIDONG 2011, p. 133.

[7]   'The Xiaguan District Procuratorate of Nanjing Promotes "Lawyer's Presence" System', <http://news.xinhuanet.com/legal/2007-01/31/content_5676587.htm>, accessed 1 February 2012.

[8]   'Jiangsu Haimen, Implementing System of Lawyer's Presence during Interrogation of Criminal Suspects', <http://news.jcrb.com/jiancha/jcdt/200810/t20081008_78867.html>, accessed 1 February 2012.

[9]   'Attending Presents An Opportunity for "Lawyer's Right to Presence"', <http://news.cnxianzai.com/2010/12/304109.html>, accessed 1 February 2012.

[10]   'Suspects May Have Lawyers Present during Interrogation, Beijing Becomes the Eighth City to Develop the System', <http://newspaper.jfdaily.com/xwcb/html/2010-12/07/content_-468746.htm>, accessed 1 February 2012.

6. CONCLUSION

Chen Weidong, Taru Spronken and Chai Yufeng

The creation and existence of a legal system is born out of the knowledge that comes from extensive experience and not from theorists sitting round a table drafting laws. It comes into being through social practice and continually develops and evolves. Every existing system is the result of the interplay of multiple factors, including political, economic, social, cultural, historical and geographical conditions.[1] Looking at the various problems in China concerning the application of the exclusionary rule, we are not trying to apportion blame or criticism to any person or organisation. The issue is not the law-breaking behaviour of one specific investigator or judicial authority that has caused miscarriages of justice as in the case of Zhao Zuohai, and others. Nor is it about the defects of single rules. The root of the problem lies in China's current justice system, and its social culture which cannot easily accept the exclusionary rule. This means that Chinese judges are required to identify the truth in all cases, and realise substantive justice. They are reluctant to let these aims be outweighed by procedural justice, and therefore the development path of the exclusionary rule will be a gradual one. Starting with a blank slate, there has been a gradual improvement and transformation of China's exclusionary rule. The promulgation and implementation of the 'Two Evidence Provisions' and the revised Criminal Procedure Law (CPL) are based on the real situation of current judicial practice in China. They reflect the goodwill of the legislative authorities and their aspiration to provide more detailed evidentiary rules and improve the exclusionary rule. Furthermore, they showcase the firm resolve of the people's courts, the people's procuratorates and the public security authorities to implement the exclusionary rule.

On the other hand, China and Europe, especially the Netherlands, are similar in their mode of litigation, which means that they can learn from each other as regards the exclusionary rule. Following on from the comparison in chapter 2, we believe that after the implementation of the new CPL in 2013,

---

[1] CHEN WEIDONG, *The Journey to Procedural Justice,* China Law Press, 2005.

China firstly needs to do more to protect the independence of the judiciary, as a premise of putting the exclusionary rule in to practice. After that, in terms of supporting measures, China also needs to perfect its case law in order to define torture, and to attempt to gradually define the core issues of illegal collection of evidence, so as to make all illegally obtained evidence eligible for exclusion, and to identify the boundaries between statutory and discretionary exclusion.[2] At the same time, practical and effective complaint mechanisms and procedural safeguards should be established in the pre-trial stage, especially in the investigation stage, in order to protect the defence rights of suspects and lawyers. This is one of the most important issues required to fulfil the spirit of 'no person may be forced to prove his or her own guilt' in Article 50 in the new CPL. Next to this establishing a system where lawyers are present during interrogations will provide safeguards against undue pressure on suspects. Finally, China must strengthen communication and cooperation with international human rights groups, so that we can scrutinize and construct a criminal justice system at the supra-national level,[3]and fulfil the requirement in Article 2 in the new CPL relating to 'respecting and protecting human rights' in order to achieve the spirit of the Universal Declaration of Human Rights and other relevant international treaties.

Just as a country's criminal justice system is like scales, balancing the punishment of crime and the safeguarding of human rights, so the exclusionary rule is like the weights loaded on either side. The revised Criminal Procedure Law is by no means the end of the development of the exclusionary rule in China, but rather a new start. We hope that by seizing the opportunity of evidence exclusion, China will find its way to realise procedural justice in criminal procedure.

---

[2] In the interpretation of the new CPL by the Legislative Affairs Commission of the NPC Standing Committee, the understanding of 'extorted confessions by torture' in Art. 54 follows The Convention against Torture and Other Cruel, Inhuman or Degrading Treatment or Punishment. In future, we need clarification in order to improve the application in legal practice.

[3] For example, in November 1991, the Information Office of the State Council published a white paper on 'The Human Rights Condition in China'. In April 2009, the Information Office of the State Council published the 'The National Human Rights Action Plan (2009-2010)', which is the first plan relating to human rights published by the Chinese government. Exchanges and cooperation between China and the international community is strengthening yearly. See <http://news.xinhuanet.com/ziliao/2003-01/22/content_702907.-htm>, accessed 2 April 2012.

PART II

DETENTION CENTRE REGULATIONS

1. MOVING TOWARDS MODERN DETENTION CENTRE REGULATIONS

Gerard de Jonge

1. WHY DETENTION CENTRE REGULATIONS ARE IMPORTANT

1.1. HOW A SAD INCIDENT CAN TRIGGER INNOVATIONS – THE 'HIDE AND SEEK' CASE

The fact that sad incidents can lead to important innovations is demonstrated by the so-called 'hide and seek case', well known in China, but less so in other countries. Therefore it seems appropriate to give a summary of this incident for the uninformed reader, referring to coverage in the *China Daily* online newspaper.[1]

A young man, suspected of having committed an offence, was detained in Jinning (Yunnan province) on 30 January 2009. Little more than a week after his admission to the detention centre he was admitted to hospital, where he died four days later from brain damage. The Jinning public security bureau maintained that Li was fatally injured while playing 'hide-and-seek' with other inmates, one of whom supposedly reacted angrily when his hiding place was uncovered by Li. This statement has aroused much media attention across the nation. After an initial false report by prison authorities and an unsuccessful investigation by a special committee including members of the public, the Yunnan Provincial Procuratorate announced that Li was actually beaten to death by 'prison bullies'. More cases of deaths in police custody can be found in the online archive of the *China Daily* that notices that police, over time, have cited 'a litany of suspected causes of death including "falling out of bed", "suddenly drinking cold water" and "playing hide-and-seek with other inmates"', absurd as these may seem. Sometimes a suspect death in custody attracts the attention of the international media. The death of Xue Jinbo in a police cell in Wukan (Guangdong province) in December 2011 is a

---

[1]   <http://www.chinadaily.com.cn/china/>, accessed on 2 March 2012.

recent example.[2] The alleged ill treatment of the famous artist Ai Wei Wei whilst being interrogated by security officers was immediately reported abroad.[3] Incidents like these, if not investigated promptly and effectively, can lead to serious social and political unrest and to a decline of public trust in governmental institutions. It is therefore in the interest of both the citizens and the government to analyse the causes of these unfortunate events and to develop legal and practical mechanisms to prevent further inhuman treatment of persons who as suspects are deprived of their liberty and placed under the control of security officials.

The authorities did not fail to react to the public unrest caused by the 'hide and seek' incident and other cases involving death or ill treatment of detainees in detention centres and endorsed academic research into the causes of this kind of incidents and put forward suggestions for the improvement of detention centre legislation and the monitoring system. The Center for Criminal Procedure and Reform (CCPR) of the Renmin University of China School of Law (RUC) responded to this by starting a research project that, as is explained in the introductory chapter of this book, features three distinct approaches: 1) an in-depth analysis of the theoretical and practical implications of the exclusion of evidence that is illegally obtained; 2) the improvement of interrogation techniques and 3) revision of detention centre regulations to improve the material and procedural protection of detainees. The first two issues are dealt with in chapters 2 and 3. The updating of detention centre regulations is the subject of this chapter but it is obvious that the three approaches are strongly interrelated: taken together they aim to reduce and ultimately eliminate the risk of maltreatment of suspects by police interviewers, by their fellow inmates or by detention centre personnel. If the results of this threefold research bear fruit, the 'hide and seek' incident could end up having a salutary effect on the quality of criminal procedure and the position of suspects.

Maastricht University in the Netherlands has carried out a study of international standards concerning the treatment of both pre-trial and sentenced prisoners, as both convicted prisoners (who have less than one year to serve) and suspects are held in detention centres. The results of this study are presented in paragraphs 2 and 3 of this chapter.

---

[2] This incident was, for instance, widely covered in the Dutch press. *De Volkskrant* (translated: *Peoples' Daily*) of 15 and 16 December 2011, cited citizens of Wukan who openly doubted whether Xue died, as the police had said, of a heart attack, suspecting that he had in fact been beaten to death by the police during interrogation.

[3] Report in *De Volkskrant* of 3 March 2012, where Ai Wei Wei claimed that he had been threatened during police interviews and that his lawyer had been threatened as well.

The RUC study plan involved an evaluation of a pilot lay visitors scheme in a detention centre in Liaoyuan, Jilin Province and a pilot complaints mechanism in the detention centre in Wuhu, Anhui Province. The results of this fieldwork (described in paragraph 6) have contributed a great deal to the work on the draft detention centre regulations that are presented in the first annex to this chapter.

1.2. SUSPECTS ARE 'LEGAL CITIZENS' AND SHOULD BE TREATED AS SUCH

Persons detained by the police in order to be interrogated about crimes they may have committed are quite often viewed by the public as convicted 'criminals', demonstrating, the tendency to favour the 'presumption of guilt' over the 'presumption of innocence' that is one of the basic principles of criminal procedure. Few show compassion to detainees who often find themselves in dire situations, while most people are indifferent about how detainees are treated, especially in countries or regions where the struggle for economic survival is the main daily concern. Proposals for reform of detention centre regulations cannot therefore count on much public support where living conditions of free citizens are tough. Initiatives for reform cannot be expected to come from the police themselves where they feel constant pressure to deliver 'results' in the form of signed confessions, to be obtained as quickly as possible, lest the applicable performance indicators are not met. In these circumstances the police investigators may be tempted to resort to the exertion of illegal pressure, varying from verbal threats to physical abuse, on suspects who keep silent or do not readily confess, and they will continue to do so if they are not subsequently corrected by the courts of law (by excluding thus obtained evidence) or by their superiors.[4] As most interrogations take place in interview rooms in detention centres, the management of these centres is responsible for the safety of 'their' detainees. As a consequence, the director or warden can be held accountable for possible ill treatment of detainees during interrogations on the premises of his institution. This means that detention centre regulations must contain provisions that protect suspects during police interviews and say what

---

[4]   UN *Code of Conduct for Law Enforcement Officials* adopted by General Assembly resolution 34/169 of 17 December 1979 Art. 5: 'No law enforcement official may inflict, instigate or tolerate any act of torture or other cruel, inhuman or degrading treatment or punishment, nor may any law enforcement official invoke superior orders or exceptional circumstances such as a state of war or a threat of war, a threat to national security, internal political instability or any other public emergency as a justification of torture or other cruel, inhuman or degrading treatment or punishment'.

procedures are applicable in cases of alleged or suspected ill treatment of detainees during interrogations.

Detainees, as shown in the cases mentioned in paragraph 1.1 above, are also in need of protection against violent acts from fellow-prisoners as well as detention centre personnel. It is again the management and ultimately the director who should be held accountable for physical and mental harm to detainees. Their safety and security should actively be protected. The concept of *dynamic security* – embedded in the European Prison Rules (EPR)[5] – offers guidance here. Rule 51.2 says: 'The security which is provided by physical barriers and other technical means shall be complemented by the dynamic security provided by an alert staff who knows the prisoners who are under their control.' In the official commentary to this Rule it is said: 'Security also depends on an alert staff who interact with prisoners, who have an awareness of what is going on in the prison and who make sure that prisoners are kept active in a positive way. This is often described as dynamic security and is much more qualitative than one which is entirely dependent on static security measures'.

The concept of dynamic security is useless, however, when the applicable regime allows only for formal contacts between detainees and staff, where only commands are given to the detainees and normal human contact between detainees and their keepers is nigh impossible.

What counts, for the general public, as well as for the authorities responsible for the treatment of detainees, is that they should be made aware of the fact that deprivation of liberty of a person does not automatically imply his or her 'civil death'. Detainees and prisoners remain 'legal citizens', which means that they retain all rights that are not lawfully taken away by the decision to place them in police (remand) custody or by the decision to sentence them. In sum, viewing detained suspects as human beings with rights helps to combat inhuman and illegal treatment. As soon as officials see them as worthless criminals who deserve little or no compassion, detainees are vulnerable to abuse.

1.3. THE FUNCTION OF DETENTION CENTRES AND THE TREATMENT OF DETAINEES

In most countries detention centres or remand centres have a simple function. That is to retain persons who are suspected of having committed a

---

[5]   Council of Europe Committee of Ministers, Recommendation Rec(2006)2 of the Committee of Ministers to member states on the European Prison Rules (adopted by the Committee of Ministers on 11 January 2006 at the 952nd meeting of the Ministers' Deputies).

(serious) offence and to keep them available for (further) investigation and for court hearings. Pre-trial detention as such may never be used to press a suspect to confess or to give testimony in cases involving other suspects. In this sense, a detention centre is not an investigative tool.

Many national jurisdictions require that remand detention should be used as a measure of last resort and should not last longer than strictly necessary. This means that, if bail is a realistic option, it should be granted and if not, that pre-trial detention should end when the investigators cannot gather sufficient proof against the suspect within a reasonable time. In practice, suspects are not always granted bail where it would be reasonable and practicable. The investigating authorities, often, as a matter of routine, prolong the pre-trial detention (initial police detention and arrest) to (and sometimes beyond) the legal maximum by what McConville calls 'creative' interpretation of the rules.[6] These practices have the effect that too many people are kept in detention much longer than strictly necessary. It goes without saying that an excessively long stay in an overcrowded dormitory is a perfect precondition for the development of 'hide and seek' situations, for aggression between detainees, suicides, suicide attempts and strained relations with personnel. The latter can easily result in imposing disciplinary sanctions on frustrated and angry inmates. This way, detention centres run the risk of becoming places of suffering and punishment, which was never their purpose. To maintain good order in detention centres it is essential that detainees feel safe and consider the regime, or 'detention climate', to be fair. Only then will daily life in detention centres become bearable for the detainees, management and staff.

The British criminologist Liebling has shown that what really matters in prison is what prisoners feel most strongly about. One of the key factors was *fairness*, defined by her as 'free from dishonesty or discrimination. To be treated clearly, consistently, impartially, in conformity with rules and standards, with access to redress, and courteously'.[7]

1.4. LEGAL GUARANTEES FOR FAIR TREATMENT AND PROTECTION AGAINST ILL TREATMENT

Comprehensive, clear and practicable detention centre regulations can greatly contribute to fair treatment of detainees and to their protection against ill treatment. These regulations should leave as little room as possible for arbitrary decisions. Where decisions or behaviour of management and staff

---

[6] McConville et al. 2011, p. 45.
[7] Liebling & Arnold 2005, p. 271.

are considered as arbitrary, unjust or unlawful, the detainees involved, without fear for reprisals, should have the right to complain formally and have their complaint effectively dealt with by competent higher authorities. Alleged cases of torture and other forms of physical or mental ill treatment should be handed over to outside investigating authorities that are not connected with the detention centre where the alleged incident would have taken place. One of the most effective ways to guarantee the safety of detainees is to allow for and encourage transparency of detention centres by introducing 'lay visitor' schemes and regular monitoring by external bodies, whose reports are accessible to the public.

Detention centre regulations should be formulated in such a way that they are 1) understandable for management staff and detainees alike and 2) practicable in the sense that they reflect and regulate daily practice. The protective effect of such regulations works both ways: management and staff clearly understand their duties and the limits of their powers and are in no doubt that they are accountable to their superiors and to the general public. Detainees clearly understand their rights and obligations, which draws a clear distinction between legal and illegal practice.

Having said this much about the importance of clear and practical detention centre regulations, the question remains: which international standards are relevant to those tasked with drafting new detention centre regulations? In the next two paragraphs I will summarise the most important UN and European standards in this area. As we will see, most of these provisions apply to unconvicted prisoners and sentenced prisoners alike while some international rules and regulations specifically concern untried suspects.

2. UN DETENTION STANDARDS

Over the course of time the United Nations have developed several minimum standards for the treatment of persons who are deprived of their liberty as suspects or convicted persons on two levels, namely, as 'hard law' in treaties and as 'soft law' in international agreements, with a lower legal status such as resolutions, guidelines and recommendations, adopted by the General Assembly of the UN. Minimum standards set in the treaties are considered to carry the force of law in the national jurisdictions of the States that acceded to them; while 'soft law' documents offer guidelines for national penitentiary legislation, policy, jurisprudence and administration.

2.1.   DETENTION STANDARDS AS PART OF, OR BASED ON UN TREATIES

2.1.1.   The International Covenant on Civil and Political Rights (ICCPR)

The ICCPR was adopted in 1966 and entered into force in 1976.[8] In the context of this chapter it is important to note that Article 7 of this treaty states: 'No one shall be subjected to torture or to cruel, inhuman or degrading treatment or punishment'. Article 10 explicitly addresses detainees and prisoners where it says:

> 1. All persons deprived of their liberty shall be treated with humanity and with respect for the inherent dignity of the human person.
> 2. (a) Accused persons shall, save in exceptional circumstances, be segregated from convicted persons and shall be subject to separate treatment appropriate to their status as unconvicted persons;
> (b) Accused juvenile persons shall be separated from adults and brought as speedily as possible for adjudication.
> 3. The penitentiary system shall comprise treatment of prisoners, the essential aim of which shall be their reformation and social rehabilitation. Juvenile offenders shall be segregated from adults and be accorded treatment appropriate to their age and legal status.

Though not very specific it provides sound basic principles to guide national legislation and policy in this field by requiring humane treatment for all categories of persons who are deprived of their liberty, no matter what the legal basis for their detention. It provides for juveniles as well as for adults, suspects and convicted prisoners alike. Provided their country has signed the *First Optional Protocol* to the ICCPR,[9] persons who are or have been deprived of their liberty and claim that Article 10 has been violated can send a 'communication' (complaint) to the Human Rights Committee in Geneva which, after having considered the case, will forward its 'view' on the matter to the State Party and the complainant.

2.1.2.   The International Convention on the Rights of the Child (CRC)[10]

Though minors are not to be detained in the detention centres (*kanshousuo*) it cannot be ruled out that children who are suspected of having committed

---

8   Signed by China 5 October 1998 but not yet ratified to date.
9   Adopted 1966, entered into force 1976; not signed by China.
10   The CRC was adopted in 1989 and entered into force in 1990. It was ratified by China in 1992.

an offence will be held there in exceptional circumstances. Article 37 of the CRC that says:

> States Parties shall ensure that:
>
> (a) No child shall be subjected to torture or other cruel, inhuman or degrading treatment or punishment. Neither capital punishment nor life imprisonment without possibility of release shall be imposed for offences committed by persons below eighteen years of age;
> (b) No child shall be deprived of his or her liberty unlawfully or arbitrarily. The arrest, detention or imprisonment of a child shall be in conformity with the law and shall be used only as a measure of last resort and for the shortest appropriate period of time;
> (c) Every child deprived of liberty shall be treated with humanity and respect for the inherent dignity of the human person, and in a manner which takes into account the needs of persons of his or her age. In particular, every child deprived of liberty shall be separated from adults unless it is considered in the child's best interest not to do so and shall have the right to maintain contact with his or her family through correspondence and visits, save in exceptional circumstances;
> (d) Every child deprived of his or her liberty shall have the right to prompt access to legal and other appropriate assistance, as well as the right to challenge the legality of the deprivation of his or her liberty before a court or other competent, independent and impartial authority, and to a prompt decision on any such action.

It should be noted here that China made the following reservation to this article:

> 'Where at any time there is a lack of suitable detention facilities, or where the mixing of adults and children is deemed to be mutually beneficial, the Government of the People's Republic of China reserves, *for the Hong Kong Special Administrative Region* (emphasis added), the right not to apply Article 37 (c) of the Convention in so far as those provisions require children who are detained to be accommodated separately from adults'.

This means that in other parts of China minors should never be detained together with adults.

2.1.3. *The Convention against Torture and Other Cruel, Inhuman or Degrading Treatment and Punishment (CAT)*

The second UN treaty that must be mentioned here is the CAT, adopted in 1984 and which entered into force in 1987.[11] This treaty defines *'torture'* in Article 1 as:

---

[11]   Ratified by China in 1988.

'(...) any act by which severe pain or suffering, whether physical or mental, is intentionally inflicted on a person for such purposes as obtaining from him or a third person information or a confession, punishing him for an act he or a third person has committed or is suspected of having committed, or intimidating or coercing him or a third person, or for any reason based on discrimination of any kind, when such pain or suffering is inflicted by or at the instigation of or with the consent or acquiescence of a public official or other person acting in an official capacity. It does not include pain or suffering arising only from, inherent in or incidental to lawful sanctions'.

Article 2 obliges State Parties to this treaty to 'take effective legislative, administrative, judicial or other measures to prevent acts of torture in any territory under its jurisdiction'.

An *Optional Protocol* to the CAT (OPCAT), adopted in 2002 and entered into force in 2006,[12] requires that the State Parties that have ratified it allow the Subcommittee on Prevention (SPT) free access to all places where persons are deprived of their liberty, report on their findings and make recommendations to States Parties concerning the protection of persons deprived of their liberty against torture and other cruel, inhuman or degrading treatment or punishment. Another important feature of the OPCAT is that it obliges State Parties to maintain, designate or establish one or several independent *national preventive mechanisms* for the prevention of torture at the domestic level.

2.1.4. Detention Regulations Based on the Rome Statute of the International Criminal Court[13]

National legislators who are looking for model, 'state of the art' detention centre regulations may find these on the website of the *International Criminal Court* as Chapter 6 ('Detention matters') of the *Regulations of the Court*, elaborated in Chapter 5 ('Detention matters') of the *Regulations of the Registry*.[14] The ICC Detention centre, run by UN officials and inspected by the Red Cross,[15] is located in The Hague, The Netherlands and operates, as to be expected, from a UN facility, in conformity with the highest international human rights standards for the treatment of detainees, such as the United

---

12 Not acceded by China.

13 Not acceded by China.

14 <www.icc-cpi.int/NR/rdonlyres/A57F6A7F-4C20-4C11-A61F-759338A3B5D4/140149/-ICCBD_030106_English1.pdf>, accessed 19 March 2012.

15 Agreement between the International Criminal Court and the International Committee of the Red Cross on Visits to Persons deprived of Liberty Pursuant to the Jurisdiction of the International Criminal Court, Date of entry into force: 13 April 2006, Publication of the *Official Journal*.

Nations Standard Minimum Rules. The ICC detention regulations are similar to those of the ad hoc tribunals like the International Criminal Tribunal for the Former Yugoslavia (ICTY), which detains its suspects in the same UN detention unit (UNDU) in The Hague though in a separate part of it. The UNDU is an international remand centre, only for detaining suspects waiting for their cases to be tried in the first instance or in appeal by the ICC or the ICTY. If they have been sentenced to a term of imprisonment they will be transferred to a prison in a host state that has volunteered to execute the sentence. After sentencing and before transfer to the host state, the regulations of the UNDU remain applicable to the convicted person. After transfer to a host state the penitentiary laws and regulations of the host state are applicable, with the exception of rules concerning early release and pardon, about which the president of the ICC keeps control.

The ICC detention regulations are tuned to the specific task of the ICC, which is clearly demonstrated by Court Regulation 101.1, which states: '1. A Chamber seized of the case may, at the request of the Prosecutor, order that access to the news be restricted, if it is considered necessary in the interests of the administration of justice, in particular, *if unrestricted access could prejudice the outcome of the proceedings* against that detained person or the outcome of any other investigation' (italics added). For the rest, these regulations cover the same subjects as de UN Standard Minimum Rules do, but in an updated, more explicit form.

2.2. DETENTION STANDARDS IN UN NON-TREATY DOCUMENTS

The UN has adopted several non-treaty documents with minimum standards for the treatment of persons who are deprived of their liberty. Special standards have been developed for juvenile detainees and prisoners. Because the detention centre regulations that are the subject of this chapter concern primarily adult detainees, UN non-treaty standards concerning juveniles will be dealt with only briefly.[16]

2.2.1. *Standard Minimum Rules for the Treatment of Prisoners (SMR) and Some Connected Documents*

The UN SMR dates from 1955. The present, amended version was adopted in 1977. The SMR offer minimum standards for the treatment of untried and

---

[16] The relevant non treaty UN guidelines for the treatment of detained children are to be found in the *United Nations Rules for the Protection of Juveniles Deprived of their Liberty* (1990), the so-called Havana Rules.

sentenced prisoners alike. They handle in some detail the material treatment of inmates (accommodation, hygiene, clothing and bedding, food, exercise and sport, medical services, work) and also the keeping of good order in penal institutions (discipline and punishment, instruments of restraint, the use of force). The SMR also contain guidelines on some rights and freedoms for detainees and prisoners, such as contact with the outside world (correspondence, family visits) and the right to make requests and complaints. A separate chapter addresses issues concerning the treatment of special categories, such as sentenced prisoners, mentally ill prisoners, prisoners under arrest or awaiting trial and civil prisoners. The SMR also offer guidelines to institutional personnel and provide standards for inspecting the way institutions are administered.

The UN SMR served initially as a model for the *European Prison Rules* which are summarized below. The UN SMR were also directional for the *Kampala Declaration on Prison Conditions in Africa*, adopted in 1996 under the aegis of the African Commission on Human and Peoples' Rights. Though the UN SMR has not been updated since 1977, they have to be read in context with various other UN documents. Worth mentioning here are the *Code of Conduct for Law enforcement Officials* of 1979, the *Principles of Medical Ethics relevant to the Role of Health Personnel, particularly Physicians, in the Protection of Prisoners and Detainees against Torture and Other Cruel, Inhuman or Degrading Treatment or Punishment of 1982* and the *Body of Principles for the Protection of All Persons under Any Form of Detention or Imprisonment.*

2.2.2. The Istanbul Protocol

In view of the prevention of incidents concerning ill-treatment mentioned in the very first paragraph of this chapter, the UN *Istanbul Protocol* deserves special attention here. This protocol is a comprehensive *Manual on the Effective Investigation and Documentation of Torture and Other Cruel, Inhuman or Degrading Treatment or Punishment* published in 2004 by the Office of the United Nations High Commissioner for Human Rights in Geneva.[17] In addition to chapters on relevant international legal standards on relevant ethical codes, this protocol offers detailed instructions on how to investigate in an effective way alleged cases of torture and other forms of ill treatment.

---

[17] <www.ohchr.org/Documents/Publications/training8Rev1en.pdf>, accessed 18 March 2012.

In paragraph 78 this protocol states that the reasons for effective investigation and documentation of torture or other ill-treatment include the following:

> a. Clarification of the facts and establishment and acknowledgement of individual and State responsibility for victims and their families;
> b. Identification of measures needed to prevent recurrence;
> c. Facilitation of prosecution or, as appropriate, disciplinary sanctions for those indicated by the investigation as being responsible and demonstration of the need for full reparation and redress from the State, including fair and adequate financial compensation and provision of the means for medical care and rehabilitation.

The *Istanbul Protocol* also provides for detailed procedures for an effective 'torture investigation'. The main elements of that are 1) the establishment of a special impartial investigation mechanism; 2) interviewing the alleged victim and other witnesses; 3) securing and obtaining physical evidence; 4) obtaining medical evidence and 5) the use of photography to document the injuries of persons alleging that they have been tortured. The investigating commission should always issue a *public* report within a reasonable period of time. The State should reply *publicly* to the commission's report and, where appropriate, indicate which steps it intends to take in response to the report.

3. EUROPEAN DETENTION STANDARDS

Alongside the (minimum) UN standards for the treatment of persons (such as detainees and prisoners) who are deprived of their liberty, the Council of Europe (CoE) has set comparable standards, adapting and fine tuning them in line with European criminal justice systems and the penitentiary policy and practice of CoE Member States.[18] The toughest minimum standards are to be found in documents with treaty-status. Many more criteria are laid down in documents with 'soft law' status, as discussed below.

---

[18] A list of relevant COE document can be found in: *Council of Europe, Penitentiary questions – Council of Europe conventions, recommendations and resolutions*, Strasbourg 2009. An evaluation of the significance and impact of this document is presented in MURDOCH 2006.

3.1. DETENTION STANDARDS AS PART OF OR DERIVED FROM EUROPEAN TREATIES

3.1.1. The European Convention for the Protection of Human Rights and Fundamental Freedoms (ECHR)

All provisions of the ECHR apply to detained and imprisoned persons. The ECHR makes a distinction between *absolute rights* and freedoms that can never be derogated from (like the right to life, the prohibition of torture and the right to a fair trial) and *relative rights* (such as the right to respect for private and family life, to freedom of thought, conscience and religion and to freedom of expression) that can be restricted by public authorities, provided this is in accordance with the law *and* is necessary in a democratic society in the interests of national security, public safety or the economic well-being of the country, for the prevention of disorder or crime, for the protection of health or morals, or for the protection of the rights and freedoms of others.

Any person, non-governmental organisation or group of individuals claiming to be the victim of a violation of these rights and freedoms by a public authority, after having exhausted the national legal remedies, is entitled to send an 'application' (complaint) to the *European Court of Human Rights* (ECtHR) in Strasbourg (France). The decisions of the Court, that may include damages to be paid to the victim, are binding to the State Parties to the Convention concerned and have the force of precedent for other State Parties to the Convention. Murdoch notes that right after the ECHR entered into force 'substantial numbers of complaints challenging violations of Convention guarantees were brought by persons deprived of their liberty'[19] and this is still the case.

Most prisoners' complaints regard alleged violations of Article 3, the prohibition of torture or inhuman or degrading treatment or punishment. The Court decides on a case by case basis whether the complainant had been ill-treated. The Court has held on many occasions that ill-treatment must attain *a minimum level of severity* if it is to fall within the scope of Article 3 of the Convention. The assessment of this minimum level of severity depends on all the circumstances of the case, such as the duration of the treatment, its physical and mental effects and, in some cases, the sex, age and state of health of the victim. Furthermore, in considering whether a treatment is 'degrading' within the meaning of Article 3, the Court will have regard to whether its purpose was to humiliate and debase the person concerned and whether, as far as the consequences are concerned, it adversely affected his or her

---

[19] MURDOCH 2006, p. 20.

personality in a manner incompatible with Article 3. Although the question whether the purpose of the treatment was to humiliate or debase the victim is a factor to be taken into account, the absence of any such purpose cannot conclusively rule out a finding of violation of Article 3.[20] Measures depriving a person of his liberty may often involve an inevitable element of suffering or humiliation. Nevertheless, the suffering and humiliation involved must not go beyond the inevitable element of suffering or humiliation connected with a given form of legitimate treatment or punishment.

One of the most important outcomes of the many decisions the Court has taken on this subject is that the State Parties to the Convention have a *positive obligation* a) to prevent situations wherein ill-treatment can occur and to protect actively persons who are in the power of police, judicial or penitentiary authorities. The Court in its jurisprudence demands further that where alleged ill-treatment has allegedly occurred, this shall lead to a prompt, effective and public investigation by an independent authority.[21]

The ECtHR does not shy away from criticizing countries that generate an excessive amount of complaints about overcrowded and thus unsafe and inhuman prison conditions. An example of this is the decision in the case of *Orchowski v. Poland* concerning the violation of Article 3 of the Convention caused by severe overcrowding of the cells in different remand centres and prisons where he had been held. The Court castigated Poland, stating: '(…) that it is incumbent on the (…) Government to organise its penitentiary system in such a way that ensures respect for the dignity of detainees, regardless of financial or logistical difficulties (…). If the State is unable to ensure that prison conditions comply with the requirements of Article 3 of the Convention, it must abandon its strict penal policy in order to reduce the number of incarcerated persons or put in place a system of alternative means of punishment'.[22]

The ECtHR has also addressed the problem of (sometimes lethal) inter-prisoner violence. It has held in various case that the State (i.e. the management of detention centres or prisons) is responsible for the safety of detainees and prisoners vis-à-vis their fellow inmates, in the Chinese context often referred to as the problem of the '*prison bully*'. The Court holds the opinion that the right to life, guaranteed in Article 2 of the Convention, enjoins the State not only to refrain from the intentional and unlawful taking of life, but also to take appropriate steps to safeguard the lives of those within

---

[20] See ECtHR 19 April 2001, *Peers v. Greece*, no. 28524/95, paras. 67-68, para. 74 and ECtHR 24 October 2001, *Valašinas v. Lithuania*, no. 44558/98, para. 101.

[21] MURDOCH 2006, p. 127-136.

[22] ECtHR 22 October 2009, *Orchowski v. Poland*, no. 17885/04, para. 153.

its jurisdiction. 'This involves a primary duty on the State to secure the right to life by putting in place effective criminal law provisions to deter the commission of offences against the person backed up by law-enforcement machinery for the prevention, suppression and punishment of breaches of such provisions. It also extends in appropriate circumstances to a positive obligation on the authorities to take preventive operational measures to protect an individual whose life is at risk from the criminal acts of another individual (...)'. And: 'It is incumbent on the State to account for any injuries suffered in custody, which obligation is particularly stringent where that individual dies (...)'.[23] In the case of *Preminiy v. Russia* the Court imposes an obligation on the Contracting States 'not only to refrain from provoking ill-treatment, but also to take the necessary preventive measures to preserve the physical and psychological integrity and well-being of persons deprived of their liberty (...). At the same time the Court has consistently interpreted that obligation in such a manner as not to impose an impossible or disproportionate burden on the authorities (...)'. In this case, where a remand prisoner was severely ill-treated by his cellmates the Court reiterated that State responsibility is engaged by a failure to take reasonably available measures which could have had a real prospect of altering the outcome or mitigating the harm to the applicant (...) In this kind of case the Court therefore has to establish whether the authorities knew or ought to have known that the detainee was suffering or at risk of being subjected to ill-treatment at the hands of his cellmates, and if so, whether the administration of the detention facility, within the limits of their official powers, took reasonable steps to eliminate those risks and to protect the first applicant from that abuse.[24]

One can safely conclude that the decisions of the ECtHR on the complaints concerning conditions of detention have had and still have a huge impact on the quality of the treatment of detained suspects and imprisoned offenders in the 47 Member States of the Council of Europe, who are, without exception, signatories to the Convention on Human Rights.

3.1.2. European Convention for the Prevention of Torture and Inhuman or Degrading Treatment or Punishment (1987)

This Convention has established the European Committee for the Prevention of Torture and Inhuman or Degrading Treatment or Punishment (CPT). The

---

[23] ECtHR 14 March 2002, *Paul and Audrey Edwards v. The United Kingdom*, no. 46477/99, paras. 54-56.

[24] ECtHR 10 February 2011, *Preminiy v. Russia*, no. 44973/04, paras. 83-84.

CPT examines by means of regular, follow up and ad hoc visits to all 47 Member States of the COE, the treatment of persons deprived of their liberty with a view to strengthening, if necessary, the protection of such persons from torture and from inhuman or degrading treatment or punishment. The CPT has unlimited access to any place where persons are deprived of their liberty, including the right to move inside such places without restriction. It may interview in private persons deprived of their liberty and may communicate freely with any person whom it believes can supply relevant information. After each visit, the CPT draws up a report on the facts found during the visit and transmits this, along with any recommendations it considers necessary, to the government of the State Party on whose territory the visit was made. The CPT reports are published on the CPT website, unless the State concerned objects to this. On the basis of its (numerous) visits the CPT has formulated minimum standards for the treatment of persons who are deprived of their liberty. These are published in the document '*CPT Standards*', which is updated on a regular basis.[25] In the context of this chapter on detention centre regulations, the first two chapters of CPT Standards on '*Law enforcement agencies*' and '*Prisons*' have special relevance for the regulations for the detention centres that are the subject of this chapter. The following quote from this document illustrates very well the main concerns of the CPT here:

> 'The CPT attaches particular importance to three rights for persons detained by the police, namely, the right of the person concerned to have the fact of his detention notified to a third party of his choice (family member, friend, consulate), the right of access to a lawyer, and the right to request a medical examination by a doctor of his choice (in addition to any medical examination carried out by a doctor called by the police authorities). They are, in the CPT's opinion, three fundamental safeguards against the ill-treatment of detained persons which should apply from the very outset of deprivation of liberty, regardless of how it may be described under the legal system concerned (apprehension, arrest, etc.)'.[26]

3.1.3. The Charter of Fundamental Rights of the European Union

This Charter, which dates from the year 2000, is binding for all 27 Member States of the EU. Though sometimes with different wording, it covers most of the provisions already laid down in the European Convention for the Protection of Human Rights (like the prohibition of torture) and has as yet no special relevance for detainees and prisoners because all EU Member States are also parties to the ECHR.

---

25 <www.cpt.coe.int/en/docsstandards.htm>.
26 Council of Europe, *CPT Standards*, CPT/Inf/E (2002) 1 – Rev. 2010, § 36, p. 6.

3.2. DETENTION STANDARDS IN EUROPEAN NON-TREATY DOCUMENTS

3.2.1. Council of Europe Recommendations

Minimum standards for the treatment of (remand) prisoners have been laid down in three important recommendations of the COE. These are:

- Recommendation (2006)2 on the European Prison Rules;
- Recommendation (2006)13 on the use of remand in custody, the conditions in which it takes place and the provision of safeguards and abuse;
- Recommendation (2012)5 on the European Code of Ethics for Prison Staff.

Being the most up to date set of standards to date, the drafters of new detention centre arrests have paid due attention to the European Prison Rules, that regard the treatment of the more than 1,8 million (!) prisoners[27] in the 47 Member States of the COE of which about 630,000 are detained in the 27 states that are also EU members. Without underestimating the importance of the other Rules, it fairly can be said that the Rules on admission procedures, access to legal aid and health care, on the right to complain and on inspection and monitoring represent key standards for detention centre or prison regulations in all modern criminal justice systems.

The Recommendation on the use of remand in custody, which is of particular interest for detention centre regulations such as those debated here, is closely connected to the Recommendation on the European Prison Rules (EPR), where it says in Article 35: 'The conditions of remand in custody shall, subject to the Rules set out below, be governed by the European Prison Rules'. The EPR are a more 'state of the art' European version of the UN Standard Minimum Rules.

It is in the interests of justice and of the suspects involved, that pre-trial detention shall be used sparingly and shall not last longer than strictly necessary. In terms of Article 22 of the Recommendation on the use of remand custody, this means that 1) in any case its duration shall not exceed, nor normally be disproportionate to, the penalty that may be imposed for the offence concerned; 2) in no case shall remand in custody breach the right of a detained person to be tried within a reasonable time; 3) any specification of a

---

[27] Total of untried and sentenced prisoners. Source: International Centre for Prison Studies London; <www.prisonstudies.org>. All EU member states are member states of the COE as well.

maximum period of remand in custody shall not lead to a failure to consider at regular intervals the actual need for its continuation in the particular circumstances of a given case 4) it is the responsibility of the prosecuting authority or the investigating judicial authority to act with due diligence in the conduct of an investigation and to ensure that the existence of matters supporting remand in custody is kept under continuous review and 5) priority shall be given to cases involving a person who has been remanded in custody.

The most recently adopted recommendations concern the ethics of prison staff. In this recommendation, the term 'prison' is used to describe institutions reserved for holding persons who have been remanded in custody by a judicial authority or who have been deprived of their liberty following conviction. In the context of this chapter on the detention centre regulations the following provisions of this recommendation are worth mentioning:

6. Prison staff shall endeavour to maintain positive professional relationships with prisoners and their family members.
9. Prison staff shall carry out all legal instructions properly issued by their superiors, but they shall have a duty to refrain from carrying out any instructions which are seriously and manifestly infringing the law and to report such instructions, without having to fear sanctions.
10. Prison staff shall at all times respect and protect everyone's right to life.
11. In the performance of their daily tasks, prison staff shall respect and protect human dignity and maintain and uphold the human rights of all persons.
12. Prison staff shall not inflict, instigate or tolerate any act of torture or other inhuman or degrading treatment or punishment, under any circumstances, including when ordered by a superior.
26. Prison staff shall respect the presumption of innocence of prisoners who have not been convicted or sentenced by a court.

Another COE recommendation that deserves to be mentioned here is:

- Recommendation (2008)11 on the European rules for juvenile offenders subject to sanctions or measures.

This recommendation defines in Article 21.1 the term 'juvenile offender' as any person below the age of 18 who is alleged to have or who has committed an offence. Part III of this recommendation contains detailed (minimum) standards for the treatment of juveniles who are deprived of their liberty. This documents underlines in Article 52.1, that 'As juveniles deprived of their liberty are highly vulnerable, the authorities shall protect their physical and mental integrity and foster their well being'. In Article 59.1 it states that juveniles shall not be held in institutions for adults, but in institutions specially designed for them. The provisions regarding detention conditions largely reflect those of the European Prison Rules.

4. DETENTION LAW AND PRACTICE IN THE EUROPEAN UNION

4.1. NO COMMON EU DETENTION LAW AS YET

Foreigners who have visited the EU and have, to some degree, become acquainted with the various national institutions of its Member States will readily admit hat it is often difficult to conceive the EU as a truly united region. Perhaps the EU over time will evolve into some sort of federal political system, but for the time being, national sovereignty is still cherished by most of the Member States. The result of the reluctance to give up national sovereignty on certain issues is that the formally supported harmonisation of and cooperation between the criminal justice systems of the EU Member States is progressing at a very slow pace. Until now priority has been given to cooperation in the field of cross-border criminal investigation and prosecution. Only recently have the EU Member States started to be interested in each other's prison systems and detention regulations. The European Commission (the executive committee of the EU) is well aware of the fact that detention conditions and periods vary widely between EU countries. This can have a negative impact on the mutual recognition of judicial decisions if judicial authorities refuse to extradite or hand over accused or convicted persons because detention conditions in the requesting EU member stated are sub-standard. The introduction in 2004 of the European Arrest Warrant (a legal tool to smoothen the transfer of arrested suspects in the EU-region) and the transfer of sentenced prisoners[28] prompted the European Commission in 2011 to publish a 'green paper' on the application of EU criminal justice legislation in the field of detention.[29] This paper invited all persons and entities with an interest in this subject to respond to 10 specific questions about EU detention issues. The answers to

---

[28] On the basis of the Council Framework Decision 2008/909/JHA of 27 November 2008 on the application of the principle of mutual recognition to judgments imposing custodial sentences or measures involving deprivation of liberty (to be implemented by 5 December 2011).

[29] European Commission, *Green Paper. Strengthening mutual trust in the European judicial area – A Green Paper on the application of EU criminal justice legislation in the field of detention*, 30 November 2011 (<http://ec.europa.eu/justice/newsroom/criminal/opinion/-110614_en.htm>, accessed on 27 March 2012).

the questionnaire[30] will be decisive for further action of the European Commission in this field and may well lead to directives on detention regulations. Following on from this, the European Commission commissioned a research project on Member States' material detention conditions as well as on early/conditional release and earned remission provisions and sentence execution modalities to be carried out by the Institute of International Research on Criminal Policy (IRCP) of the University of Ghent (Belgium). That institute collated information on key legislation and policy which impacts on prison conditions in 24 of the 27 EU Member States.[31] 'The results' the ICRP says, 'not only provide a good account of Member States' legal systems, they also show the extent to which EU Member States have incorporated obligations arising from European and international norms and standards and/or jurisprudence from the European Court of Human Rights.' At the end of each chapter on the situation in a member state, all relevant national penitentiary laws and regulations are listed in an appendix. This research does not compare those national detention laws and regulations but only checks whether the Member States have adopted all international commitments related to human rights of prisoners in their legislation and practice. This broad overview shows that many (but not all) legally binding and not legally binding commitments have been incorporated in the different EU jurisdictions. 'However', the authors say, 'this doesn't tell us anything about the actual situation in practice, which is not always in line with what law and/or policy prescribe(s)'.[32] One of many examples of this is the Republic of Estonia, which despite having adopted all commitments relating to the core principles underpinning prison health care, including the legally binding commitment requiring that primary health care is provided to an equivalent standard to that available in the community, in practice, has a very different situation. 'The UN Committee against torture expressed some concerns about the health and medical services in detention facilities in its report of 2007, especially regarding the lack of adequate food and the lack of appropriate treatment, especially with regards to HIV and TBC infected detainees'.[33]

Up to date comparative research on the penitentiary legislation of the EU Member States is scarce. An exception is the study of Lazarus, who compared prisoners' rights in England and Germany. Where 'in Germany prisoners' rights were formed in a political and legal culture shaped by constitutional

---

[30]   These have been published on the website of the COE: <www.coe.int>.
[31]   VERMEULEN ET AL. 2011.
[32]   VERMEULEN ET AL. 2011, p. 37.
[33]   VERMEULEN ET AL. 2011, p. 305-306.

rights, characterized by faith in fundamental rights' she found no 'clear legal principles guiding the exercise of prison administration and defining prisoners' rights in English law'.[34] 'European' detention law and practice do not exist, as the legal cultures of the various EU states will only slowly converge.

5. THE RELEVANCE OF UN AND EUROPEAN DETENTION STANDARDS FOR THE CHINESE PENITENTIARY SYSTEM – LEGAL CULTURE AND THE PROBLEM OF TRANSFERABILITY

The previous paragraphs show that there is a wealth of – often overlapping – international detention standards available for the guidance of national legislators, policy makers and judicial authorities who are involved in reform projects. The key question is however, whether or not these international detention standards have universal applicability and can be transferred without much effort into all national criminal justice systems. Most international detention standards have been developed in a western socio-political context, which attaches great importance to personal freedoms of citizens and the protection of those freedoms against state intervention. In a socialist society like the Chinese one, collective interests will prevail over individual concerns,[35] which is an attitude that will be reflected in legal thought and practice. This means that international detention standards that fit into, say, the Dutch or Spanish penitentiary systems, could well miss their mark in the Chinese political, legal and practical reality. Not all western concepts can be easily transferred to legal systems in non western societies. The following example may illustrate this transferability problem.

Whereas in China pre-trial detention and arrest are enforced in the same facility under the authority of the police force, the situation in the EU is different. In the EU, suspects can be held for only a short time in police cells for initial interrogation and, when an extension of their detention is deemed necessary by the judicial authorities, they have to be transferred to remand prisons that are run under the authority of civil servants (the national prison service) who have no investigating powers themselves, but leave this to the police, the public prosecutor and/or the investigating judge. This state of affairs differs strongly from the Chinese situation where the detention centre

---

[34] LAZARUS 2004, p. 248-250. Older studies on prison systems and comparative studies in the European region are: CÉRÉ 2002; VAGG 1994 and MUNCIE & SPARKS 1991.
[35] ISAÏA 1978, p. 54.

(*kanshousuo*) is a police station and remand centre in one, managed by the police, who are investigating the cases of the detained suspects, and are supervised by a special branch of the office of the procurator, that is an investigative organ as well. Where in the EU the 'keepers' of pre-trial detainees have no formal interest in the way the cases of the suspects/-detainees are being investigated, in China the managers of the detention centres are investigators themselves. In this way, detention centres are investigating tools. This brings up the question of what defines the regime in a *kanshousuo* more – fair treatment of the detainees or the gathering of proof against them? The *European Prison Rules* try to solve this problem by stating in Rule 71: 'Prisons shall be the responsibility of public authorities separate from military, police or criminal investigation services'. The rationale for this is given in the commentary which says:

> 'This Rule requires prisons to be the responsibility of public authorities, separate from military, police or criminal investigation services. Prisons are places that should be placed under the control of the civil power. Imprisonment is part of the criminal justice process and in democratic societies people are sent to prison by independent judges'. (...)

> 'The Committee of Ministers of the Council of Europe has recommended that "There shall be a clear distinction between the role of the police and the prosecution, the judiciary and the correctional system"'.

It is clear that this Rule 71 has little meaning for the present Chinese penitentiary system and it would be not difficult to find other international detention standards that do not fit with the Chinese system. In assessing the value of international detention standards for national jurisdictions one should be wary of the idea of 'one size fits all'. It needs sufficient if not full knowledge of a national legal culture and system before an outsider can judge whether international norms should or could be implemented in that jurisdiction. To quote Lazarus again:

> 'The comparative examination of human rights generally, and particularly prisoners' rights, is inextricable from the drive towards globalisation. For those who champion universal human rights, the defence of local values represents a dilemma. The protection of cultural diversity is a recognised human rights goal. But human rights (involving belief in universally shared values) and cultural diversity (demanding the recognition of difference) can seem antithetical. Comparative human rights researchers have to navigate this environment carefully, ensuring that their normative commitment to human rights does not lead them either to downplay the complexity and diversity of local environments, or represent (or re-construct) cultural differences in opposition to human rights values'.

The author has tried to sketch the pathway to new, human rights oriented detention centre regulations.[36]

6. EMPIRICAL RESEARCH IN CHINA AND STUDY VISITS TO EUROPE

To get a realistic picture of what kind of reforms were needed the CCPR designed, organised and evaluated three pilot programmes: a pilot inspection system in Liaoyuan, Jilin Province and an experimental prisoners' complaints procedure in the detention centre of Wuhu, Anhui province.[37] The results of the evaluations of these pilot projects provided the drafters of the detention centre regulations with valuable factual information about various aspects of the material and legal position of the inmates of detention centres. The content and outcome of these pilots are summarized below.

6.1. THE PILOT ON INSPECTION OF DETENTION CENTRES BY LAY VISITORS IN LIAOYUAN

From November 2006 to September 2008 the CCPR, the People's Procuratorate and the Public Security Bureau of Liaoyuan jointly carried out a research project on a pilot inspection system in the local detention centre of Liaoyuan, Jilin province.[38]

6.1.1. Background and Objectives

The background of this project was to detect causes of ill treatment of detainees and to propose remedies to prevent this. Another reason to start this pilot was that if the Chinese government considers ratifying the *Optional Protocol to the Convention against Torture* (OPCAT), it will be obliged to establish an independent inspection system. This is stated in Article 17 of the OPCAT: 'Each State Party shall maintain, designate or establish, at the latest one year after the entry into force of the present Protocol or of its ratification or accession, one or several independent national preventive mechanisms for

---

[36] LAZARUS 2004, p. 9.

[37] The pilot in Wuhu is on-going; when this chapter was written only an interim evaluation was available.

[38] Centre for Criminal Procedure and Reform, Renmin University of China School of Law, *Research Paper on Pilot Trials on Inspection of Places of Detention*, [final paper; unpublished], [Beijing] 27 August 2008. The research team was led by Professor CHEN WEIDONG; MEMBERS: CHENG LEI, LIAN LEWEI, YANG DONGLIANG, GAO TONG and LIU ZHONGQI.

the prevention of torture at the domestic level. Mechanisms established by decentralized units may be designated as national preventive mechanisms for the purposes of the present Protocol if they are in conformity with its provisions'.

The main objectives of this research project were: 1) to enhance the transparency of the places of detention; 2) to promote the improvement of detention conditions; 3) to promote better treatment of detainees and 4) and to raise the level of legal protection of detainees, all in order to prevent and reduce the occurrence of torture and the extraction of confessions through torture. The research targeted untried and sentenced inmates as well as enforcement officials, including investigators and prison guards.

6.1.2. Research Method

Before the pilot project began, the CCPR project team studied documentary materials concerning the average number of detainees in the detention centre, the cost of their upkeep, the number and working hours of prison guards, sanctions taken against enforcement officials guilty of ill treatment of detainees during the previous 8 years, and the number of complaints of detainees processed in the previous year. After this, the prison guards, (police) investigators, prosecutors and (defence) lawyers were asked to fill out questionnaires concerning their attitude towards the inspection system. Another part of the pre-pilot research was the interviewing on a one-to-one basis of prison guards, prosecutors, lawyers and judges about the problems of ill treatment (torture) and detention conditions. Before starting the pilot the project team visited the detention centre itself to test the envisaged inspection procedure.

Then, on the basis of an assessment of their competences, Liaoyuan Public Security Bureau and Liaoyuan Procuratorate liased with Liaoyuan People's Congress and other organizations to recommend potential 'lay visitors'. Liaoyuan Procuratorate then selected 20 candidates to undertake inspection visits.

The 20 selected laypersons who would act as 'inspectors' were trained in the legal and practical aspects of making and reporting back on visits. Their (protocol led) inspections were carried out in pairs. They were entitled to visit the detention centre of Liaoyuan without prior notice at any time of the week. For security reasons prosecutors and staff could accompany the inspectors during the inspections. Members of the project team accompanied the inspectors. The inspectors were entitled to visit almost *all* places in the detention centre where detainees were held, and were entitled to interview two randomly chosen detainees during every visit, albeit in the presence of a prosecutor. These interviews focused on two issues, namely the basic living conditions in the detention centre and the protection of their legal rights. During their (20) inspections the lay visitors filled out reports using forms provided by the project team.

6.1.3. Outcome

The project had to deal with several *limitations* which one should keep in mind when reading the results of the pilot. The number of inspections was limited to 20 in six months; the number of detainees was modest; the number of completed questionnaires was small and it was not possible to assess whether the inspection reports have led to improvements in the conditions of detention and the legal protection of detainees in the Liaoyuan detention centre. A further handicap was that – without having a control group in another region – the situation in Liaoyuan could not be compared with the situation in other detention centres. Nevertheless, the research produced information that can be used in the process of reforming the detention centre regulations.

An important outcome of the pilot was that the inspectors were quite explicit in pointing out many shortcomings in the living conditions of detainees.[39] This resulted in quite a long list of recommendations for improvements but also to some unexpected observations. Where, on the one hand, the research team found in their pre-pilot research that the budget of the detention centre for decent food and drink for detainees was below the state standard, 15 of the 20 inspectors rated the food and drink conditions in the detention centre as 'quite good' and held the opinion that a difference should be made between what is normal food and drink in the compulsory setting of a detention centre and what is normal in the outside world. This seems to indicate that the majority of these pilot-inspectors tended to see detainees, notwithstanding their status as *suspects,* as 'criminals' who did not deserve the same treatment as civilians, just because they had been detained.

The inspectors found that most detainees had been informed on their procedural rights, but found at the same time that more than half of those interviewed, mostly poorly educated detainees had little, or no understanding

---

[39] They noted unhygienic conditions in the dining hall; the unavailability of boiled water, the small size of the cells (30 square meters for 12-22 detainees); the absence of a sick-bay; the temporary impossibility of outdoor exercise caused by building activities, added to not being allowed to be out of the cells; few books and no newspapers in the library; unhygienic garbage disposal; insufficient medical staff and equipment; insufficient number of medical tests available; not all detainees receiving physical tests immediately after admission to the detention centre.

of their litigious rights or how to exercise them. This finding demonstrates the importance of free and timely access to legal assistance.

Another outcome of this pilot was that the number of complaints received by the prosecutors rose substantially during the pilot, compared to the number of complaints received in preceding years. Two topics were prominent: complaints about 'prison bullies' and complaints about the extension of the pre-trial detention. When interviewed on the subject of ill-treatment, some detainees claimed to have received beatings during interrogations, and others, while in their cells, by other prisoners ('tyrants' or 'bullies'). This led the pilot-inspectors to recommend that the authorities put up a physical separation between interrogators and suspects; that a simple physical check-up by a doctor takes place before and after interrogation; and that they install monitoring equipment in the cells.

What puzzled the researchers is that the inspectors had hardly any comments on the level of legal protection of detainees. The project team attributed this finding to a *lack of basic legal knowledge* on the part of inspectors and also of detainees. The project team stated that this should be remedied, by focusing on the legal knowledge in the training programmes for future inspectors.

6.2.   THE PILOT OF THE WUHU PRISONERS' COMPLAINTS MECHANISM

In the context of reviewing detention centre regulations and the development of legal and practical tools for the prevention of ill treatment of detainees, the Centre for Criminal Procedure and Reform of Renmin University has designed a pilot project for the improvement of the existing prisoners' complaint mechanism. The project team identified three main problems to be solved.[40] The first problem is that detainees have little knowledge about the existing complaint mechanism that presently is set out in Article 42 of the *Supervisory Rules on Detention Centres of the People's Procurates*. Secondly, the existing procedure is not deemed effective and thirdly, there are signals that detainees do not dare to lodge complaints out of fear of reprisals by guards. This would explain the small number of complaints that are commonly received by the prosecutor. In the framework of this pilot a new

---

[40]   The information on this pilot project is based on an account of the Seminar on the Complaint Handling Mechanism for Detainees in Detention Centres held on July 24 in Wuhu and the presentation done by Sun Hao 'Detainee Complaint Mechanisms in Jail', during a round table meeting with prosecutors working in the Wuhu *kanshousuo* and members of the local (lay) Complaints Handling Committee on 8 November 2011.

complaints procedure will be tested out. The new complaints regulation, drafted by the People's Procuratorate of Wuhu & the Public Security Bureau of Wuhu, obliges the detention centre to inform the detainees of their legal rights and the treatment they are entitled to. Detainees have the right to lodge a complaint (orally or in writing) if they think these rights are infringed upon or are denied to them. Written complaints can be dropped in a special complaints box that is accessible to detainees and for the sake of confidentiality should not be placed in full view of staff and guards who might show themselves resentful towards complainants. Close relatives of detainees and also their lawyers are entitled to submit complaints on their behalf. Complaints shall be handled within 14 days if the *Complaints Handling Committee* is not involved (cases between inmates handled by the disciplinary police) and within one month if the Committee is involved (see below). All parties involved will receive a written and motivated decision and they have the right to ask decision-makers to review their decision again. In future, it is hoped that it will be possible to appoint high-level committees to handle appeals.

Complaints against investigating officers and staff must be handled by the prosecutor. If the complaints concern attempts to obtain evidence by illegal means (ill treatment or torture) these shall be handled by the procurators' office with reference to the *Code of Criminal Procedure* and the Rules on several issues concerning exclusion of illegally obtained evidence in criminal cases. Disciplinary police (= guards?) shall deal with complaints of detainees about other detainees and complaints about conditions of detention. A new feature to be tested is the involvement of a *Complaints Handling Committee*, whose members are selected by the People's Procuratorate's Supervision Department, the Public Security Bureau and the People's Court. This Committee is charged with advising the procurator's office on how to handle complaints. If the procurator does not follow the recommendation of the Committee, the case will be forwarded to the Procuratorial Committee to decide. If a complaint is upheld a disciplinary sanction can be imposed on the person that acted incorrectly.

The intended outcome of this pilot is to draft a new complaints procedure that can be trusted by detainees, staff and prosecutors alike, and can serve as an effective tool for the protection of prisoners against unfair or ill treatment. The research team sees this pilot as closely linked with the lay visitors project that was completed in Liaoyuan (see previous paragraph). The pilot began in July 2011 and is to run until July 2012, in the detention centre of Wuhu, with a maximum capacity of 700 detainees, 80 staff and 5 prosecutors, which is the average for a detention centre *kanshousuo*. At the time the text of this book was in press the pilot was still ongoing. A mid-term evaluation of the pilot yielded the following results.

To facilitate the complaints pilot, letterboxes and pen and paper were made available in all cells. Each detainee is provided with a booklet that spells out his rights and duties. Only the prosecutor is entitled to empty the letterboxes. All complaints received are registered to supervise the time limits for handling them. The mid-term evaluation cannot yet offer an answer to whether the new procedure is effective or not.

6.3.   STUDY VISITS MADE BY CHINESE ACADEMICS AND PROFESSIONALS TO EUROPE

Funded by the EU and coordinated by the *Great Britain China Centre* in cooperation with *The Rights Practice*, both London-based, researchers of Renmin University Law School, professionals involved in the Chinese criminal justice system and legislators, paid several study visits to EU Member States.[41] The cooperation between the Renmin University School of Law and the Department of Criminal Law of Maastricht University had the effect that Dutch detention law and practice received the special attention of its Chinese counterparts. They visited a major Dutch police detention centre in the city of Maastricht and one in neighbouring Belgium, and they were instructed about the legal position and detention conditions of suspects that temporally[42] were detained there before being transferred to a remand prison. Chinese delegations visited extensively the remand prison in the city of Sittard and a prison for unconvicted and convicted prisoners in the city of Rotterdam. Chinese researchers were received by the director of the Governmental Inspection Authority for the Enforcement of Criminal Sanctions in The Hague. They were extensively instructed on the Dutch Penitentiary law and by-laws and on the complaints committees and appeals committees that have been functioning since 1977, to the satisfaction of all parties involved. In the course of numerous meetings in the Netherlands and in China, the usefulness of international detention standards for the Chinese was discussed.

---

41   In October 2006 a senior delegation comprising 11 senior police, legislators, a judge and academic researchers travelled to the UK, Hungary and Lithuania for a two week study visit to learn more about police interrogation techniques and EU mechanisms for torture prevention.

6.4. THE OUTCOME: A DRAFT TEXT TO BE DISSEMINATED

All the foregoing has resulted in the draft text for improved detention centre regulation that is added as an annex to this chapter. This draft text reflects to a great extent the modern international minimum rules for the treatment of persons who, as suspects or convicted offenders, are deprived of their liberty, adapted to Chinese socialist legal culture and practice. The aim of the drafters of this new version of the detention centre regulations is that they be discussed, not only by academics but especially by those professionals who are responsible for the decision to detain (alleged) offenders, by investigators, procurators, defence lawyers, legislators and also the general public.

Of course there is still a long way to go before political consensus can be reached about a final text, if at all possible, because resistance can be expected from officials who hold the opinion that the present situation is perhaps not ideal but not as bad as some say it is. Improving the treatment of imprisoned offenders has never been an item than generates wide public support anywhere in the world. Suggestions for spending a larger part of the budget on 'criminals' do not make officials very popular, rather the contrary. Investigators and prison guards will find it difficult to accept that their behaviour will be scrutinized by the outside world and that prisoners can complain with a fair chance of success about the way they are treated. Professional conservatism can only be overcome when sceptics can be convinced that offenders still have civil rights, that ill treatment of prisoners affects the trust in the state administration, that criminal cases can be solved without resorting to rough, illegal interrogation methods and that it is almost impossible to reintegrate offenders in free society when they have acquired a negative attitude towards governmental officials when they have been the object of unfair and inhuman treatment during their detention. And, last but not least, fair treatment of inmates will contribute immensely to the good order in any penitentiary institution, which makes it a lot easier for guards, staff and management alike to work there. It would of course make no sense if new detention centre regulations such as those presented here were adopted and suddenly imposed on unprepared investigators, guards and all others who work with detainees. New rules need to be introduced to those whose are expected to respect them gradually, step by step, by organising seminars, and on the job training.

BIBLIOGRAPHY

CÉRÉ 2002
CÉRÉ, J.-P. (ed.), *Panorama européen de la prison,* Paris/Budapest/Torino: Éd. L'Harmattan, Coll. Sciences Criminelles, 2002.

ISAÏA 1978
ISAÏA, H., *La Justice en Chine*, Paris: Economica, 1978.

LAZARUS 2004
LAZARUS, L., *Contrasting Prisoners' Rights – A Comparative Examination of England and Germany*, Oxford: Oxford University Press, 2004.

LIEBLING & ARNOLD 2005
LIEBLING, A. & ARNOLD, H., *Prisons and Their Moral Performance – A Study of Values, Quality and Prison Life*, Oxford: Oxford University Press, 2005.

MCCONVILLE ET AL. 2011
MCCONVILLE, M., CHOONGH, S., CHOY, P., WAN, D., CHUI, E., HONG, W., DOBINSON, I. & JONES, C., *Criminal Justice in China – An Empirical Inquiry*, Cheltenham: Edward Elgar Publishing Limited, 2011.

MUNCIE & SPARKS 1991
MUNCIE, J. & SPARKS, R. (eds.), *Imprisonment – European Perspectives*, New York: Prentice-Hall, 1991.

MURDOCH 2006
MURDOCH, J., *The Treatment of Prisoners – European Standards*, Strasbourg: Council of Europe Publishing, 2006.

VAGG 1994
VAGG, J., *Prison Systems – A Comparative Study of Accountability in England, France, Germany, and the Netherlands*, Oxford: Clarendon Press, 1994.

VERMEULEN ET AL. 2011
VERMEULEN, G., KALMTHOUT, A., VAN, PATERSON, N., KNAPEN, M., VERBEKE, P. & BONDT, W., DE, *Material Detention Conditions, Execution of Custodial Sentences and Prisoner Transfer in the EU Member States*, Antwerp/-Apeldoorn/Portland: Maklu Publishers 2011.

2. EXPERT PROPOSAL FOR A DRAFT DETENTION CENTRE LAW

Cheng Lei

1. INTRODUCTORY NOTE

The reform of detention centres in China has been a major concern in recent years. The management of detention centres is still governed by a set of administrative regulations – the *Regulations on Detention Centres* – which were adopted in 1990. Consequently, many of the provisions fall far behind current developments in practice. Given that the Chinese government advocated the improvement of detention centre legislation in late 2008, creating a law on detention centres has now become a necessity. Led by Professor Chen Weidong and with the strong support of colleagues at Maastricht University in the Netherlands, the Procedural System and Judicial Reform Research Centre of Renmin University in China has drafted this Expert Proposal for Detention Centre Law. We hope that with this first draft law prepared by scholars from civil society, we can make a contribution to the on-going attempts to improve the detention centre legislation.

To prepare for this academic proposal, we have, as described in previous chapters, carried out multiple field surveys and referred to international rules and relevant laws relating to detention management in various countries. We do not expect it to be an ideal guideline for legislation but rather a proposal that features both idealism and effectiveness, whilst at the same time taking into consideration the reality of the Chinese criminal justice system.

2. THE TEXT OF THE PROPOSED DRAFT DENTENTION CENTRE LAW

Table of Contents

Chapter One: General Provisions

Article 1: Purpose

According to the Constitution, this law is designed to protect the legal rights of detainees and regulate management of detention centres in order to ensure smooth criminal proceedings.

Note:

The law of detention centres involves the basic rights of detainees, which should be regulated by law according to the rule of law and the Law on Legislation of China. The Regulations on Detention Centres, which currently regulate detention centres in China, are administrative regulations whose legal status is too low to meet the requirement of 'rule of law'. To 'Ensure smooth criminal proceedings' here means on the one hand that the detention centre shall ensure that all detainees are safe, that they cannot flee and that they participate in the proceedings in accordance with law; on the other hand it shall ensure that the detention is carried out according to law, and that the rights and the treatment of detainees are protected.

Article 2: Function

A detention centre is a criminal lockup facility of the State. It is charged with holding suspects and defendants subject to arrest and detention in accordance with the Criminal Procedure Law.

Before an offender is handed over for the enforcement of his or her criminal punishment, if the remaining term of his or her sentence is less than three months, the criminal punishment shall be carried out at a detention centre instead. Prisoners sentenced to the death penalty awaiting execution and foreign detainees awaiting deportation are detained at a detention centre.

Note:

This Article defines who can be held in a detention centre. The majority of detainees are persons under prosecution who are not yet convicted, although a small proportion are prisoners with a remaining prison term of less than three months, those sentenced to the death penalty awaiting execution, or foreign detainees awaiting deportation. A detention centre's main function is to hold remand prisoners (weijuefan in Chinese). Detention centres are also authorized by the Criminal Procedure Law to hold certain groups of convicts. Prisons and detention centres are the two main detention facilities in China, leaving aside the facilities for administrative detention. The former belongs to the Ministry of Justice while the latter is run by the police. All convicts should, in principle, serve their prison sentences in prisons but for some convicts who have only three months of their sentences left to serve, it does not make economic sense to have them transferred to prison for such a short period. As a result, the law authorises detention centres to administer penalties for this group of convicts on behalf of prisons. Convicts and suspects are, of course, held separately within detention centres and are subject to quite different regimes.

Article 3: Location and Management

A detention centre is set up in each administrative area above county level and is managed by the local agency of the Detention Management Bureau.

Note:

At present, all detention centres in China are managed by the public security authorities. This arrangement has created a situation where there is, to a certain degree, an overlap of investigation and detention, which therefore impairs the neutrality of detention centres. This Article suggests the separation of detention centres from the public security authorities by creating an independent custody service responsible for the management of detention centres.

Article 4: Humane Treatment

All detainees shall receive humane treatment and their dignity shall be respected. No detainee shall be subjected to torture and other cruel, inhuman or degrading treatment or punishment.

Possible cases of torture, degrading or inhuman treatment of detainees that come, in whatever way, to the knowledge of detention centre personnel shall be investigated promptly by an independent authority as prescribed by law.

Note:

This provision implies the positive obligation of the management of detention centres to provide decent and safe living conditions in detention centres and to guarantee the fair treatment of detainees in every respect. At the same time it urges the authorities to be alert to possible ill-treatment of detainees and to take appropriate action whenever this occurs.

Article 5: Legality and Proportionality

Detention centres are managed in accordance with the law. Persons who are deprived of their liberty in a detention centre retain all rights that are not lawfully taken away from them.

Restrictions placed on persons referred to in Article 1 shall be legal, the minimum necessary, proportionate, and shall be applied for the shortest possible duration.

Note:

This article reflects the notion that detainees are not automatically deprived of their civil or political rights by the fact of their detention.

Article 6: Equal Application

1. No detainee shall be subjected to discrimination of any kind, irrespective of his or her race, colour, gender, language, religion or religious beliefs, political or other opinions, nationality, ethnicity or social background, property, birth or other status.

2. Special protection for pregnant women, breast-feeding mothers, minors, the elderly, and people with physical disabilities shall not be deemed to be discrimination.

Article 7: Remedy of Rights Violation

1. A detainee shall be entitled to lodge complaints against infringements of his or her personal rights as elaborated in Article 2 of this Law.

2. Such a complaint shall be investigated and handled in a prompt, effective and confidential manner.

Note:

This article empowers detainees to contest alleged unjust decisions and actions of personnel, or harmful behaviour of fellow detainees. The existence of an effective complaints system can prevent unfair and ill treatment of detainees.

Article 8: External Supervision

All detention centres shall be subject to legal supervision by the people's procuratorates and monitoring visits by citizens.

Note:

Detention centres in China have been known for their closed nature and lack of external supervision. Procurators in China are given the status and the duty of legal supervision. At every detention centre there are designated procurators responsible for supervising detention police to ensure that they work within the law. Detention centre procurators and detention police belong to two different systems and thus represent a type of external supervision. This proposal advocates continued enhancement of the supervision function of procurators, as well as external supervision by members of society and the public.

Article 9: Guaranteed Independence of Detention Centres

The lawful execution of power by detention centres is protected by law and shall not be interfered with by any organisation or individual. Governments at all levels shall provide the necessary conditions and facilitate the operation of detention centres.

Article 10: Definitions

1. Detention Centre: facility for holding pre-trial detainees and prisoners with a remaining prison term of less than three months or prisoners sentenced to the death penalty pending execution, or foreign detainees awaiting deportation.

2. Detainee: a) person who is deprived of his or her freedom due to arrest (Juliu in Chinese) or detention (Daibu in Chinese) according to the Criminal Procedure Law; b) a prisoner with a remaining prison term of less than three months; c) a person who is sentenced to the death penalty pending execution; d).a foreign prisoner awaiting deportation. e) criminal suspects and defendants subject to compulsory measures, as well as criminals with fixed-term sentences.

3. The Elderly: People who are over 70 years old.

4. Torture: any act by which severe pain or suffering, whether physical or mental, is intentionally inflicted on a person for such purposes as obtaining from him or a third person information or a confession, punishing him for an act he or a third person has committed or is suspected of having committed, or intimidating or coercing him or a third person, or for any reason based on discrimination of any kind, when such pain or suffering is inflicted by or at the instigation of or with the consent or acquiescence of a public official or other person acting in an official capacity. It does not include pain or suffering arising only from, inherent in or incidental to, lawful sanctions.

Chapter Two: Establishment, Management and Staffing

Article 11: Establishment and Closure

1. The establishment or closing down of a detention centre shall be based firstly on a proposal by the Detention Management Bureau of the people's government above county level, secondly review by the department responsible for management and staffing of establishments within the

people's government, and finally approval from the people's government at the same level.

2. The establishment or closing down of a county or city level detention centre shall also require filing an application to the people's government at a higher level.

3. No organization or individual shall be allowed to arbitrarily designate the use of any particular place as a detention centre.

4. In principle, a detention centre shall be set up in each administrative area above county level.

Note:
This provision outlaws extra-legal detention centres.

Article 12: Principle of Infrastructure Construction

The construction of a detention centre shall be incorporated into the master plan of the city in which it is located. It should also take into account architectural properties and the particular requirements of its surroundings, be part of a unified plan and be in an accessible location.

Article 13: Construction Scale

The size of a detention centre should be based on realistic forecasts, taking into account factors such as population, political and geographical conditions, crime rate and development plan for a particular criminal jurisdiction. Furthermore, the governing judicial administrative agency should first submit the construction plan to the local government and then to the judicial administrative agency at the provincial level for approval.

Article 14: Construction Standard

The required construction standard of detention centres shall be determined on the basis of joint consultations between departments of administration, reform, development, construction and finance under the State Council, in accordance with law.

Article 15 Grading System

1. The quality of a detention centre is reflected in its grade.

2. Grading criteria shall be formulated by the Detention Management Bureau, under the State Council.

3. The evaluation of a detention centre shall be carried out strictly according to certain standards and should follow the principle of seeking truth from facts, combining regular inspections with performance evaluation.

4. A detention centre can be awarded one of four grades, namely, One, Two, Three or Sub-standard, following an evaluation process to be carried out annually.

Note:
The creation of a Detention Management Bureau is one of the major innovations that are introduced by this law. The function and powers of this Bureau will be articulated in a special by-law.
There are over three thousand detention centres across China. Depending on their location, the conditions and the levels of law enforcement in different detention centres vary markedly. As a result, there is a clear need for uniform control through the evaluation management system set forth in this Article, so as to ensure that all detainees are equal before the law and that the enforcement of law is consistent.

Article 16: Staffing and Manpower
A detention centre shall determine the required staffing of police manpower based on actual need. However, every detention centre shall have a ratio of at least one policeman to five criminal suspects, defendants, or criminals.

Note:
'Police' refers here to detention guards, who do not carry out investigations, which is an essential distinction from the police of the public security authorities.

Article 17: Recruitment, Appraisal and Training of Detention Centre Staff
1. The recruitment of guards shall be done by observance of national rules which require public examinations, strict performance appraisal, and selection based on merit.
2. The judicial and administrative departments at all levels shall hold at least one professional examination a year for detention centre police, and conduct training sessions on a regular basis to improve the quality of professional performance and law enforcement.

Article 18: Exclusive Management Responsibility
The responsibility for managing the operation of detention centres lies exclusively with full-time custody officers and no other staff shall be authorized or appointed for such purpose.

Note:
This article implies that the management of detention centres is the exclusive responsibility of the detention police force under the control of the Detention

Management Bureau mentioned in Article 15 of this law. Consequently, the public security authorities cannot participate in the management of detention centres.

Article 19: Work Records

All detention centres shall establish a stringent work record mechanism, which adopts the format, standard and content prescribed by the Detention Management Bureau under the State Council.

Chapter Three: Admission

Article 20: Detention Location

1. Criminal suspects and defendants in criminal detention or under arrest shall be held by the detention centre in the location where the investigation is being undertaken.

2. The public security authorities, the State security agency, prisons, people's courts and people's procuratorates above county level may request temporary custody of a detainee whom they have pursued, caught and are finally escorting, at a detention centre in a different location from where the investigation is being carried out. Such temporary custody shall not exceed 48 hours.

Note:

A criminal suspect should normally be detained in the local detention centre of the place where the alleged crime is committed. However, in practice, many criminal suspects are captured in other places. Since the Criminal Procedure Law stipulates that captured criminal suspects shall be immediately delivered into detention centres, those suspects may be held in temporary custody in the detention centres where they are captured, as it might take a long time to transfer them to the detention centre where the alleged crime was committed.

Article 21: Certificate of Admission

1. A detention centre shall admit a detained or arrested suspect or defendant if it is presented with a detention or arrest warrant in accordance with the Criminal Procedure Law.

2. An offender who is to be imprisoned awaiting execution of his or her punishment following conviction shall be admitted with a valid written judgment or ruling from the people's court;

3. An offender who has been detained before conviction and is to remain imprisoned to serve his or her sentence after conviction shall be admitted with a copy of the bill of prosecution from the people's procuratorate together with the written judgment, the ruling, the notice of execution and

the registration form issued by the people's court showing that the case is closed.

4. When the public security authorities, the State security agency, the prisons, the people's courts or the people's procuratorates above county level, request that a detention centre provide temporary custody to a detainee whom it has pursued, and caught, and is now escorting, the detention centre shall admit the detainee only upon submission of either a detention warrant, an arrest warrant, a wanted warrant, or an official letter from the above county-level agency and subsequent approval from its competent authority.

5. A detention centre shall not admit a detainee without receiving the above-mentioned supporting documents, or if the seal on the documents is unclear, or if the information provided in the documents is incorrect.

Article 22: Cross-Region Detention

1. For a detention centre in one administrative area to admit a detainee from another administrative area above county-level, it shall be presented with a detention warrant or an arrest warrant, as well as the approval by the competent authority of the detention centres in the two areas.

2. If a suspect or prisoner, who was already admitted to one detention centre, has to be exceptionally transferred to a detention centre in another region, the former detention centre shall send the suspect or prisoner to the latter institution bearing the cross-region detention transfer approval form and the other legal documents mentioned in Article 21. In addition, it shall record the transfer in the admission registration form.

Article 23: Hand-Over of Detainees

1. When the authority in charge of a case hands over a suspect or defendant, it shall indicate the lmaximum legal detention time on the supporting documents, except in the case of temporary custody.

2. If a case concerns crimes concerning State Security or terrorism, the authority in charge of the case shall notify the detention centre in writing of this fact, when it hands over the suspect or defendant.

Note:

Second paragraph: according to the revised Criminal Procedure Law 2012, lawyers should, in principle, meet freely with detainees (their clients). The law however specifies that such meetings require prior approval in two types of cases namely, those endangering state security and those concerning terrorism. When drafting this proposal, we took the view that as these two types of cases concern state interests, the meetings should therefore be restricted.

Article 24: Medical Examination

1. A suspect, defendant or prisoner shall be examined by medical staff within 24 hours of being admitted to a detention centre.

2. If the person is found to have an injury, such information shall be noted down and the authority which hands him or her over shall be required to present within 24 hours a signed and sealed statement by a medical doctor, confirming that the person concerned had previously suffered no injuries when he or she was delivered to the detention centre.

3. If a severe injury is found by the medical staff of the detention centre, the hand-over authority shall take the criminal suspect, defendant or criminal to a people's hospital above county-level for diagnosis and should obtain proof of such diagnosis from the hospital. Without a legitimate reason, the authorities cannot refuse to take the detainee to hospital for diagnosis or refuse to provide proof of injury. If it does refuse, the detention centre may reject admission and make a log of the situation in its records.

4. The medical staff shall immediately inform the management in writing of detainee injuries discovered at admission. The management will send a copy of this information to the procurator. If the procurator cannot exclude the possibility that the injuries were caused by ill-treatment of the victim, he must have the case investigated without delay.

5. In any of the following circumstances, a detention centre may reject the admission of a detainee, or keep him or her in separate detention, or transfer him or her to a hospital, and immediately report to the authority in charge of the case:

(1) if he or she is suffering from mental illness or an acute infectious illness;

(2) if he or she is suffering from other types of serious illness, or his or her life is at risk, or he or she is unable to take care of him or herself during detention;

(3) if she is a pregnant woman or a woman who is breastfeeding her baby, aged less than one year old;

If after admission a detainee is found to be in one of the above-mentioned circumstances and is therefore unsuitable for detention, the detention centre shall notify the authority in charge of his or her case in writing, in order to change the compulsory measure, or to arrange administration of the punishment outside the detention centre. A copy of the written notice shall be kept in the detainee's file.

Note:

A medical check-up right at the point of, or just after, admission helps combat ill-treatment of persons who previously have been held by the investigating authorities. If injuries are found, the medical staff will report this to the management of the detention centre. The management has to hand over this information in full to the prison prosecutor, who has to decide whether to start a criminal investigation or not.

Article 25: Security Check

1. Upon admission of a suspect, defendant or prisoner, the detention centre shall search the person and check in his or her belongings.

2. All detention centres shall allow a suspect, defendant or prisoner to bring basic necessities into the cell if such goods have been security checked; non-necessities, cash and other articles which may affect the safety of the detention centre shall not be brought into the cell and shall be placed in safe custody on the detainee's behalf. Prohibited articles shall be confiscated and turned over to the State Treasury.

3. If criminal evidence and suspicious articles are discovered among a detainee's belongings, the detention centre shall note the information down, ask him or her to sign the record, and forward the sealed record to the authority in charge of his or her case.

4. Female guards shall be responsible for assessing the safety of female suspects, defendants and prisoners.

Notes:

The security check mainly refers to checks performed by detention police on the detainee and the articles belonging to him or her upon arrival at the detention centre. The purpose of this is to prevent any security risks incurred by bringing prohibited articles, such as knives and guns, into the cells.

Article 26: Admission Receipt

A detention centre shall provide an admission receipt to the authority in charge of the case after admitting a criminal suspect, defendant or criminal.

Article 27: Notification

1. Immediately after admission, all criminal suspects, defendants and criminals shall be informed, in a language they understand, of the regulations governing detention centre discipline and of their rights and duties in the detention centre.

2 Upon request, detention centres shall provide detainees with a booklet or brochure to inform them of the rights of detainees. This information shall also be available in the library of the detention centre too and shall be freely accessible by all inmates.

Article 28: Registration

Upon admission the following details concerning each detained criminal suspect, defendant and criminal shall be recorded on a registration form:
(1) information concerning the identity of the detainee;
(2) the reasons for commitment to detention and the authority behind it;
(3) the date and hour of admission;
(4) an inventory of the personal property of the detainee;
(5) any visible injuries and complaints about prior extortion of confessions by torture, threats, seduction, deception or other illegal means;
(6) any information about the detainee's health that is relevant to the physical and mental well-being of the detainee or others; and
(7) other items specified by law.

Article 29: Detainees' Files

1. After admitting a criminal suspect, defendant or criminal, a detainee's file shall be prepared by the detention centre. The file shall include: proof of admission, detainee admission registration form, photos and film, health examination form, property safekeeping registration form, certificate of change of custody, performance during detention, treatment of illness, and release certificate.
2. A detainee, his or her close relatives and lawyer shall be entitled to review his or her file during detention and request to correct the file. If the file concerns State secrets, prior approval shall be obtained from the authority in charge of his or her case and the detention centre governor.
3. The detainee shall be given a copy of his or her file when he or she is released.
4. All detention centres shall keep detainees' files in good order and shall only use them when they are needed for detainee management and criminal case handling.

Article 30: Special Procedure for Admitting Criminals

1. Within 24 hours of admission of a suspect or sentenced offender, notification of the location where sentence will be served shall be given to the person's family or guardian.
2. Admission of persons who are foreign nationals or who have no nationality shall be reported to the Detention Centre authority of the same level within 24 hours.

Chapter Four: Management

Section 1: Transition Management

Article 31: Principle

1. All detention centres shall introduce a transition management system for physical and mental assessment and instruction of newly admitted detainees.
2. The transition period shall not exceed 15 days. During this period, the detainees may be held in cells that are separate from the ordinary cells.

Note:

Transition management refers to the practice, where new detainees are placed in some special cells so that detention police can observe their behaviour more closely and provide more specific attention and care to help them adapt to life in the detention centre and to understand the rules. In the majority of cases, a detainee may spend a maximum of 15 days in a transition cell and will be transferred to an ordinary cell once he is used to living in the detention centre.

Article 32: Transition Cell

1. A detention centre may set up transition cells to hold new detainees in order to achieve collective transition management.
2. If there is no transition cell, or there are a number of detainees allegedly involved in the same crime, (and it is thus unsuitable to hold them in the same room), the detainees may be held in ordinary cells. But transition management shall be applied.
3. Transition cells for women shall be managed by female police.

Article 33: Transition Management

1. Detention centre police shall pay particular attention to the supervision and observation of new detainees who are held in either transition or ordinary cells, to prevent security problems and to ensure that detailed observation records are kept.
2. Detention centre police shall interview new detainees within 24 hours of their admission in order to become familiar with their basic circumstances, the nature of the case they have been committed for, their thoughts regarding their situation, and to inform them of their lawful rights and the regulations governing detention centre discipline. In particular, new detainees shall be informed how to deal with illness, appeals, filing charges, and other common issues. They shall also be informed that bullying of or by other detainees will not be tolerated, and what action they can take if they are bullied.

3. Transition management shall last a minimum of 7 days and may be longer in exceptional circumstances. The maximum time a new detainee spends in a transition cell is 15 days.

Article 34: Transition Management Report
At the end of each case of transition management, detention centre police shall assess the performance of a new detainee during this period.

Section 2: Principle of Separate Custody

Article 35: Risk Assessment
A detention centre shall make a comprehensive assessment of a detainee by considering the nature of the crime he or she is alleged to have committed, his or her character, physical health and mental state, the risk he or she poses to the outside world, and his or her performance during the transition management to determine how he or she will be detained and managed.

Article 36: Principle of Separate Custody
1. A detention centre shall adopt separate custody and control methods for criminal suspects, defendants and criminals, male and female detainees, adults and juveniles, criminal suspects and defendants involved in the same case.
2. Female detainees shall be accommodated in particular detention centres or in particular sections of a detention centre and shall be under the direct control and care of female police.

Article 37: Principle of Separate Custody and Separate Control in Special Circumstances
1. Based on the results of risk assessment, a detention centre may decide to keep detainees with different levels of risk in separate custody.
2. In light of the actual situation, due account shall be taken of the need to detain and manage detainees involved in violent offences separately from those involved in non-violent offences, detainees of intentional crime separately from detainees of crimes of negligence, and detainees involved in sex crime separately from detainees involved in other types of crime.
3. Detainees who suffer from infectious illnesses shall be quarantined in custody for the period of infection.
4. A detention centre shall set up particular cells for collective detention of vulnerable persons like the elderly, the weak, the sick and the physically disabled.

Section 3: Guards and Detention

Article 38: Armed Guard

1. Officers from the people's armed police force shall guard the perimeter of detention centres.

2. The management of the detention centres shall provide guidance on the duty performance of such officers of the people's armed police force.

Note:

The main function of armed police is to ensure that detainees do not flee from the detention centre. They do not enter the detention centre, but keep guard on or outside the surrounding walls.

Article 39: The Responsibilities of the Armed Police

1. Armed guards posted at the perimeter of detention centres are charged with preventing detainees from escaping, committing physical assault or damage, causing riots or revolts. They are also responsible for preventing and clamping down on activities aimed at attacking detention centres, seizing and rescuing detainees, performing armed escort, pursuit and capture, and assisting detention centres in preventing and responding to disasters and accidents.

2. The officers of the people's armed police force based at a detention centre shall have guard posts at the detention centre gates, fences, walls and watchtowers.

Article 40: Collaborative Mechanism between Detention Centres and the Armed Police

A detention centre shall establish a way of collaborating with the armed police force based at the detention centre.

Article 41: Duty Shifts

1. Detention centres shall introduce a 24-hour monitoring and inspection system and a contingency response mechanism.

2. Monitoring and inspection staff shall stringently carry out duty shifts, and report and deal with identified problems in a timely and proper manner to the management of the detention centre.

Article 42: Management

1. At a detention centre, the senior police officer and assistant officers are in charge of cell management and communication with detainees.

2. Strict prohibition on Detainees managing other Detainees.[1]

Article 43: Access Pass for Prisons and Detention Centres

1. All detention centres shall adopt an access pass system for the areas of detention. Anyone who enters or exits a detention area shall wear an access pass.

2. Except for detention centre police and procurators working at the detention centre, persons who need to enter and exit detention areas for other work-related reasons, shall require a temporary access pass.

Article 44: Searches

Regular or ad hoc searches of detainees, cells and other places shall be carried out to remove articles which might be used by detainees to escape, commit physical assault or suicide, or cause damage. Any suspicious signs or signs of damage shall be investigated immediately and be dealt with in accordance with law.

Note:

The manner in which detainees can be searched is twofold: 1) the search of clothing and the surface of the (naked) body and 2) the search of the natural orifices of the body. The last type of search shall be ordered only when there is a serious suspicion that the detainee is hiding contraband and should only be performed by medical staff.

Article 45: Types of Instruments of Restraint

Detention centre staff may apply instruments of restraint including standard handcuffs, shackles and standard police restraint belts.

Article 46: Use of Instruments of Restraint

1. If facts show that a detainee is in any of the following circumstances, and detention centre staff have substantial reason to find the use of instruments of restraint necessary, such instruments of restraint may be used, but based on a legitimate need and the actual situation:

---

[1]   Reference: Art. 19 of the Rules for the Implementation of the Regulations on Detention Centres, the Ten Rules for Regulating and Cracking Down on 'Prison Bullies' at Detention Centres.

(1) if a detainee poses danger to others;

(2) if a detainee might commit suicide, escape, engage in violence, and cause rioting;

(3) if a detainee seriously violates detention centre management rules and sabotages control orders;

(4) if a detainee is being brought to see a doctor, to an interrogation, to trial, or being taken out of a detention centre and being escorted;

(5) other circumstances that should justify use of instruments of restraint.

2. If the use of instruments of restraint is justified in circumstances listed in (2), (3) and (5) of the preceding paragraph, an approval from the detention centre governor shall be obtained. In an emergency, the instruments of restraint may be applied first and the situation shall then be immediately brought to the notice of the detention centre governor.

3. Instruments of restraint shall be applied for more than 7 days but their use may be extended to 15 days with approval from the detention centre governor. Once the circumstances specified in the preceding paragraph no longer apply, instruments of restraint shall not be used further.

4. The use of instruments of restraint and the underlying reason for their use shall be recorded in the personal file of the detainee.

Article 47: Temporary Control Measures

1. When the use of instruments of restraint is insufficient to prevent harm, a detainee may be temporarily confined physically to a cell bed by handcuffs, shackles, leg irons, and rope straps , subject to obtaining approval from the detention centre governor. The decision and underlying reasons for restraint should be recorded in the personal file of the detainee.

2. Temporary control shall generally last no longer than 24 hours. Its extension shall require an approval from the public security authorities and be for a maximum of 3 days. As soon as the danger is no longer present, it shall be immediately stopped immediately.

3. When such temporary control measures are adopted, the detention centre doctor shall examine the controlled detainee every four hours. If the detainee's health is found to be unsuitable for temporary control measures, such measures shall be terminated immediately.

4. Detention centre staff shall present a written report to the procurator's office (based at the same institution) immediately after the adoption of temporary control measures. If the procurator deems it improper and advises against such use, the detention centre shall immediately rectify the situation and report back to the procurator's office once this has been done.

Article 48: Weapons

1. Unless in exceptional circumstances, detention centre police shall not carry lethal weapons within the detention centre perimeter.

2. Personnel on duty from the detention centre police or the people's armed police force may, in any of the following circumstances, which cannot be controlled without the use of weapons, use weapons in accordance with the relevant regulations of the State:

(1) if any detainee is assembling a crowd to make a riot or revolt;

(2) if any detainee is escaping or resisting arrest;

(3) if any detainee is committing physical assault or destruction with a lethal weapon or other dangerous articles to endanger the safety of another person's life or property;

(4) if any detainee is being seized and rescued by force; or

(5) if any detainee is seizing a weapon by force.

3. Personnel who have used weapons shall report the situation in accordance with the relevant regulations of the State.

Section 4: Management of Detainees' Property

Article 49: Property Given during Meetings[2]

1. Goods brought by detainees' close relatives shall be given to detainees after being subject to examination and registration by detention centre police.

2. Detainees shall be entitled to obtain a 'Property Safekeeping Registration Form' and formal receipt stubs.

3. Visitors shall not give detainees food and medicines, unless such goods cannot be obtained within detention centres through normal channels.

Article 50: Money for Living Expenses and Cash Management

1. A detention centre shall open an account for every detainee. The cash carried by a detainee on admission as well as the cash he or she receives during detention shall be deposited in his or her account. All detainees shall be entitled to check and use their accounts.

2. All detainees shall be entitled to use their accounts to purchase basic every-day necessities and non-hazardous consumer goods.

3. Detention centres manage their accounts using traditional book-keeping. Coupons are not allowed. Any purchases made by a detainee shall bear his or her signature.

---

[2]   Reference: Art. 37 of the Rules for the Implementation of the Regulations on Detention Centres, Art. 32 of the Detention Law of Taiwan, and Art. 31 of the European Prison Rules.

Note:

A small shop is set up in detention centres to provide basic every-day necessities for detainees. The price should be consistent with the market price.

Article 51: Handling of Property

If a detainee's property is not suitable for being kept or cannot be kept in a detention centre, the institution shall ask the detainee to dispose of such property or ask his or her family to take it back home. If the detainee refuses to do so, or it is impossible to inform his or her family, or his or her family refuses to take such property back after being informed, such property may be dealt with promptly with the approval of the detention centre's competent authority.

Article 52: Compensation for Lost or Damaged Property

If a detainee's property is damaged or destroyed when being taken into custody by a detention centre, he or she shall receive compensation equivalent to the value of such property.

Article 53: Return of Property

Upon release, all property belonging to a detainee that was taken into safe custody shall be checked and returned (or alternatively transferred to prison and other places of detention).

Section 5: Request for Interrogation

Article 54: Interrogation Warrant

The public security authorities, the State security agency, the people's procuratorates, and the people's courts shall present an interrogation warrant to support their request to interrogate a detainee. Only if the authority handling the case presents a detention or arrest warrant, or a change of custody warrant shall the detention centre put its seal on the authority's interrogation warrant.

Article 55: Registration System

All detention centres shall establish a registration system for requests to interrogate detainees. All details shall be registered, such as the name of the agency and the individual making the interrogation request, the name of the detainee and the time at which the interrogation begins and ends.

Article 56: Arrangements

1. The authority in charge of a case shall present an interrogation warrant bearing the detention centre's interrogation seal and valid identification documents when it requests an interrogation with a detainee. There should be at least two interrogators present during each interrogation.

2. A detention centre shall reject the request if it does not follow the afore-mentioned rules.

Article 57: Place of Interrogation

1. Interrogation shall take place in interrogation rooms within the detention centre. Such rooms physically separate interrogators from detainees.

2. Detention centre staff shall intervene if interrogators engage in any acts which are against the rules, and shall not hesitate to terminate the interrogation if necessary. If a detainee behaves irregularly during an interrogation, interrogators shall inform detention centre police of the situation.

Note:

According to the Criminal Procedure Law, the interrogation of detained criminal suspects should take place in detention centres. There are interrogation rooms in every detention centre where the police officers and the criminal suspects are separated by iron bars. They enter and exit the interrogation room through different channels and have no physical contact with each other. Such a set-up effectively prevents the extortion of confessions by torture.

All detention centres have the obligation to protect detainees from torture. Therefore they have the supervisory power which enables them to check whether interrogations carried out by investigators are legal. This Article provides that detention police have the power to terminate an interrogation when necessary.

Article 58: Timing of Interrogation

A detention centre shall not arrange an interrogation session at a time that would affect the detainee's schedule, in terms of rest, mealtimes and medical treatment.

Article 59: Audio and Video-taping

When the authority in charge of a case interrogates a detainee, the detention centre may audio or video-tape the process.

Note:
According to the Criminal Procedure Law, interrogations of criminal suspects in cases involving the death sentence or life imprisonment must be audio or video-taped. The internal rules of the Supreme People's Procuratorate require that all interrogations of public officials in cases of alleged corruption or other public-duty related crimes should be audio and videotaped.
For other cases, the law says that the interrogation 'may' be audio or video-taped. It is not compulsory to have all the interrogations audio or video-taped.

Section 6: Leaving The Detention Centre Temporarily

Article 60: Proof

1. A detainee shall need permission from the public security authorities, the State security agency, the people's procuratorates, or the people's courts above county- level if he or she is temporarily removed from a detention centre in order to identify, verify and perform other evidence-collection activities to facilitate investigation, prosecution and trial, or to have a long-distance video interrogation, or to attend a trial or hear a judgment at the people's court, or to see a doctor, or to engage in civil legal acts which must be performed by him or her, such as if his or her spouse, parents or children are terminally ill or have died, or if the detainee is required for marriage registration.

2. Persons who have come to remove a detainee from the detention centre shall carry with them the approval form of the authority in charge of the case, the certificate with the detention centre's special seal, and their valid identification documents. In addition, they shall obtain approval from the detention centre governor. There shall be at least two persons present to escort one detainee. The maximum leave from detention centres is 48 hours and the process of exit and re-entry should be recorded in the detainee's file.

3. A detention centre shall refuse to cooperate if the two rules mentioned above are not observed.

Article 61: Registration System

A detention centre shall introduce a registration system for temporarily removing detainees from the detention centre. The system should keep records of institutions which take detainees away, the name of the persons sent to do the job, the name of the detainee being moved, and the time at which the process begins and ends.

Article 62: Time Log

1. The authority in charge of the case shall prepare a log of the suspect's activities outside the detention centre, including the time that the detainee is taken in and out, and this will be signed and sealed by the detainee.

2. A detainee shall not be taken out of a detention centre for more than 48 hours. Extending the time in exceptional circumstances shall require the approval of the detention centre governor.

Article 63: Medical Examination

When a detainee is brought back to a detention centre by the authority in charge of his or her case, he or she shall be offered a physical examination. If he or she is found to have a physical injury or to have any hidden articles on his or her person, he or she shall be dealt with in accordance with this law.

Note:

'Be dealt with in accordance with law' in this Article refers to the circumstances specified by the law and detention centre related regulations that detention procurators and the supervision department of public security authorities should investigate accordingly if a detainee is found to have a physical injury. In addition, a detainee may receive disciplinary action if he possesses drugs, firearms and other prohibited articles.

Article 64: Escort

1. A detainee being taken to hospital or sent to serve sentence in prison shall have an armed escort.

2. Female detainees shall be taken care of by female police while being escorted.

Section 7: Discipline, Reward and Punishment

Article 65: Daily Evaluations of Detainees

Detention centres shall have a detainee evaluation system and link evaluation results with rewards and punishments.

Article 66: Detainees Providing Crime Clues

1. If a detainee confesses to other criminal acts which have not been known previously to the judicial agency, the detention centre shall forward such information to the authority in charge of the case.

2. If a detainee discloses information concerning criminal acts or provides important clues of alleged crimes of other criminals, the detention centre shall forward such information to the case jurisdiction authority. The

authority shall inform the detention centre in writing of its efforts to investigate such information.

Article 67: Rewards

A detainee shall be commended and rewarded if he or she:

(1) observes the code of conduct, studies diligently, and obeys the management;

(2) contributes to ensuring the order and safety of the detention centre; or

(3) demonstrates other types of good behaviour.

Note:

'Other good behaviour' means that if a detainee behaves well in a detention centre, his or her behaviour will be pointed out to the judge who will take this into consideration in sentencing.

Article 68: Voluntary Surrender and Contributions

A detention centre shall collect relevant evidence and report to its competent authority in writing to advise that the authority in charge of a detainee's case recommends that the people's court gives the detainee a lighter or mitigated punishment or exempts him or her from punishment in accordance with law, or applies for commutation of punishment and release on probation if he or she:

(1) has given a truthful confession of his or her other criminal acts which have not been previously known to the judicial agency;

(2) has reported another person's criminal act which has then been ascertained to be true, or has provided important clues to help resolve other cases;

(3) has successfully persuaded or prevented others from committing physical assault or suicide, escaping, causing a riot, or engaging in other criminal activities; or

(4) has made other types of contribution.

Note:

Articles 66-68 do not suggest that all detention centres have an obligation or responsibility to facilitate case resolution. Due to the provision in the Criminal Law which stipulates that a defendant may be given a lighter or mitigated punishment if he confesses to his crime or discloses another person's crime, if a detainee voluntarily requests to confess or make other types of contribution, the detention centre should accept such request and forward it to the case handling department even though it does not have an obligation to pro-actively seek crime clues. In other words, the detention police should not actively seek to uncover crime related information but may passively receive crime clues.

Article 69: Handling of Alleged Criminal Acts Committed in Detention Centres

If a detainee allegedly commits a criminal act during detention, the institution shall inform the procurator based in the detention centre of the situation in a timely manner and transfer the case to the authority in charge of case handling; however the detention centre shall be responsible for investigating any crimes committed by a criminal within the detention centre perimeter.

Note:

According to current law and practice, the detention centre should be responsible for investigating criminal acts carried out by detainees (e.g. killing other detainees) inside the detention centre. This Article mainly relates to the convenience of investigation and the promptness of evidence collection.

Article 70: Punishment

1. A detention centre may give a detainee a warning, an admonishment, an instruction to show true repentance or enforce solitary confinement if he or she is in any of the following circumstances; if the detainee's act amounts to a crime, he or she shall be held criminally responsible:

(1) if a detainee creates a disturbance, causes a fight, or disrupts order in detention;

(2) if a detainee intentionally destroys the property of the detention centre or of other people;

(3) if a detainee beats and bullies others;

(4) if a detainee plots or attempts to escape; or

(5) if a detainee engages in other behaviour that seriously violates the regulations governing detention centre discipline.

2. Any warning, admonishment, or instruction to show true repentance shall be given to a detainee once detention centre police have decided and reported such decision to the governor

3. Prior to administering the punishment of solitary confinement, the detention centre police shall apply to the governor in writing for approval.

4. The period of solitary confinement lasts between five to ten days.

5. During the period of solitary confinement, a detainee is not allowed any communication with the outside world other than with his or her lawyer.

6. A detainee in solitary confinement should have natural light in the cell and at least one-hour's walk a day in the open air, weather permitting.

Note:

The 'instruction to show true repentance' means that the detention police officer is required to explain to the detainee how to follow the detention centre rules and to stress the need to reflect on his or her behaviour.

Article 71: Objection to Punishments

If a detainee wishes to object to a punishment in detention, he or she may submit a complaint to the detention centre governor or the procurator. If, after review, the procurator finds the punishment is unjustified, the prosecutor may choose to supervise the actions of the detention police (according to current supervision regulations) in order to deal with the matter.

Chapter Five: Rights and Treatment

Section 1: Personal Rights

Article 72: Ensuring Personal Safety and Upholding Dignity

All detention centres shall take the necessary steps to protect the personal safety and human dignity of detainees.

Article 73: Rights during Transfer

1. When detainees are being moved to or from a detention centre, they shall be kept from public view as far as is possible and proper safeguards shall be adopted to protect them from any form of indignity, intrusive curiosity or publicity.

2. The transport of detainees shall be carried out in conveyances with adequate ventilation and light, and which would not subject them in any way to unnecessary physical hardship.

3. When detainees are being transferred to other detention facilities, or to hospital due to injury, or physical or mental health problems, the detention centre shall notify close relatives as soon as possible.

Article 74: Termination of Excess Detention

A detainee shall be entitled to appeal to the detention centre police, the procurator based in the detention centre and the authority in charge of his or her case to terminate his or her detention if it exceeds the legal limit.

Article 75: Right to Protect Reputation and Right to Privacy

1. A detainee's right to privacy shall be protected in a detention centre. His or her reputation shall not be damaged and he or she shall not be subjected to humiliating treatment.

2. Any interview of a detainee by the press, as long as it is permitted by the detention centre governor, shall require the detainee's prior consent. A detainee shall not be forced into being interviewed by the press.

Section 2: Conditions of Detention

Article 76: Living Space
1. The personal safety of detainees shall be guaranteed in their living space. The per-capita living area shall be a minimum of three square meters.
2. All detention centres shall ensure that every detainee has a separate bed.
3. All cells shall meet the required sanitary standards and offer adequate ventilation, light, and protection against damp, heat and cold.
4. All cells shall be subject to regular inspections and timely repairs so as to prevent potential damage from disasters such as fire hazard, amongst others..
5. Inside the cells, detainees shall have access to adequate sanitary facilities that are clean and tidy. Particular attention shall be paid to respecting the privacy of female detainees.
6. An alarm system shall be installed in all cells so that detainees can contact the guards in a timely manner.

Note:
At present, a majority of the old detention centres in China are like dormitories, in which around ten detainees are held in one cell. Since 2011, relevant rules require new detention centres to have a number of single cells and to ensure that each detainee in the cell has his or her own separate bed, instead of sharing one large bed This reform will help minimize conflicts between detainees and better protect the right of privacy, the right of rest and the personal dignity of detainees.

Article 77: Access to Showers
In the interest of general hygiene, detention centres shall ensure that every detainee has a bath or shower, at a temperature suitable to the climate, at least twice a week (or more frequently if necessary for the season or the region).

Article 78: Personal Hygiene
1. Adequate cold and hot water and toiletries shall be provided so that every detainee can keep his or her body clean and healthy.
2. Detainees shall have access to the necessary implements to keep their hair (including beards and moustaches) clean and tidy, so that they are able to maintain their looks and dignity.

3. Detainees may have haircuts as and when required. Male detainees may shave daily.

Article 79: Clothing and Bedding

1. Detainees may bring their own clothing or bedding into the detention centre. Detainees who do not have adequate clothing and bedding of their own shall have these provided free of charge.

2. Clothing and bedding provided by the detention centre shall be adequate, clean, and suitable for the climate. Such clothing and bedding shall not be in any state which is degrading or humiliating or harmful to the health of detainees. In addition, such items shall be changed as often as is required.

3. All detention centres shall provide detainees with conditions to wash and dry their clothing on a regular basis to ensure cleanliness.

Article 80: Dressing with dignity

Detainees who are removed from a detention centre to appear in court or for other reasons shall be allowed to wear their own clothing or clothing that does not draw particular attention to them.

Article 81: Food

1. Detainees shall be provided daily with sanitary and clean food and a healthy diet.

2. Due attention shall be paid to detainees' special dietary requirements.

3. A special diet shall be prepared for a detainee who is unwell if so instructed by the doctor.

4. Clean drinking water shall be available to detainees at all times.

Article 82: Purchasing Food

Detainees may purchase food with their own money in the shop at the detention centre.

Article 83: Smoking

Detainees may purchase cigarettes, cigars and pipe tobacco, but shall only smoke at designated times and places.

Article 84: Outdoor Activities

If weather and other conditions permit, every detainee shall perform at least two hours of outdoor activities daily. He or she may do proper exercise if it is suitable for his or her health.

Article 85: News, Books, and Recreational Activities

1. Detainees are entitled to have regular access to news by listening to radio, watching TV, and reading newspapers and books.

2. Every detention centre shall have a library for the use of detainees, which is adequately stocked with a wide range of books. Efforts shall be made to encourage detainees to make full use of the library.

3. Detainees shall be allowed to subscribe to newspapers, magazines and other news media at their own expense.

4. Detainees may attend all kinds of recreational activities that do not hamper the safety and good order of the detention centre. The programme for such activities shall not be cancelled or restricted without reason.

Article 86: Right to Rest

A detention centre shall protect the right to rest of detainees and ensure that detainees have sufficient time to sleep.

Article 87: Religion

1. Freedom of religion of detainees shall be respected. Detainees may practise their religion by praying, reciting prayers or confessing sins etc in a lawful manner.

2. Detainees may have in their possession articles for religious purposes allowed by law and may use them.

Section 3: Right to Health Care

Article 88: Health Care Provision

1. The quality of medical healthcare for criminal suspects, defendants and prisoners shall be of the same standard as basic healthcare services in society at large.

2. The competent authority shall promptly arrange medical insurance for detainees who do not have any public medical insurance of their own.

3. The medical healthcare of detainees shall be integrated into the public health and epidemic prevention program of the local area in order to achieve an equivalent level of care as that enjoyed by local citizens.

Article 89: Medical Wards

1. A detention centre shall set up a medical ward, clinic, or even a small hospital. Or alternatively, the institution may have a local hospital which is able to offer outpatient services or establish a branch hospital.

2. Arrangements shall be made to put in place a medical hygiene and illness prevention system.

Article 90: Allocation of Medical Resources[3]

1. As a rule, every detention centre shall have at least two qualified doctors. Arrangements shall be made to ensure that a qualified doctor is available at all times in the detention centre.

2. The detention centre shall work closely with the local public health administrative department and hospitals, and particularly the department of mental health in order to facilitate the diagnosis and treatment of detainees who have mental health problems.

3. Every detention centre shall have the necessary medical equipment and a stock of the most frequently used medicines.

4. Every detention centre shall organize regular physical examinations for detainees and prepare health examination forms.

Article 91: Purchasing Medical Services

Criminal suspects, defendants and criminals serving their sentences in a detention centre may apply to have private medical treatment at their own expense.

Article 92: Medical Treatment

1. If a detainee falls ill, the detention centre shall offer prompt treatment; if a detainee is seriously ill and the authority in charge of the case decides to change the compulsory measure imposed on him or her, the matter shall be handled according to relevant rules.

2. If a detainee requires treatment outside the detention centre, the decision shall be approved by the detention centre governor. If a criminal suspect or a defendant is hospitalized for treatment, the detention centre shall inform the authority in charge of his or her case, and close relatives. If such detainee were serving a sentence in the detention centre, his or her relatives shall be informed. In addition, armed police shall work on shifts to guard the hospitalized detainee in order to prevent escape, suicide and other unexpected events.

3. Detainees who injure or harm themselves will not be granted pre-trial bail or residential surveillance. The detention centre shall of course provide timely treatment for them.

Article 93: Duties of the Detention Centre Doctor

1. Medical doctors working at detention centres shall perform the following duties:

---

[3] Reference: Art. 26 of the Regulations on Detention Centres, and Art. 41.1-41.4 of the European Prison Rules.

(1) observe the normal rules of medical confidentiality;

(2) diagnose physical or mental illness and take all measures necessary for treatment of such conditions;

(3) record and report to the detention centre management and procurator any sign or indication that detainees may have been ill-treated;

(4) deal with the use of drugs and medication of detainees who are unwell;

(5) isolate detainees suspected of suffering from infectious or contagious conditions for the period of infection and provide them with proper treatment; and

(6) determine the fitness of each detainee to engage in work and to perform exercise.

2. The detention centre doctor or his medical staff shall regularly inspect and advise the detention centre governor and the procurator based in the institution on:

(1) the quality, preparation and serving of food;

(2) the temperature, sanitation, lighting and ventilation of the cells;

(3) the cleanliness of the detainees' clothing and bedding

(4)the observance of rules of physical exercise which is not organized by professionals; and

(5) other matters in relation to the health of detainees and criminals serving sentences.

Section 4: Contact with the Outside World

Article 94: Meeting with Close Relatives

1. If a criminal suspect wants to meet with a close relative during the investigation stage, he or she shall ask approval from the authority in charge of the case;

2. Suspects and defendants may meet with close relatives in the prosecution and the trial stage.

3. Persons suspected of crimes concerning State secrets shall ask for approval from the authority in charge of the case to meet with close relatives.

4. Prisoners serving sentences may meet with family members in the detention centre.

Article 95: Meeting Requirements

1. Meetings shall take place in specially designated meeting rooms set up by detention centres, which shall not include any physical barriers to separate the detainee from his or her visitors.

2. Every detainee shall be allowed one meeting per month with close relatives, and no more than three visitors at a time. Each meeting shall not exceed one hour.

3. If in exceptional circumstances a detainee needs to meet with more than three close relatives for longer time and more often, he or she must obtain approval from the detention centre governor.

4. Meetings may be audio or video-taped and investigators or detention centre police may be present at such meetings.

5. No one shall interfere with the display of intimacy between a detainee and his or her close relatives.

Article 96: Notification of Serious Illness or Death of A Close Relative and Visiting Rights

1. A criminal suspect, defendant or detainee shall be immediately informed of the news of serious illness or death of a close relative.

2. If possible, the detention centre may allow the detainee to visit or attend the funeral of a close relative, either alone or with the escort of detention centre police and armed police.

3. If a detainee is suffering from either serious injury or illness, has been moved to another institution for treatment, or has died, the detention centre shall immediately inform the next of kin.[4]

Article 97: Mail

1. All outgoing and incoming mail shall be inspected; any correspondence found to impede investigation, prosecution, trial or execution of criminal punishment shall be confiscated and transferred to the authority in charge of the case.

2. Correspondence between detainees and the detention centre's competent authority, judicial agency and lawyers shall be immune from inspection and confiscation.

Section 5: Right to Legal Assistance

Article 98: Meeting with Lawyers and Counsel

1. After the first interrogation with the investigative authorities, or from the day on which compulsory measures are adopted, a criminal suspect may meet with a lawyer.

---

[4] Reference: Art. 29 of the Regulations on Detention Centres, Art. 36 of the Rules for the Implementation of the Regulations on Detention Centres, Rule 44 of the Standard Minimum Rules for the Treatment of Prisoners, and Art. 24.6-24.9 of the European Prison Rules.

2. The detention centre shall check if the lawyer has the necessary qualifications, certification from a law firm and an appointment letter or an official letter of legal aid.

3. If the criminal suspect or defendant has different counsel for the prosecution and trial stage, the detention centre shall check all documentation including identification, appointment letter, and the legal approval form from the people's procuratorate and the people's court regarding the meeting.

Note:

According to the Criminal Procedure Law, a criminal suspect should hire a lawyer from the first interrogation by the investigative authorities or from the day on which compulsory measures are adopted. This Article is based on the provision of the Criminal Procedure Law.

Article 99: Meeting Requirements

1. Meetings between a suspect or a defendant and his or her lawyer and other counsel shall take place in the designated meeting room of the detention centre.

2. Monitoring of such meetings shall be carried out within sight but out of hearing.

3. Such meetings may take place between 9 am and 4 pm.

4. A detention centre may set up a meeting schedule taking into account its specific circumstances but it shall not impose any obstacle to such meetings.

Article 100: Information Relating to Persons Meeting with Detainees

When a person puts in a request to meet with a detainee, details of name, occupation, age, domicile, reason for meeting, name of detainee and their relationship shall be provided.

Article 101: Prohibition of Meetings

The governor of a detention centre shall not agree to a request for a meeting in any of the following circumstances:

(1) if the information provided at the point of making the request is incorrect;

(2) if the criminal suspect, defendant or detainee serving sentence refuses to meet with the person and issues a written notice;

(3) if the criminal suspect, defendant or detainee serving sentence is suffering from mental health problems or an acute infectious disease; or

(4) any other scenarios in which a meeting would be inappropriate.

Note:

The 'other scenarios' specified in item (4) of this article include sudden security emergencies during an interrogation, such as riots at the detention centre or earthquakes.

Article 102: Termination of Meetings

During meetings the relevant rules of the detention centre shall be observed. If such rules are broken, the detention centre may terminate the meeting.

Article 103: Telephone Calls

1. With the detention centre governor's approval, a detainee may use a designated landline telephone to call his or her relatives, guardian or lawyer.
2. All telephone conversations in the detention centre shall be monitored and if it is found that the purpose of such phone calls is to hamper the investigation, prosecution, trial or execution of criminal punishment, the institution shall be entitled to terminate the phone call.
3. Detention centre staff shall inform detainees of the content outlined in the preceding paragraph, in advance of any phone calls being made.

Article 104: Legal Aid

If a criminal suspect, a defendant or a detainee serving sentence applies to a detention centre to hire a lawyer or to request legal aid, the detention centre shall forward the application to the authority in charge of his or her case or the particular people's court within 24 hours.

Section 6: Political, Economic and Cultural Rights

Article 105: Right to Vote and Right to Be Elected

All detainees who are over 18 and physically fit have the right to vote and the right to be elected, in accordance with law. All detention centres shall take necessary measures to guarantee the realisation of such rights, except for those who have been deprived of their political rights according to law, or whose right to vote and right to be elected have been terminated by the people's court and the people's procuratorate in accordance with law.

Article 106: Freedom of Speech and Freedom of The Press

Detainees who have not been deprived of their political rights shall enjoy the freedom of speech and press in accordance with law. They shall not be discriminated against and persecuted due to any lawful ideas expressed by them. A detention centre shall not interfere with the freedom of the press enjoyed by detainees.

Article 107: Right to Work

1. Subject to safety requirements and as long as it does not hamper criminal proceedings, a detention centre may organise detainees to do a certain amount of work.

2. The work provided will enable the detainee to at least maintain the previous earning potential and standard of living, after release from detention.

3. A detention centre shall provide the required vocational training for detainees who participate in work.

Article 108: Labour Remuneration and Protection

1. Detainees shall receive reasonable remuneration for work done.

2. National laws and regulations concerning labour protection shall prevail.

3. Accounts and stringent procedures shall be set up to manage labour remuneration and expenses of detainees.

Article 109: Creative Activities

If a detainee engages in creative activities to do with science, literature or art, in the detention centre, any material gain from such activities shall be protected.

Article 110: Right to Education

1. Every detention centre shall establish a detainee education system.

2. The education provided should be tailor-made to the specific needs of detainees, placing particular emphasis on such areas as the rule of law, ethics, culture and skills.

3. The education programme shall take into account the views, behaviour and psychological characteristics of detainees focusing on their individual needs, engaging them using sound arguments and a results-oriented approach.

4. The education programme should offer a combination of group and individual study.

5. Detainees may sit public examinations for higher education.

6. All detention centres shall provide the necessary facilities for detainees to study and sit examinations.

Chapter Six: Going outside the Detention Centre

Article 111: Procedure

When a detainee is transferred from the detention centre to another penitentiary facility, a copy of his personal file will be sent to that facility.

Article 112: Circumstances Required for Release

Based on the notice of release issued by the people's court, the people's procuratorate, the public security authorities or the State security agency, a detention centre shall implement the release procedure and issue a certificate of release if any of the following circumstances exist:

(1) if, after a detainee has been detained, the investigative authorities find that he or she should not have been detained, or the people's procuratorate rejects the application for his or her arrest and asks for his or her immediate release;

(2) if, after a detainee has been arrested, the investigative authorities find that he or she should not have been arrested and asks for his or her immediate release;

(3) if the people's procuratorate decides to exempt a detainee from being prosecuted or not to prosecute a detainee, and the investigative authorities ask for his or her release;

(4) if a detainee is found not guilty or is exempted from criminal punishment by the people's court, and the detention centre is informed of the release decision; or

(5) if a convicted detainee in a detention centre has served his or her sentence in full.

Article 113: Registration and Handling of Property

1. When a detainee is moved out of a detention centre, the institution shall update the detention registration form to include the exit approval reference number, time of departure and transfer destination.

2. Upon release, all property held in safe custody shall be returned to the detainee in person, except in circumstances where certain items of clothing have been destroyed in the interests of general hygiene. Furthermore, the detainee shall sign and seal the Property Safekeeping Registration Form and return the deposit stub to the detention centre.

Article 114: Pre-release Examination

Prior to leaving the detention centre detainees shall have a physical examination and have their belongings examined to ensure they are not taking out mail or other items on behalf of other detainees.

Article 115: Notice on Release of Convicts Having Served Their Sentences in Full

If a convict has served sentence in full, the detention centre shall, at 30 days' advance notice, notify the county-level public security authorities and the regional judicial administrative department holding the household registration document, of the convict's upcoming release.

Article 116: Release Notification and Handling of Special Situations

1. A person who has served his or her sentence shall be informed of the need to go through the household registration procedure at a police station in the region where his or her household registration was originally kept, together with delivery of his or her certificate of release within a specified time.

2. If a convict who is served his or her release form is seriously ill, the detention centre shall family members to accompany him or her back home.

Chapter Seven: Supervision of Detention Centres

Section 1: Supervision by The Procurators Based in The Detention Centre

Article 117: Positioning and Establishment of Duties

1. The people's procuratorate dispatches a sufficient number of procurators to each detention centre to supervise and oversee the institution.

2. The duties of such procurators include ensuring correct enforcement of national laws and regulations relating to criminal sanctions and control measures, protecting detainees' legitimate rights and interests, accepting and handling detainees' petitions, complaints and accusations, maintaining the good order of detention centres, and guaranteeing smooth criminal proceedings.

3. Procurators dispatched by county and district procuratorates are appointed and managed by prefecture-level people's procuratorates. All procurators based in county detention centres under the jurisdiction of the prefecture-level procuratorate shall serve no more than one year in the position.

Note:

In China, the function of procurators is to act as legal supervisors authorised by law. They are responsible for supervising investigation, trial and execution of penalties, including law enforcement at detention centres. Each detention centre has designated procurators to supervise the law enforcement activities of its detention police. Such procurators are not responsible for detention, nor do they carry out investigation. Their sole duties are to supervise detention centres to ensure that they perform their designated function, receive complaints lodged by detainees and deal with law-breaking behaviour of detention police.

Article 118: Approaches to Supervision and Limitations of Power

1. The procurators mentioned in Article 117 are based at detention centres. They should have offices in the sections earmarked for untried detainees as well as in the sections designated for sentenced offenders.
2. The information system of the detention centre's control management shall be linked to that of the detention centre procurator.
3. Procurators based in detention centres are entitled to investigate illegal and criminal acts within law enforcement. For minor offences, they are entitled to issue a Notice on Correcting Illegal Acts. 4. If the institution fails to respond within 15 days of receiving such Notice, the procurator based in the detention centre has the right to recommend that the management staff be replaced by their superior authority.

Section 2: Complaint Handling Procedure

Article 119: Subject and Content of A Complaint

1. A detainee has the right to lodge a complaint if his or her personal and litigation rights, and the treatment he or she receives in daily life are infringed upon, denied or restricted illegally whilst being placed in detention.
2. The detention centre shall inform detainees of the legal rights and treatment they are entitled to during detention in a clear and understandable manner.

Note:

Detention centres in China have long been plagued by poor complaint channels, insufficient complaint mechanisms and extremely low levels of reported complaints. In order to improve the complaint mechanism, Renmin University of China has worked closely with Maastricht University to design a complaint handling pilot scheme, which was trialled in the detention centre at Wuhu, Anhui province of China. This section showcases the results of the Wuhu pilot model.

Article 120: Acceptance and Handling of Complaints

1. The governor of the detention centre shall accept and handle complaints lodged against law enforcement officers working at the detention centre and immediately notify the procurator, stationed at the detention centre, of such complaints.
2. Detention centre guards shall accept complaints lodged against staff from the investigative authorities and forward them to be handled by the procurator stationed at the detention centre.
3. Detention centre guards shall accept and handle complaints lodged by a detainee against other detainees.

4. The People's Procuratorate's Supervision Department at the detention centre together with the Public Security Bureau and the People's Court select delegates to form a Complaints Handling Committee charged with handling appeals against decisions made by the above-mentioned staff regarding complaints. The Committee may also include representatives from the general public and professionals.

5. The Committee is charged with holding hearings to review complaints and putting forward recommendations to the procurator office at the detention centre to handle complaints. If the Prison and Reformatory Procuratorial Department decide not to accept the recommendations made by the Committee, the case should be forwarded to the Procuratorial Committee for further deliberation and resolution.

Article 121: How to Lodge Complaints

1. A detainee can lodge a complaint orally or in writing.

2. A complaint box shall be placed in the detention centre in a place which is accessible and where detainees lodge their written complaints in confidence.

3. Detainees may also lodge complaints orally by asking the guard to arrange an appointment with the procurator stationed at the detention centre.

4. The person who accepts an oral complaint shall make a written record which should be signed by the detainee.

5. Detention centre staff shall directly forward complaint letters or written records to the relevant institution or person responsible for handling complaints. No other individuals within the detention centre have the right to access such records and should not be informed of the existence of such documents.

Article 122: Notification and Facilitation of Lodging Complaints

The detention centre shall put up notices in clear and simple language to inform detainees of their right to lodge complaints and the correct channels for doing so. Pens and paper shall be provided in cells to facilitate the filing of written complaints by detainees.

Article 123: How Detention Centre Procurators Accept Complaints

1. During working hours, a detainee may press the call button in his or her cell to request a meeting with the procurator stationed at the detention centre.

2. The procurator shall carry out a tour of the cells at least twice daily.

Article 124: Lodging Complaints on Behalf of Detainees

1. With the approval of the investigative authorities, a detainee may meet with his or her close relatives during pre-trial detention and ask the relative to lodge a complaint on his or her behalf. The lawyer hired by the detainee may also lodge a complaint on his or her behalf.

2. After meeting with his or her client in the detention centre, the lawyer may lodge a written or oral complaint to the guard on behalf of his or her client. The guard is responsible for handling or forwarding the complaint to other authorities or individuals. Lawyers or close relatives may also lodge complaints at the reception hall of the detention centre.

Article 125: Complaint Handling Time

1. Complaints lodged by detainees shall be handled by relevant parties within 14 days.

2. Complaints lodged with the Complaint Handling Committee shall be handled within one month. The decision shall be presented in writing, and shall include a clear statement of the underlying reasons for the decision.

3. Parties involved – the detainee who lodges the complaint, the person who lodges the complaint on the detainee's behalf and the person against whom the complaint is lodged shall be informed of the decision.

Article 126: Remedy Against Decisions after Complaint Handling

If the detainee who lodges the complaint or the person against whom the complaint is lodged does not accept the decision made by the handling party, he or she may apply for review by the Complaint Handling Committee, unless the decision is made by the Committee itself. The Committee may review the case by means of hearing, investigation and reading relevant materials.

Article 127: Investigation into Complaint Handling

Those handling complaints may apply non-compulsory investigation methods, such as interviews, enquiries or an analysis of transferred data to investigate whether the reasons for the complaint are justified. The person being investigated is under obligation to cooperate. If necessary, the People's Procuratorate's Supervision Department at the detention centre may conduct a joint investigation together with the procuratorate's Department of Dereliction of Duty and Tort.

Article 128: Handling of Complaints Relating to Illegally Obtained Evidence

The People's Procuratorate's Supervision Office at the detention centre and other relevant departments shall refer to the Criminal Procedure Law, the

'Rules on Several Issues Concerning Exclusion of Illegally Obtained Evidence in Criminal Cases' and other relevant laws and judicial interpretations in handling complaints about illegally obtained evidence.

Article 129: Safeguarding Confidentiality and Protecting Detainees Who Lodge Complaints

Parties charged with handling complaints shall ensure that the process is kept confidential. The detainee who has lodged a complaint shall not suffer negative consequences for doing so.

Article 130: Legal Obligation of the Person against Whom The Complaint is Lodged

If the investigation finds that the complaint is justified, the subject who handles the complaint shall send a correction notice to the person against whom the complaint is lodged, and instruct him or her to correct his or her unlawful behaviour within a finite period of time. In addition, based on the severity of his or her law-breaking behaviour, the person shall receive proportionate disciplinary punishment, administrative measures or even go through a criminal procedure to assume criminal responsibility.

Section 3: Procedure for Investigating Deaths at Detention Centres

Article 131: Notification of A Death inside A Detention Centre

If a detainee dies at a detention centre, the governor shall immediately inform procurators based at the detention centre and the next of kin of the news, and 'freeze' the scene (i.e. keep it unchanged) where the death took place.

Article 132: The Person in Charge of An Investigation into The Death of a Detainee

After being informed of the news, procurators based at the detention centre shall immediately report the death to the person in charge of the detention department of the procuratorate, whose management shall be responsible for investigating the cause of death.

Article 133: Taking over the investigation at the scene

The procurator based at the detention centre shall arrive at the scene within two hours of receiving the news. If he or she is unable to do so, the procurator shall ask his or her colleagues in the detention department of the procuratorate to take over the investigation at the scene of the death.

Article 134: Onsite Investigation of The Cause of Death of A Detainee

1. The procurator based at the detention centre and a forensic expert shall inspect and examine the scene, all items and persons present and the body of the dead detainee so as to collect relevant physical and written evidence in a prompt manner. Photographing or filming the scene from all angles can be done to provide physical evidence.

2. Particular attention shall be paid to whether the scene could have been falsified, altered or damaged in any way; the location and features of the body, any items, and traces (including fingerprints, footprints, blood stains, hairs, bodily fluid and human tissue) left at the scene shall be collected and extracted. Written records for inspection and examination of the scene shall also be prepared.

3. Particular attention shall also be paid to collecting and extracting suspicious blood stains, hairs, bodily fluids, fingerprints, footprints, and other traces of the deceased and others, as well as any forgotten objects left behind at the scene, or tools that might be related to the injury of the victim. In addition, suspicious tools, toxic products and containers kept at the scene should be collected. Attention should be paid to whether the epidermis and other human tissue is to be found under the deceased detainee's fingernails.

Forensic tests shall be performed in a timely manner on any material collected and extracted including blood stains, sperm stains, hairs, bodily fluids, fingerprints, footprints, human tissue, and other biological evidence, traces or objects.

Article 135: Selection of Experts To Identify Cause of Death

1. If the procurator fails, after examination, to identify the cause of death, or the next of kin are sceptical about the identified cause of death, the assistance of qualified experts shall be requested in order to ensure that the cause of death is correctly identified.

2. The detention centre may also select an expert to identify the cause of death.

3. The family of the deceased detainee may select a different expert, who is selected randomly from a roster. The person in charge of the detention department of the people's procuratorate shall chair the selection process and the detention centre governor and the family of the deceased are entitled to be present during the autopsy.

Article 136: Independence of Experts Called In to Identify Cause of Death

Experts shall be entitled to identify the cause of death independently. They shall not be replaced arbitrarily once they have been selected.

Article 137: Autopsy

1. Experts have the right to decide on whether or not to carry out an autopsy.

2. If carrying out an autopsy goes against the religious beliefs of the deceased or is objected to by the next of kin, the person in charge of the detention department of the people's procuratorate shall make the final decision in light of the circumstances of the case.

Article 138: Family's Right to Be Present

The next of kin of the deceased detainee is entitled to be present when the body is examined and an autopsy is performed, or to appoint experts with relevant knowledge to be present.

Article 139: Notification of Death outside A Detention Centre

If a detainee dies outside a detention centre, the governor of the detention centre shall immediately report the death to the procurator based at the institution and the detainee's next of kin. The procurator shall arrive at the scene within two hours.

Article 140: Investigation of A Death outside A Detention Centre

If a detainee is confirmed to have died of illness, the procurator based at the detention centre shall investigate what activities the detainee participated in before leaving the detention centre. If it is believed that the death was caused by other reasons, the procurator shall launch an investigation.

Article 141: Investigation Report

When the investigation into the cause of death has been carried out, the procurator shall present a Cause of Death Investigation Report and the experts shall present a Cause Of Death Identification Report which should be sent to the detention centre and the next of kin of the deceased.

Article 142: Result of the Investigation

If it is found that the death is not caused by illness or accident, the person in charge of the detention department shall immediately establish a case and launch an investigation.

Article 143: Petition

The detainee's family may file a petition to a superior level people's procuratorate if it is not satisfied with the results of the investigation. The body of the deceased shall not be cremated and shall be overseen by the procurator based at the detention centre during the petition period.

Article 144: Treatment of The Body

The body may be cremated once the investigation has come to an end, if the family of the deceased agrees. If the family refuses to cremate the body, it shall pay for the cost of keeping the corpse.

Section 4: Detention Monitoring System

Article 145: Institutions Set up to Visit Detention Centres and other Official Visitors

1. A national or local detention visiting committee is composed of representatives from the Standing Committee of the National People's Congress and from the people's congress at the local level.

2. Relevant experts such as medical doctors, lawyers and social scientists are selected as visitors to conduct regular and ad hoc inspections and visits to detention facilities.

3. Social groups, democratic parties and private institutions may conduct regular and ad hoc visits after consultation and agreement with local detention authorities.

Note:

Though China ratified the United Nations Convention against Torture as early as 1986, it has yet to ratify the UN's Optional Protocol to the Convention Against Torture OPCAT (entered into force in 2006). In the past, detention centres in China were, for a long time, run in a closed environment, making it hard to implement the visiting scheme set forth in OPCAT. In 2007, Renmin University in China began to experiment with establishing a custody visiting system in China. Thanks to three years of research and experimentation, we put in place the first-ever visiting system in the Liaoyuan Detention Centre, in which representatives of the public conduct regular visits to the detention centre without prior notification. The effects have been phenomenal. In 2011, the Supervision Bureau of the Ministry of Public Security recognized the effects of this reform by issuing a nation-wide law enforcement notice – the Work Rules for Detention Centre Special Supervisors on Inspection and Supervision, which marked the official launch of the reform in over 3,000 detention centres across China.

Currently most detention centres in China accept public visits on a regular basis. During a visit, the visitors may have access to any place inside the detention centre and speak with detainees confidentially to understand how they are treated. In the follow-up visiting report, visitors may propose advice for improvement. The detention centre should make improvements accordingly and provide feedback to the visitors.

The establishment of the custody visiting system bolsters the opening up of detention centres, promotes the civility of law enforcement, and lays the foundation for China to ratify the OPCAT.

Article 146: Procedure

1. The visitors shall check whether the rights of detainees are protected, they receive fair treatment, the conditions of detentions are sufficient and whether the detention regulations are enforced as intended.

2. The visitors work in pairs during their regular or ad hoc visits.

3. They have free access to all parts of the detention centre, may view all relevant records, and may talk in private with detainees whom they choose, unless the detainee refuses to have such face-to-face talks.

The visit shall not involve anything to do with the criminal case under investigation.

Article 147: Reports on visits

1. When a visit ends, visitors shall prepare a visit report and submit that report to the detention visiting committee. The committee shall communicate advice for improvement listed in the report to the detention centre's competent authority.

2. If problems identified in the report cannot be replied to effectively and promptly, the visiting committee shall be entitled to make the report public.

3. Visitors shall be entitled to receive feedback on the implementation of their recommendations.

Article 148: Visitors' Obligations

1. Visitors shall respect personal privacy of detainees, and keep details concerning case prosecution progress and other matters gained through visits completely confidential, unless such details are to be included in the visit report.

2. Visitors shall not deliver goods and exchange information for detainees. They shall be required to observe relevant detention centre rules and be subject to a security inspection upon entering the institution.

Article 149: Appointment and Training of Visitors

The competent authority shall formulate standard rules governing the appointment and training of visitors.

Chapter Eight: Detention of Special Groups

Section 1: Detention of Foreign Nationals

Article 150: The Right of Detained Foreign Nationals to Communicate with Diplomatic or Consular Representatives

Upon admission, detainees who are foreign nationals shall be informed of the right to contact and communicate with the diplomatic or consular representative of their country.

Article 151: Permission for Foreign Nationals to Meet with People and Correspond By Mail

Permission shall be obtained from the Public Security Bureau or the State security ministry or bureau at the provincial level, autonomous region or municipality, if detainees want to meet with and correspond by mail with close relatives living in Hong Kong SAR, Macao SAR, Taiwan and foreign countries, or if foreign detainees want to meet with or send mail to their close relatives, guardians or embassy or consulate staff in China.

Article 152: Handling of Deported Foreign Detainees

If a foreign detainee is sentenced to deportation, the detention centre shall inform the Exit and Entry Administration of the Ministry of Public Security at 10 days' advance notice, that the criminal is to be deported according to the sentence.

Section 2: Detention of Minors, Women and People with Physical Disabilities

Article 153: Purpose of Detaining Minors

The purpose of detaining minors in a detention centre is to provide care, protection and education so as to help them feel remorse, to reform their behaviour and to enable them to return to society. They shall be kept separate from adult detainees and prisoners.

Article 154: The Physical Environment required for Detaining Minors

Institutions used to detain minors shall be fit for purpose, i.e. they should be equipped with facilities to help, educate and reform minors, whilst at the same time considering their needs as regards health, privacy, social interaction and cultural and recreational activities.

Article 155: Protection of The Physical and Mental Health of Minors

Every detention centre shall provide care and assistance as far as the health, psychology, healthcare, education and professional guidance of minors is concerned, by giving consideration to age, gender and personality, in order to offer sufficient protection of their physical and mental well-being.

Article 156: The Right of Minors to Receive An Education

1. If a minor detainee has not finished his or her compulsory education, the detention centre shall provide him or her with compulsory education in the detention centre.

2. For a minor who is above the age of compulsory education but still wishes to continue his or her studies, the detention centre shall offer proper education courses.

3. Minors who are no longer detained shall not be discriminated against when returning to full-time education and going back to school.

Article 157: The Right to Receive Vocational Training

1. Minor detainees shall be entitled to receive vocational training to prepare them for future employment.

2. Minors who are no longer detained shall not be discriminated against when they are seeking employment.

Article 158: The Right to Work and Get Paid

1. As long as their security, personal development and mental health is safeguarded, minor detainees may have paid work relating to vocational training in the local community. The purpose of such work is to prepare them for a normal professional life after release.

2. Minor detainees who work shall be entitled to receive fair remuneration. The remuneration shall be kept in a safe deposit and shall be returned to them when they are released.

Article 159: The Right to Engage in Cultural and Recreational Activities

Minor detainees have the right to two hours of cultural and recreational activities per day. All detention centres shall provide a suitable venue, facilities and equipment for minors to enjoy such activities.

Article 160: Minors Who are Unwell and Who Do not Have Guardians

1. Timely medical treatment shall be offered to minors who are unwell. Their guardians or close relatives shall be informed of their illness.

2. Proper care shall be given to detained minors who do not have guardians.

Article 161: Special Treatment of Ethnic Minorities

Specific cultural and folk traditions of detainees who are ethnic minorities shall be respected. In addition, they shall be treated with decency.

Article 162: Special Treatment of Female Detainees

1. The special needs of female detainees shall be considered and special care shall be given to them in their daily life and work.

2. Measures taken to protect female detainees due to their special status shall not be deemed to be discrimination.

Article 163: Management of Female Detainees

1. All detention centres shall have a proportionate amount of female staff.

2. Female staff are responsible for the management and physical examination of female detainees.

Article 164: Special Treatment of the Elderly

1. Proper care shall be given to elderly detainees, taking into account their age and physical state.

2. Elderly detainees may engage in work if it is not detrimental to their health.

3. Detainees who are too old and unwell shall be exempted from working.

Article 165: Special Treatment of People with Physical Disabilities

1. Detainees with physical disabilities shall be given special care and provided with disabled access facilities if required.

2. Detainees with physical disabilities may perform work if it is not detrimental to their health.

Section 3: Detention of People with Mental Health Problems, Drug Addiction, AIDS and Other Infectious Diseases

Article 166: Detention of mentally ill persons

1. Detainees with serious mental illness shall be held separately from other detainees. They shall be jointly managed by police and the detention centre doctor.

2. If a detainee has a mental breakdown requiring urgent treatment and is therefore unfit to be held in a detention centre, the institution shall immediately inform the investigative authorities of the situation and transfer him or her to hospital.

Article 167: Detention of People with Drug Addiction

If a detention centre finds a detainee to be addicted to drugs, the institution shall promptly inform the investigative authorities of the situation and ask the public security authorities to make a decision on community rehabilitation or compulsory isolated rehabilitation.

Article 168: Detention of People with AIDS and other transmittable Diseases

1. Detainees who suffer from AIDS or other transmittable diseases shall be held separately from other detainees. They shall be jointly managed by police and the detention centre doctor.

2. If a detainee suffers from an acute infectious disease, needs isolated treatment and is therefore unsuited to be held in a detention centre, the institution shall inform the investigative authorities, the public security authorities and the local disease prevention and control department, and the detainee will be then be transferred to a specialized hospital for treatment.

Article 169: Treatment Post-Release

When detainees who suffer from AIDS or other transmittable diseases are released, the detention centre shall offer health education and psychological counselling, and shall inform the local disease prevention and control department where the detainee lives.

Chapter Nine: Supplementary Provisions

Article 170

This law takes effect on ***.

Provisions concerning the beds of detainees bed do not have a retro-active effect.

3. SOME PERSONAL NOTES ON THE DRAFT DETENTION CENTRE LAW

Gerard de Jonge

1. A GREAT STEP FORWARD

Having contributed to the Council of Europe draft of the *European Prison Rules 2006* (EPR),[1] I am inclined to weigh up all national detention laws, regulations and practices that come to my knowledge against, what I consider to be, the most advanced standards that have been set in this COE Recommendation. This is exactly what I did implicitly and explicitly over the course of several months, during frank and open discussions on the content of proposed new pre-trial detention centre regulations with my colleagues at the Center for Criminal Procedure and Reform (CCPR) at Renmin University Law School in China. Of course China is not Europe and I am very much aware of the big cultural and political differences between our regions, so I always try to avoid the attitude of those 'human rights missionaries' who think their main task in life is to try to convert the unbelievers.[2] Even without constant referral to human rights concepts, most states currently converge in their policy and legislation on certain basic notions, such as that the authorities shall not resort to torture to attain certain ends and that states shall treat their citizens fairly, even if they happen to be suspected of having committed a crime or have been convicted and sentenced.

I am happy to say that the proposed draft Detention Centre Law presented in this chapter is not a product of abstract, unrealistic academic theorizing. This draft law is based on thorough empirical research carried out by legal scholars at CCPR who, with the full support of the local judicial and penitentiary authorities, designed and evaluated the pilot projects in Liaoyuan

---

[1] Council of Europe, *Recommendation Rec(2006)2 of the Committee of Ministers to member states on the European Prison Rules* (adopted by the Committee of Ministers on 11 January 2006 at the 952nd meeting of the Ministers' Deputies).

[2] The subject of how human rights fit in the Chinese legal system is elaborated in AHL, B., 'Exploring Ways of Implementing International Human Rights Treaties in China', *Netherlands Quarterly of Human Rights*, 2010, p. 361-403.

and Wuhu that are mentioned in the introduction to this publication. This first hand experience and research data ensure that this draft text deals specifically with current practice. The improvements proposed would stand a good chance of being accepted and even welcomed by management and staff at detention centres across China if they were to be adopted.

When I study this draft, I see with satisfaction many proposals for progressive additions and amendments to the existing regulations. I particularly approve of Chapter 7, which provides for the external monitoring of detention centres by committees of non-officials, who have free access to detention centres, can talk in private with detainees and send their inspection reports with their recommendations to the authorities that are responsible for the treatment of detainees. I mention also the proposal to introduce new procedures for handling prisoners' complaints and, last but certainly not least, the section on the handling of deaths of detainees that occur in custody. Even if only these proposals were adopted, this would mean a great step forward in the process of protecting detainees against torture and other forms of ill treatment, which, after all, is the main objective of this project.

2. THE WISH LIST OF A EUROPEAN OUTSIDER

Having thus praised the draft as it is, I would do my Chinese counterparts a great wrong if I held back my views on certain, what I consider, lacunae and problematic aspects of this Draft Law. I will only mention a few points, restricting myself to what I think are the most important issues worthy of further debate.

Detention Centres Should be Managed by Civil Authorities, not by Police

When (remand) prisons are governed by police,[3] there is a danger that the treatment of inmates depends on their willingness to cooperate with the legal process in which they are involved. In this situation, detainees who do not cooperate fully with the investigators or judicial authorities cannot expect the same treatment as cooperative detainees. This is reflected to some extent in Article 67 of the current draft, which promises rewards to detainees who cooperate with the investigation. They are even encouraged to 'snitch' on their fellow inmates (Article 66 Draft), which will no doubt lead to inter-prisoner violence. In Europe, this risk is addressed by Rule 71 of the EPR: *Prisons shall be the responsibility of public authorities separate from military,*

---

[3] The distinction made in the Draft between police investigators, disciplinary police (guards) and armed perimeter police does not make any difference: they all belong to the police corps.

police or criminal investigation services. Recently the European Committee for the Prevention of Torture (CPT) advised the Latvian authorities to reform their entire prison system such that officers of security divisions may no longer investigate criminal offences committed by prisoners outside the prison or take statements from prisoners in relation to such offences. The CPT stressed that this situation is clearly detrimental to the protection of prisoners against ill-treatment (including inter-prisoner violence) and lends itself to abuse.[4] Detention centres should not be tools for collecting evidence against inmates. This is also recognised in this new pre-trial detention centre draft by subordinating (Articles 3 and 5 Draft) all detention centres to a central Detention Management Bureau. Whilst this is to be applauded, the constitutional position of the Detention Management Bureau remains unclear, however, and the fact remains that the police still manage detention centres.

Legal Assistance to be Allowed before First Interrogation and During Subsequent Interrogations

The present draft grants defendants access to their lawyer only after their first interrogation (Article 98 Draft). If the main objective of the reform of the Detention Centre Regulations is to enhance the protection of detainees, then it is essential that they be given the opportunity to consult their lawyer *before* the first interrogation. This right is a major element of a fair trial, at least in the Member States of the Council of Europe.[5] Free access to a defence lawyer before the first interrogation can also contribute to the prevention of physical or verbal ill treatment or during interrogations. It would also be desirable to permit lawyers to be present during interrogations. If it is legally impossible to regulate this in a Detention Centre Law, this should be laid down in the Criminal Procedure Law or the legislation concerning (defence) lawyers.

Prisoners' Complaints Procedure to be Refined

The present draft makes a distinction between complaints against disciplinary sanctions (Article 71 Draft) and other complaints (Articles 119-130 Draft). The complaints procedure concerning disciplinary sanctions is summary, to

---

[4] CPT, Report to the Latvian Government on the visit to Latvia carried out by the European Committee for the Prevention of Torture and Inhuman or Degrading Treatment or Punishment (CPT) from 3 to 8 December 2009, CPT/Inf (2011) 22, para. 26 (this report can be retrieved via <www.cpt.coe.int>).

[5] See for instance ECtHR 27 November 2008, *Salduz v. Turkey*, no. 36391/02.

say the least, especially when compared to the procedure recommended in the EPR:

Rule 59. Prisoners charged with disciplinary offences shall:

a. be informed promptly, in a language which they understand and in detail, of the nature of the accusations against them;
b. have adequate time and facilities for the preparation of their defence;
c. be allowed to defend themselves in person or through legal assistance when the interests of justice so require;
d. be allowed to request the attendance of witnesses and to examine them or to have them examined on their behalf; and
e. have the free assistance of an interpreter if they cannot understand or speak the language used at the hearing.

For this reason reconsideration and elaboration of Article 71 is strongly recommended.

As to the procedure for other prisoners' complaints, the draft text is confusing with regard to the position of the so-called Complaint Handling Committee. Article 120 of the Draft attributes this Committee an advisory function 'it shall offer advice to prison procurators on how to deal with a complaint' and Article 126 grants this Committee the power to handle appeals against decisions on complaints and even the power to decide on certain complaints. The ongoing pilot project testing new complaints procedures and the handling of complaints in Wuhu will help to shed light on this issue. The findings from the evaluation of the Wuhu pilot project should be reflected in the Draft, and the articles on the handling of complaints will need to be adapted accordingly.

The composition of the Complaint Handling Committee and the procedure for appointment and dismissal of its members should also be elaborated on in this draft or in a by-law. The present draft leaves too many aspects open to interpretation, and leaves room for arbitrary appointments and dismissals. European experience has shown that Complaints Handling Committees can only be trusted when they are free to function with a high degree of independence from the penitentiary authorities.

A last article that should be reconsidered is Article 130 of the Draft, which threatens detention centre personnel with disciplinary punishments when complaints against them are upheld. This should not be an 'automatic' consequence of every complaint that is sustained. If a complaint is upheld, the successful detainee should receive fair compensation for having been treated wrongly. The official concerned should be instructed to behave correctly in the future and should only then be disciplined or even transferred when he or she does not comply with the decision of the prison procurator or the Complaints Handling Committee. If a complaint concerns alleged punishable or other illegal behaviour of prison police or other prison staff this should be dealt with by the regular external criminal justice agencies, and not by the prison procurator or the Complaints Handling Committee.

Inspection and Monitoring

One of the major innovations this Draft presents, in terms of the OPCAT, is the introduction of a 'national preventive mechanism' in the form of national or local detention visiting committees that have unfettered access and ample powers to inspect detention centres. What are missing in this draft are guarantees for the functional independence of these committees and criteria for the selection, appointment and dismissal of committee members. It would be advisable to elaborate on these in this draft or, preferably, in a detailed by-law.

The relation between the task of the visiting committees and the legal duties and powers of the prison procurator (a role unknown in non-communist states) should be fine-tuned to prevent overlapping activities and conflicting powers.

Minors not to be Held in Detention Centres

In the section on minors (Articles 154-161 Draft) it should be stated that minors should not be held in detention centres unless this is unavoidable, in which case they shall be kept separate from adult detainees and prisoners at all times. The EPR say on this:

> 11.1 Children under the age of 18 years should not be detained in a prison for adults, but in an establishment specially designed for the purpose.
>
> 11.2 If children are nevertheless exceptionally held in such a prison there shall be special regulations that take account of their status and needs.

The COE Recommendation on the European Rules for juvenile offenders, subject to sanctions or measures, adds to this:

> 10. Deprivation of liberty of a juvenile shall be a measure of last resort and imposed and implemented for the shortest period possible. Special efforts must be undertaken to avoid pre-trial detention.

59.1. Juveniles shall not be held in institutions for adults, but in institutions specially designed for them. If juveniles are nevertheless exceptionally held in an institution for adults, they shall be accommodated separately unless in individual cases where it is in their best interest not to do so. In all cases, these rules shall apply to them.

Material Detention Conditions – Personal Space

It is well known that overcrowding of penitentiary institutions is the source of a host of problems and is considered a form of ill treatment in itself. To prevent overcrowding in detention centres the law should grant each detainee a minimum personal space, often expressed in square meters per prisoner. Article 76 of this Draft sets the minimum level of just *three* square meters per capita. It should be made clear in the commentary to this article why three square meters would be sufficient. In its Commentary to Rule 18 of the European Prison Rules the Council of Europe remarks: 'The CPT, by commenting on conditions and space available in prisons in various countries has begun to indicate some minimum standards. These are considered to be 4 m^2 for prisoners in shared accommodation and 6 m^2 for a prison cell. These minima are, related however, to wider analyses of specific prison systems, including studies of how much time prisoners actually spend in their cells. These minima should not be regarded as the norm. Although the CPT has never laid down such a norm directly, indications are that it would consider 9 to 10 m^2 as a desirable size for a cell for one prisoner.'

To prevent overcrowding the management should be entitled by law to refuse admission of detainees above the formal capacity of the institution.

Special Regime for Prisoners Awaiting Execution

As long as China upholds the death penalty for certain offences it seems a humanitarian necessity to make the last days of such prisoners as comfortable as possible. Given the circumstance that persons who are sentenced to death are transferred shortly before the execution to a detention centre, the draft Detention Centre Law should pay special attention to the treatment of this unfortunate category. These prisoners should be allowed as many family visits, telephone calls and other reasonable favours as possible. Special psycho-medical care should be available to them. In short, a special regime for prisoners who are awaiting execution should be added to this draft text.

Moving Towards a Detention Centre Law

If asked my opinion, I would say that to plead for the adoption of a Detention Centre *Law* would be premature. As we know, a law, once adopted, is far more difficult to amend than lower ranking legislation. Of course, in the first instance, this draft will have to be discussed by all stakeholders and experts interested in the criminal justice system. Even if agreement were reached on textual content, it would still be hard to say how or even if the new provisions would work out in practice. It would seem to make more sense to adopt new detention centre rules in the form of an administrative regulation and, after having tested them out in practice, to evaluate the effectiveness of the new provisions. This would help to identify weaknesses and lacunae in the regulations. The results of such an evaluation could be used to finalise a draft law.

What Next?

China's ambition to accede to the Optional Protocol to the Convention Against Torture is mentioned in the notes accompanying the draft text in Chapter 2. Every state that ratifies this protocol allows the Subcommittee on Prevention (SPT), referred to in the OPCAT, to inspect all places where persons are or may be deprived of their liberty. For China this would imply, that not only the legal protection and material treatment of detainees in detention centres would be inspected, but also that of convicted persons in prisons and persons held in facilities for administrative punishment. The review of the regulations concerning the position of these last two categories would be a logical next step in the process of reforming the Chinese penitentiary legislation and practice.

PART III

ENHANCING POLICE INTERVIEWING SKILLS

SKILLS FOR INTERROGATING CRIMINAL SUSPECTS

Miet Vanderhallen and Cheng Lei

1. INTRODUCTION

The interrogation of suspects is a well documented topic in criminal investigation literature since it is regarded as one of the most critical stages of the investigation process.[1] This crucial role requires techniques which allow police officers to conduct interrogations effectively. Various interrogation techniques have been developed in order to reach a successful outcome. Within these techniques a distinction can be made between those that aim at obtaining a confession and those that focus on a search for the truth.[2]

One of the most influential confession oriented models of interrogation, the 'Reid-technique', provides police officers with techniques on how to obtain a confession.[3] Techniques derived from this model are shown to be commonly used in the United States of America (USA).[4] The 'Reid-technique' has without doubt been very important in the field of interrogation.[5] Other models have subsequently built upon the 'Reid-technique' originally published in 1986[6] and numerous police officers are currently being trained in this, according to John Reid and colleagues.[7] Training programmes have been set up in countries all over the world such as Japan, Canada, Bosnia-Herzegovina and Belgium. The most recent edition of the manual (4th edition, 2011) has been translated for educational purposes into Chinese, Japanese and Turkish.

---

[1]   BALDWIN 1993, p. 325; HOLMBERG 2004, p. 1.
[2]   HARTWIG, GRANHAG & VRIJ 2005, p. 379.
[3]   KASSIN, GOLDSTEIN & SAVITSKY 2003, p. 188; VRIJ 2010, p. 723; INBAU, REID & BUCKLEY 1986, p. xiv.
[4]   LEO 1996, p. 302.
[5]   HARTWIG, GRANHAG & VRIJ 2005, p. 382.
[6]   Among others: ZULAWSKI & WICKLANDER 2002.
[7]   <www.reid.com>.

Information-gathering techniques aimed at finding the truth have been developed as an alternative to the above-mentioned traditional confession-oriented techniques.[8] Whilst a confession-oriented approach uses an accusatory interrogation style, an information-gathering approach employs a non-accusatory, more humane (or ethical) interview style. The best known information-gathering model is the PEACE model, developed in the United Kingdom (UK). PEACE is an acronym for Plan and Prepare, Engage and Explain, Account and Clarify, Closure and Evaluation.[9] Various interview models contain similar phases and practices including the Basic Interview Technique in Belgium and the Person/Case-oriented interview model in the Netherlands.

Although some readers may find it strange to consider the process of 'interrogating' a suspect as a form of interview – and in most continental European systems the term 'interrogation' is used for questioning a suspect – we use the term 'interview' in this publication.

Both models contain guidelines on interview skills for successful interview. However, one has to consider which type of technique provides the most appropriate recommendations in terms of both safeguards (from a judicial and ethical viewpoint) as well as successful outcome.

2. SHIFTING THE FOCUS FROM CONFESSION TO SEARCH FOR TRUTH

The importance of the interview in criminal investigation is beyond any doubt. However, such importance depends partly on the strength of evidence which has already been gathered during the criminal investigation.[10] The evidential value of the interview increases when less other evidence (such as fingerprints, DNA) is found. Moreover, confession evidence is still often recognized as the queen of evidence and the best weapon of the prosecution.[11] Consequently, confession oriented models such as the 'Reid-technique' are influential all over the world. Nevertheless, there has been more and more criticism over the techniques and skills used over the years. In 1986, Joseph Grano criticized the 3rd Edition of 'Criminal interview and confessions', stating that the suggested techniques were not in line with the actual confession law.[12] In Canada, where the 'Reid-technique' forms the basis of

---

8   HARTWIG, GRANHAG & VRIJ 2005, p. 390.
9   MILNE & BULL 1999, p. 157-167.
10   VRIJ 2010, p. 723.
11   KASSIN, GOLDSTEIN & SAVITSKY 2003, p. 187.
12   GRANO 1986, p. 1497.

many of the interview techniques, concerns were recently expressed with regard to the assumptions used for lie detection as well as its coercive nature.[13]

These confession oriented techniques are often considered as unethical.[14] In general, research has shown that techniques using the presumption of guilt as a starting point can elicit a biased chain of events which increase the risk of false confessions.[15] Three important errors which can lead to false confessions can be identified in this chain.[16] Firstly, an innocent suspect can be wrongly classified as guilty through a presumption of guilt. Secondly, a suspect whom police officers think is guilty will often be questioned by use of an accusatorial approach which is psychologically coercive. Indeed, research shows that suspects perceive the interview style significantly as more dominant in comparison with victims and witnesses.[17] Thirdly, when a confession is provided, the post admission narrative is contaminated by the interviewer. In his study on the first 250 DNA exonerations from the 'Innocence Project' Garrett found that in 36 of the 38 cases of false confession, the suspect provided 'perpetrator knowledge' which could only have been communicated to them by the interviewers.[18]

In the above-mentioned chain and in particular in the accusatorial interview approach, persuasive techniques can be identified which are used to convince suspects that a confession is in their best interests.[19] Research indicates that such techniques, including minimisation,[20] presentation of false evidence, exaggeration of the strength of evidence, can all contribute to the eliciting of false confessions.[21] In addition, it has been found that the length of the interview appears to be a contributing factor for false confessions. In this regard, interviews that last for more than 6 hours are generally considered 'coercive'.[22]

Looking at the causes of miscarriages of justice in Garrett's study, false confessions are ranked third, after false identifications and wrongful forensic

---

[13] SNOOK ET AL. 2010, p. 203.
[14] GUDJONSSON 2003, p. 37.
[15] KASSIN, GOLDSTEIN & SAVITSKY 2003, p. 201; HOLMBERG 2004, p. 27-28; VANDERHALLEN 2010, p. 419-421; VANDERHALLEN, VERVAEKE & HOLMBERG 2011, p. 123.
[16] LEO & DRIZIN 2010, p. 9-21.
[17] VANDERHALLEN, VERVAEKE & HOLMBERG 2011, p. 123.
[18] ISRAELS 2012, p. 32.
[19] GUDJONSSON 2006, p. 124.
[20] Minimization refers to a technique in which the investigator mitigates the offense and downplays its seriousness.
[21] KASSIN 2008, p. 201-203.
[22] BLAIR 2005, p. 127.

evidence.[23] In approximately 20 per cent of exonerations, innocent suspects confessed. Other studies also addressed the prevalence of false confessions. Although the exact number is unknown, the existence of false confessions, as well as subsequent miscarriages of justice, is well documented. False confessions are not only proven in the USA, but case studies were also found in Canada, the UK, the Netherlands and China amongst others.[24]

2.1. LEGAL CONSEQUENCES

In the UK, miscarriages of justice have led to a legislative change.[25] The Police and Criminal Evidence Act (PACE, 1984) provided a new legislative framework for regulating the interview of suspects in custody.[26] The new legislation focused on custodial safeguards (such as the right to legal advice) and guidelines for interview, such as recording the interview. With PACE, research on interview techniques in the UK was encouraged in the early 1990s.[27] Research findings pointed to the need for improving the quality of interviews resulting in a new approach to interview called PEACE.[28] This PEACE model offered a standardised framework for interview and training. The new interviewing policy framework and training brought about a shift from a confession focused approach to a more ethical information-seeking approach which was even reflected in the evolution of the terminology[29] from 'interrogation' to 'investigative interviewing'.[30] Post PEACE research showed a decrease in the use of misleading and persuasive techniques, which supports the model as an approach which maximises the likelihood of a fair trial.[31]

In order to ensure a fair trial[32] the European Court of Human rights decided that suspects are entitled to have access to legal advice before and

---

[23] ISRAELS 2011, p. 32.

[24] KASSIN 2008, p. 194.

[25] SHAWYER, MILNE & BULL 2009, p. 24. The acquittal of the 'Guilford Four' in 1989 gave opportunities for other cases to discuss the confessions obtained, GUDJONSSON 2010, p. 168.

[26] WILLIAMSON 2006, p. 152.

[27] HOLMBERG 2009, p. 158.

[28] GUDJONSSON 2006, p. 124; SHAWYER, MILNE & BULL 2009, p. 24.

[29] 'Interrogation' is often used to refer to the questioning of criminal suspects whereas 'interview' generally refers to the questioning of victims and witnesses. 'Investigative interviewing' has been developed for the interview of victims, witnesses and suspects in the UK (GUDJONSSON 2006, p. 124). In this chapter we use the term 'interrogation' to address the questioning of suspects in different countries.

[30] SHAWYER, MILNE & BULL 2009, p. 24.

[31] SHAWYER, MILNE & BULL 2009, p. 32.

[32] ECHR, Art. 6.

during the interview.[33] Furthermore, suspects should be informed about their right to silence (caution) prior to the interview.[34] With regard to the legal advice, the court states that legal advisers can intervene during the interview in various ways.[35] The right to legal access has been confirmed by European jurisprudence.

European jurisprudence has led to legal reforms in different European countries, including Belgium and France, beginning in 2010, and in the Netherlands still ongoing today. These Europe-wide reforms address the safeguards of suspects during the criminal investigation. For example, in Belgium the new Salduz-law was implemented on 1 January 2011. The new legislation states that every person interviewed by the police needs to be informed about several rights, amongst which are the principle of *nemo tenetur* – no one is obliged to incriminate him or herself. In addition, suspects are informed of their right to silence as well as their right to access to a lawyer before (during a 30 minute confidential consultation) and during the interview. It is important to note that only adults can waive their right to legal advice. In short, procedural safeguards for suspects are now given high priority in Europe.

However, it is not only in Europe that policy makers and researchers are concerned with suspects' rights. In Canada, researchers make mention of the necessity for substantive reform regarding interview practice which is currently based upon the Reid-technique.[36] Poor interviewing has been singled out as one of the reasons for miscarriages of justice.[37] In November 2011, the case of Mr. Dixon attracted a great deal of attention in the Canadian press and put the Reid technique under scrutiny. The PEACE model was introduced as a good alternative.[38] In the USA, recently uncovered miscarriages of justice and false confessions encouraged researchers and policy makers to question the confrontational interview approach which is nowadays common practice.[39] As a more effective alternative, Kassin and

---

[33] ECtHR 27 November 2008, *Salduz v. Turkey*, no. 36391/02.

[34] ECtHR 11 December 2008, *Panovits v. Cyprus*, no. 4268/04, para. 72.

[35] ECtHR 13 October 2009, *Dayanan v. Turkey*, no. 7377/03, para. 32.

[36] SNOOK ET AL. 2010, p. 206.

[37] ST-YVES 2009, p. 94.

[38] BREAN, 'Police interrogation techniques under scrutiny due to false confessions', *National Post*, 25 November 2011. Michael Dixon was charged with burglary, a crime he did not commit. He was confronted with the accusatory tactics of the Reid technique during interrogation. After he turned out to be innocent, Mr. Dixon received nearly $50,000 for false imprisonment, false arrest and negligent investigation.

[39] KASSIN 2008, p. 207. However, a North-American survey differs with this statement because only 11 per cent (N=631) of the interrogators reported that they were trained in the Reid-technique. Moreover, high-pressure tactics were only used infrequently, according to

→

colleagues, amongst others, advocate a diagnostic interview model which is non-confrontational and yet supports police work. This refers to a scientifically supported interview model that is diagnostic for identifying innocence (and protects against false-positive errors) without a decrease in true confessions. Thus, an interview model which improves the diagnostic value of a confession is needed.[40] In this regard, the PEACE model could serve as a source of inspiration.[41] Nevertheless, some additional research is required to test these models, although preliminary research findings are encouraging.[42]

2.2. INVESTIGATIVE INTERVIEWING MODELS

The idea that procedural safeguards prevent false confessions and miscarriages of justice, is debatable. After all, the implementation of Miranda rights turned out to be insufficient to avoid miscarriages of justice. Research showed that the way in which a suspect's rights are communicated, has an impact on whether rights are waived or not.[43]

Thus, the combination of various safeguards (caution, legal assistance etc) is required as well as an information gathering interviewing model which inhibits coercive, psychological techniques.

When using an information gathering interviewing approach, an interviewer is more inclined to have an open mind and is more likely to be fair to the suspect.[44] One of the key elements is to establish rapport with the suspect in order to stimulate cooperation.[45] Furthermore, this model is characterized by empathy, friendliness, a genuine interest in the suspect and the opportunity to answer, instead of a brusque, condemnatory and aggressive approach.[46] Moreover, it is emphasized that interviewers should avoid any form of trickery.[47]

Holmberg examined suspect interviews concerning murders and sexual offences and found that an information gathering model led to more admissions compared with a more accusatorial model.[48] Suspects felt more

---

respondents. Nevertheless, this finding may be an under-estimation because the result is based upon self reporting (KASSIN ET AL. 2007, p. 388-394).

[40] MEISSNER, RUSSANO & NARCHET 2010, p. 122.
[41] SNOOK ET AL. 2010, p. 203; KASSIN 2008, p. 207-208; KASSIN, APPLEBY & PERILLO 2010, p. 39.
[42] MEISSNER, RUSSANO & NARCHET 2010, p. 122; KASSIN 2008, p. 207.
[43] REDLICH ET AL. 2004, p. 108; WRIGHTSMAN 2010, p. 172-175.
[44] HARTWIG, GRANHAG & VRIJ 2005, p. 390.
[45] HARTWIG, GRANHAG & VRIJ 2005, p. 390; HOLMBERG 2004, p. 27.
[46] HOLMBERG 2004, p. 26.
[47] GUDJONSSON 2003, p. 37.
[48] HOLMBERG 2004, p. 27-28.

respected when the interviewer used an information gathering approach. Holmberg's findings are backed up by research into benefit fraud which clearly demonstrates the advantages of an information gathering approach over an accusatorial approach.[49] Use of the PEACE interviewing technique resulted in a greater number of suspects providing full accounts, including confessions.

This information gathering approach can be found in various interviewing models, which are mostly inspired by the PEACE model developed in the UK.[50] Recent research on suspect interviews in the UK indicated that the PEACE model is widely used in practice, and most of the criticised tactics (such as minimisation) are rarely found.

Not surprisingly, the PEACE model served as a basis for interviewing models in other EU countries such as Belgium and the Netherlands.[51] These models all distinguish, whether implicitly or explicitly, three essential components within the interviewing process, namely the preparation, the completion of the interview and the evaluation.[52] With regard to each of these components, common factors can be found throughout the different models addressing 1) premises, 2) different steps of the interview and 3) skills.

Before going into the common factors of interview models, it is worth mentioning that an interview model should aim to gather reliable (i.e. consistent) and valid (i.e. accurate) information.[53] These two conditions should be the essential objectives of any interview. An interview model can be considered reliable when, hypothetically repeated the model leads to similar findings. Reliability refers to consistency, which is enhanced by the use of a stepwise method. Validity refers to accuracy and thus to truthful information. Within the interview models which are embedded in an information gathering approach, proceedings and techniques are often evidence-based[54] with a view to elicit reliable and valid information.

---

[49] WALSCH & BULL 2004, p. 319.

[50] BULL & SOUKARA 2010, p. 93-94.

[51] The PEACE model is recently also nationally adopted in New-Zealand and Norway (BULL & SOUKARA 2010, p. 82).

[52] VANDERHALLEN 2010, p. 108.

[53] VANDERHALLEN 2010, p. 125-130.

[54] Evidence-based means that these techniques are supported by scientific, empirical research.

2.2.1. Premises

In general, the above-mentioned interview models start from the premise that the interviewer needs to build a rapport with the suspect.[55] A good rapport is supposed to influence the co-operation of the suspect and the extent to which a suspect will provide accurate information.[56] The crucial role of rapport with regard to achieving a successful interview is confirmed by police officers.[57] Moreover, the interviewer needs to establish a rapport from the start of the interview and maintain it throughout.[58] It is stated that even the best interview techniques depend on the quality of the relationship between interviewer and suspect.[59] Research has showed that the working alliance, a concept strongly related to rapport, is a good predictor for interviewer's satisfaction with the statement and the overall result of the interview.[60] This study has also found that the humanitarian interviewing style and the working alliance are positively related.[61] Police officers also confirm that establishing a rapport is a necessary skill to achieving a successful interview.[62]

Manuals on interviewing skills and criminologists emphasize the importance of meeting certain conditions in order to establish a good rapport. Five common conditions can be found throughout the literature:[63] empathy, active listening, personal conversation, interpersonal skills (non verbal and verbal signals), and an informal (friendly and warm) communication style.[64] Research confirms the predicting role of empathy and a humanitarian interview style (as defined by Holmberg) for creating a working alliance between interviewer and suspects.[65] Moreover, a third predictor comprises clarification regarding the interview process.

A second common premise refers to open-mindedness as a success factor. Moreover, this open-mindedness is additionally considered as a necessary

---

[55] VANDERHALLEN 2010, p. 119; MILNE & BULL 1999, p. 40-42; VAN DE PLAS 2007, p. 37-53; ORD, SHAW & GREEN 2011, p. 15-16; VAN AMELSVOORT, RISPENS & GROLMAN 2010, p. 316.
[56] HOLMBERG 2004, p. 27-28.
[57] BULL & SOUKARA 2010, p. 83.
[58] HOLMBERG 2004, p. 27-28.
[59] ST-YVES 2006, p. 87.
[60] VANDERHALLEN 2010, p. 366.
[61] VANDERHALLEN, VERVAEKE & HOLMBERG 2011, p. 124-125.
[62] BULL & SOUKARA 2010, p. 83.
[63] VANDERHALLEN 2010, p. 156.
[64] ST-YVES also mentions the requirement of explaining goals in order to build rapport. This resembles part of the working alliance being 'an agreement on tasks and goals, and an emotional bond' (GELSO & CARTER 1985, p. 155-243).
[65] VANDERHALLEN 2010, p. 369-370.

ingredient for building a good rapport.[66] A neutral position is regarded as the best approach because it is more objective and the risk of bias is minimised. The absence or avoidance of these biases is an essential safeguard against false confessions. However, most experts agree that minimising bias, such as 'confirmation bias' and 'belief perseverance', which can lead to a 'tunnel vision' mentality in the interviewer, is a difficult task.[67] Confirmation bias refers to 'the seeking or interpreting of evidence in ways that are partial to existing beliefs, expectations or a hypothesis in hand'.[68] Once police officers are convinced of the suspects' guilt, it is very difficult to change this opinion. The latter mechanism refers to 'belief perseverance'.[69] These two, mutually strengthening, mechanisms contribute to tunnel vision.[70] Interviewers who experience tunnel vision are not able to observe the broader context and information which can be found in other directions. Due to tunnel vision coming from a preliminary hypothesis, interviewers use a dominant, accusatorial interview approach seeking to obtain a confession. Therefore, it is necessary to minimise the risk of tunnel vision in the criminal investigation stage. One protection afforded by the European Court on Human Rights is the right to legal advice (e.g. *Salduz v. Turkey*).[71]

However, since lawyers do not always play a (pro)active role and neither do they necessarily have a background in psychology, this measure is often insufficient. Consequently, to avoid the pitfalls of tunnel vision, it is important for interviewers themselves to develop alternative scenarios. A scenario is described as 'an interdependent series of statements'.[72] The best protection against tunnel vision is to use several reasonable alternative scenarios and gather information to confirm one of the alternatives.[73] The latter addresses the falsification of the original hypothesis. By investigating 'innocent' alternative scenarios during the interview, the interviewer can protect himself against looking for confirmation of the original hypothesis.

In short, police officers often develop a working hypothesis at an early stage of the criminal investigation. Despite the fact that any hypothesis is based upon incomplete and uncertain information, the very process of developing a hypothesis can lead investigators to tunnel vision. The question

---

[66] St-Yves 2006, p. 90-91.

[67] Crombag 2010, p. 390-395.

[68] Nickerson 1998, p. 175.

[69] Crombag 2010, p. 390-395.

[70] Besides confirmation bias and belief perseverance, Crombag distinguishes two additional risk factors with regard to tunnel vision: the avoidance of cognitive dissonance and conformity.

[71] ECtHR 27 November 2008, no. 36391/02.

[72] Van Koppen 2011, p. 38.

[73] At least one alternative scenario needs to be drafted.

is to what extent scenarios succeed in protecting interviewers from tunnel vision? It is stated that the first hypothesis (original scenario) and alternative scenarios need to be made explicit in order to serve as a protective measure.[74] Subsequently, any scenario need to be investigated thoroughly.[75] Moreover, is has been shown that the development of alternative scenarios, simply to follow procedural requirements, does not work properly.[76]

2.2.2. Component 1: Preparation

All interview models and researchers emphasise the importance of thorough and appropriate preparation before the interview begins.[77]

Within the preparation a distinction is made between tangible and intangible preparation.[78] Tangible preparation relates to the interview room, documents and materials needed (administrative arrangements), audiovisual recording, interpreting, timing and so on. Intangible preparation relates to the content: e.g. legal considerations, case characteristics, suspect characteristics, interview plan including objectives. Within the content preparation the interviewer needs to protect himself against tunnel vision by developing reasonable alternative scenarios as described above. However, some current interview models do not adequately offer this protection and need to explicitly state the danger of tunnel vision and include protective measures against falsification. This lack of attention threatens the validity of the information which is gathered during the interview.

In light of the recent regulation in Belgium and the Netherlands concerning the presence of a lawyer during suspect interviews, the interviewer needs to also consider the first contact with the lawyer when planning the interview procedures. The scheduling of the interview also needs to be considered beforehand.

2.2.3. Component 2: Interview

After thorough preparation and planning, the interview can begin. Within the interview itself, different steps can be distinguished. These steps need to

---

74 VANDERHALLEN, MATKOSKI & VERVAEKE 2008, p. 20-22.
75 VAN KOPPEN 2011, p. 42.
76 VAN KOPPEN 2011, p. 38-63.
77 VANDERHALLEN 2010, p. 117.
78 VAN DE PLAS 2007, p. 27-35; VAN AMELSVOORT, RISPENS & GROLMAN 2010, p. 284-285; ORD, SHAW & GREEN 2011, p. 3-14.

be executed consecutively in order to gather reliable and thus valid information.[79]

2.2.3.1. Steps

Within the interview itself, five common steps can be identified: introduction, free recall, questioning, official report and closure.[80]

In the introduction (2.2 above), it was suggested that there are four factors common to interview models.[81] Firstly, establishing rapport is often considered one of the main goals during the introduction and captures other factors which need to be addressed in the introduction phase. The second factor concerns informing a suspect of their rights. Which rights need to be communicated differs from country to country. Currently, in the UK, Belgium and the Netherlands all suspects need to be informed of the right to legal advice and the right to silence. Literature on interview models emphasizes the importance of explaining these rights to the suspect with a view to establishing rapport.[82] Besides informing the suspect of their rights and legal procedures, the interviewers need to introduce themselves, which can also help to build rapport.[83] Interviewers should clarify the aim and the procedure, as well as the reason for the interview.[84] This again helps to create a good rapport between interviewer and suspect.

Having met the above requirements, some interview models suggest that it is important to invest more in personal conversation with a view to enhancing rapport and gathering relevant information in relation to the subsequent questioning.[85] Moreover, it could be argued that by asking more personal, open-ended questions, interviewers establish a communication pattern in which the interviewer limits the time that he spends talking to 10-20 per cent of the interview time, and the suspect, who is encouraged to speak freely talks for 80-90 per cent of the interview.

According to the interview models derived from the PEACE model, interviewers need to find out what happened in the case, once good rapport has been established. Therefore, the interviewer invites the suspect to give his

---

[79] VANDERHALLEN 2010, p. 125-130.
[80] VANDERHALLEN 2010, p. 119-124.
[81] VANDERHALLEN 2010, p. 119-120.
[82] See: ORD, SHAW & GREEN 2011, p. 103.
[83] MILNE & BULL 1999, p. 41.
[84] VAN DE PLAS 2007, p. 27-35; VAN AMELSVOORT, RISPENS & GROLMAN 2010, p. 310-311, p. 331; ORD, SHAW & GREEN 2011, p. 20-21; HOLMBERG 2009, p. 156.
[85] VAN AMELSVOORT, RISPENS & GROLMAN 2010, p. 312-319.

own account, namely, to provide him with the opportunity for free recall.[86] Thus, the suspect is given the chance to provide information without being interrupted by the interviewer. Free recall is especially important in the case of co-operative suspects in order to produce the most accurate account.[87] Research on witnesses' statements shows that free recall provides the most accurate information.[88] However, it is not always likely that suspects will pass self-incriminating information after such an invitation is made. Granhag et al. found differences between experienced versus inexperienced suspects in volunteering self-incriminating information in an initial free recall phase.[89] Whereas experienced suspects provided less self-incriminating information, the importance of (the introduction of) evidence increases. In order to stimulate a suspect's free recall the interviewer needs to invite the suspect in a neutral way and repeat this invitation if necessary. During the free recall, the interviewer should listen actively and avoid any interruptions to confirm the communication pattern.[90]

Since free recall does not lead to a full account, interviewers need to complete this initial account by questioning the suspect in the next step of the interview.[91] Here the interviewer gathers additional relevant information in order to find the truth. To show the suspect that the interviewer has paid attention, the first question can go into one of the topics addressed by the suspects during his free recall.[92] The questioning phase can generally be seen as a funnel: the interviewer starts with open questioning and narrows down every topic to finish with some closed questions. Therefore a distinction can be made between appropriate (open-ended questions which stimulate elaborate answers) and inappropriate questions (closed questions which provoke short answers).[93] Inappropriate questions also refer to unsuitable questions such as multi-part questions, suggestive questions and leading questions.[94] In order to achieve a high level of questioning, the interviewer needs to consider five rules.[95]

---

[86] VAN DE PLAS 2007, p. 57-60; ORD, SHAW & GREEN 2011, p. 32; MILNE & BULL 1999, p. 41. In the Dutch interrogation model, free recall is not explicitly mentioned but interrogators are encouraged to give suspects the opportunity to provide their own account.
[87] MILNE & BULL 1999, p. 23.
[88] COLLINS, LINCOLN & FRANK 2002, p. 69-72.
[89] GRANHAG, CLEMENS & STROMWALL 2009, p. 134-135.
[90] MILNE & BULL 1999, p. 3.
[91] MILNE & BULL 1999, p. 3, p. 23; VAN DE PLAS 2007, p. 61; ORD, SHAW & GREEN 2011, p. 110.
[92] VAN DE PLAS 2007, p. 43.
[93] MILNE & BULL 1999, p. 3; ORD, SHAW & GREEN 2011, p. 111.
[94] ORD, SHAW & GREEN 2011, p. 43.
[95] ORD, SHAW & GREEN 2011, p. 28-42.

- The quality of questioning is first determined by the type of vocabulary used.
- Secondly, questions should be simple and short. Furthermore, questions should be relevant and interviewers should avoid unnecessary repetition.
- A third quality criterion concerns the pace of questioning: interviewers need to allow suspects time to consider their answers.
- Fourth, after asking a question, suspects should not be interrupted because this takes them out of the flow of the questioning and information delivery.
- Finally, the questioning should be managed by the interviewer, for example, by directing the suspect back to the topic if necessary.

Besides putting questions to the suspect, the phase of questioning is just as important from another viewpoint. After all, in the case of incomplete accounts or contradictions, the interviewer needs to challenge the suspect's account in this phase of the interview.[96] Thus, besides posing relevant questions, this phase is characterised by confrontation. The interviewer can address any contradictions through an open question inviting the suspect to give his or her own account.[97] At this stage of the interview, the interviewer will also confront the suspect with evidence. The importance of evidence has already been mentioned in relation to getting a (true) confession. Moreover, research found that one of the major reasons why suspects confess is to do with the suspect's perception of the strength of the evidence against him.[98] In this regard, the strength of the evidence is often regarded as a pivotal factor in confessions.[99] Therefore, the introduction of evidence can be crucial during interviews. Research by Walsch and Bull, found that skilful interviewers were more likely to elicit confessions by carefully deciding when and how to introduce evidence. They showed that it was not purely the amount of evidence that influenced the suspects' decision to confess or not, in contradiction to earlier research.[100] Disclosure of evidence showed the highest correlation with suspects moving towards confession during the interview.

---

[96]   BULL & SOUKARA 2010, p. 82-84.
[97]   ORD, SHAW & GREEN 2011, p. 115-116.
[98]   WALSCH & BULL 2011, p. 7.
[99]   In their study, DESLAURIERS-VARIN ET AL. found that besides the perceived evidence strength, other contextual factor such as suspect feeling guilty and receiving legal advice were related to the willingness to confess. However, one should bear in mind that transferring these findings from Canada to Europe one must take into consideration the differences in legal framework and practices regarding interrogation (WALSCH & BULL 2011, p. 6). See: DESLAURIERS-VARIN, LUSSIER & ST-YVES 2011, p. 113-145.
[100] WALSCH & BULL 2011, p. 12-14.

This 'shift to confession' is explicitly distinguishable from a confession as such, since earlier research showed that on only a few occasions were confessions made at the beginning of the interview.[101] With regard to how the interview should disclose evidence, a positive confrontational style is being promoted by researchers.[102] This raises the question of when to disclose evidence. Research showed that late disclosure of strong evidence leads to higher confessions rates in comparison to late disclosure of weak evidence or early disclosure of strong evidence.[103] [104]

However, Griffith quite rightly emphasized that all interviews in which interviewers probe the suspect's account including the exploration of motives (guilty scenario) and defences (not guilty scenario) should be acknowledged as equally effective in getting a confession.[105] Indeed, Walsch and Bull found that skilled PEACE interviewing often secured full accounts.[106] Hence, it is important to consider how skilfully interviewers conduct the interview as a whole.

The final step of interview closure can begin once the accounts have been completed. This phase should also be carefully planned and structured.[107] Ideally, the interview should end in a positive atmosphere, leaving the suspect in a positive frame of mind, regardless of outcome.[108]

In some countries (including Belgium and the Netherlands), the interviewer gives the suspect a copy of the written statement, which he or she can review and if necessary, ask to be amended, before signing. In order for the report to be accurate, great attention to detail is required when drafting the written statement during the interview. Research has found that the summaries of such statements differ in length and format (question/answer, monologue etc).[109] Written statements raise issues of accuracy and completeness – including doubts about the original questions posed, the original source of information, the first qualification of facts, leading questions, omissions of the precise language of suspects' answers and other parts which may have seemed irrelevant to the interviewer.[110] The

---

[101] BULL & SOUKARA 2010, p. 86.

[102] ORD, SHAW & GREEN 2011, p. 113-116.

[103] SELLERS & KEBBELL 2009, p. 156-158.

[104] It should be noted that testing the confession on the basis of perpetrator knowledge is a condition sine qua non when a confession is obtained.

[105] GRIFFITHS 2008, p. 72.

[106] WALSCH & BULL 2010, p. 305.

[107] ORD, SHAW & GREEN 2011, p. 117-118.

[108] MILNE & BULL 1999, p. 46-47; VAN AMELSVOORT, RISPENS & GROLMAN 2010, p. 333.

[109] MALSCH ET AL. 2010, p. 2405-2406.

[110] MALSCH, HAKET & NIJBOER 2008, p. 2018-2019.

quality of the statements can therefore be improved by accurate and comprehensive note-taking during the interview.[111] It is well-documented that when interviewers only write up the official report (statement) at the end of the interview, up to 1/3 of the relevant information can be lost.[112]

To improve the quality of written statements, there are two additional recommendations, apart from improved note-taking. Firstly, when the interview is conducted by two interviewers, tasks can be divided.[113] Secondly, the way the interview is structured means that it can accommodate simultaneous statement writing.[114] When the lead interviewer (or the sole interviewer in some cases) uses regular summaries (for example after free recall), these can also form the basis of the written statement. In this way, there is minimal loss of eye contact during interview. During free recall, the lead interviewer may be involved in note-taking as previously mentioned. It is therefore crucial that interviewers improve the quality of note-taking by dividing tasks, using summaries and being mindful to be accurate and comprehensive.[115]

Finally, a full picture of the interview can only be obtained by ensuring it is recorded. In the UK all suspect interviews are recorded with audio-tapes and the number of videotaped interviews is also growing. The latter is also happening in the Netherlands and Belgium where the advice is to videotape suspect interviews for serious offences. In the UK, the taping of suspect interviews has led to scrutiny and greater accountability in the practice of interview because the quality of interview evidence can be assessed after the event.[116] Scrutiny of recordings can help to indentify contamination of perpetrator knowledge during interviews, hence Israel's conclusion that recording is one of the key protection measures against false confessions.[117]

Moreover, recording has additional added value since it has made a significant contribution to identifying skills deficits and to making recommendations for training in the UK.[118]

---

[111] See: FISHER & GEISELMAN 1992; ORD, SHAW & GREEN 2011, p. 52.
[112] DANIELL 1999.
[113] ORD, SHAW & GREEN 2011, p. 52, p. 112; VAN DE PLAS 2007, p. 63.
[114] VAN DE PLAS 2007, p. 63.
[115] ORD, SHAW & GREEN 2011, p. 52.
[116] SHAWYER, MILNE & BULL 2009, p. 29.
[117] ISRAELS 2012, p. 32.
[118] WILLIAMSON 2006, p. 152-153.

2.2.3.2. Skills

In order to interrogate a suspect successfully, therefore, it is crucial to have a set of required communication skills, the most important being: summarising, questioning, confrontation, reflection, and active listening. After the initial implementation of the PEACE model, police officers were asked to indicate which interview skills they considered most important.[119] Police officers mentioned preparation, knowledge of topic, rapport, listening, questioning, flexibility, open-mindedness, compassion and empathy.

Besides these skills, interviewers must be responsive towards suspects and must put the model into practice in a flexible way. Research has shown a significant and positive correlation between the responsiveness of suspects and the behaviour of interviewers (namely, communication, establishing rapport, open-mindedness, flexibility).[120] Skills recommended by the PEACE model were examined in a large evaluation study conducted by Clarke and Milne in 2001 after the PEACE training was introduced. They found that the interview skills of interviewers had improved significantly since the pre-PACE studies. Nevertheless, improvement was still needed in the areas of rapport building, active listening and summarising. These findings led to a revised PEACE training programme, and a more comprehensive and appropriate system (i.e. Five-tier strategy), to bring standards to a higher level in the UK.[121] A further study was then conducted showing skills relating to serious offences to have improved.[122] More recently, Soukara and Bull examined tape-recordings of suspect interviews which showed that interviewers generally used the non-coercive skills outlined in PEACE.[123] The most frequently used were disclosure of evidence, leading questions and repetitive questions. In at least 50 per cent of cases, emphasizing contradictions, positive confrontation and challenging of the suspect's account could be identified. Techniques such as minimisation and intimidation were not or almost not used in any of the interviews. It can be said therefore, that the introduction of the PEACE model and subsequent training has enhanced skilful information gathering interview practices in the UK. This was also found in a sample study showing that advanced training did improve the skills of interviewers.[124]

---

[119] BULL & SOUKARA 2010, p. 83.
[120] BULL & SOUKARA 2010, p. 88.
[121] SHAWYER, MILNE & BULL 2009, p. 34.
[122] WALSCH & BULL 2010, p. 7.
[123] BULL & SOUKARA 2010, p. 86.
[124] GRIFFITHS & MILNE 2006, p. 187.

2.2.4. Component 3: Evaluation

Despite the number of studies which evaluate the current state of the art techniques in the interview room, police culture does not embrace the idea of continuous monitoring by means of supervision, expert feedback or coaching. In the interview model, the third component addresses the evaluation of the interview in terms of both outcome and process. The significant effort put into the outcome evaluation which directs the interviewers towards one or more clues, is in stark contrast to the poor attention paid to the process evaluation. The monitoring process of interviews needs improvement in the UK, and even more so in the Netherlands and Belgium in particular.[125]

Thorough training including the implementation of a good follow-up system is indispensable to guaranteeing high-quality interview.[126] Supervision, including expert feedback is suggested as one of the processes which can improve individual performance.[127] Research shows that individual follow-up leads to better results in interviewing children in comparison with collective follow-up.[128] However, even in cases of collective follow-up, interview quality is significantly improved, when compared with a group where there has been no-follow up.

Training and follow-up can therefore be viewed as crucial for qualitative interviews. The key to improving interview skills is practical skills training and evaluation of the interview process.[129]

3. INTERVIEW TRAINING

According to Meissner and Lassiter a consensus exists amongst various scholars concerning five necessary key reforms in practice and policy with regard to interview.[130] These are: the recording of all interviews, the prohibition of the use of psychologically manipulative interview techniques, the protection of vulnerable suspects, the guarantee of appropriate administration of rights, and the training of law enforcement investigators, which are all required to reduce the number of false confessions. There is general agreement, in many countries, that enhancement of interview skills through training is essential for improving interview quality.[131] In the UK,

---

[125] CLARKE & MILNE 2001; CLÉMENT ET AL. 2009, p. 75-76.
[126] VANDERHALLEN 2010, p. 150.
[127] POWELL, FISHER & WRIGHT 2005, p. 34-38.
[128] DOMMICENT ET AL. 2008, p. 258-259.
[129] ORD, SHAW & GREEN 2011, p. 137.
[130] MEISSNER & LASSITER 2010, p. 225.
[131] WILLIAMSON 2006, p. 354.

even though there has already been extensive improvement of training, there is still an ongoing focus on training reform. For example, the Professionalization Investigation Programme (PIP) has only recently been implemented, in addition to the five-tier strategy of extensive training.[132] In Belgium, over the past decade much effort has gone into training which has evolved from being solely theoretical towards being much more practical.[133] However, although there has been a degree of harmonisation of these basic training programmes as far as the training material is concerned, a study has revealed that there are still major differences in basic interview training in terms of materials and practice by means of role play etc. At the advanced training level, harmonisation of interview training is undoubtedly still lacking.[134]

The fact that police officers themselves acknowledge the necessity for specialised training, as well as the importance of interview in finding the truth without resorting to trickery, is a good reason to professionalise the training process.[135] Although some police officers have a constructive attitude, the majority have difficulty adopting a different ethos towards interview through re-training. Researchers certainly encountered difficulties in changing attitudes and skills of detectives, particularly the most experienced ones. In order to overcome these difficulties, it makes sense to train new recruits or detectives. However, research demonstrates that with good training, the skills of even the experienced interrogators can be improved.[136]

It is important to understand that a change in police practice to a new model of interview requires a mentality shift which begins during training. Trainers therefore have to deal with the resistance they encounter and balance it with use of other ingredients in order to achieve a successful outcome. Firstly, it is crucial to have enough opportunity to practice using role play, with trainees rotating between the roles of interviewer, witness, and observer. It is even more effective to set up an exercise in which civilian respondents take on the role of suspect,[137] ideally based upon real cases. Furthermore, it is very important to be given critical feedback.

Finally, it may be helpful here to explain underlying scientific theories.

---

[132] SHAWYER, MILNE & BULL 2009, p. 34.

[133] CLÉMENT ET AL. 2009, p. 75-76.

[134] According to MOSTON and FISHER, some countries provide rarely interrogation training for police officers which stresses the worldwide need for training (MOSTON & FISHER 2007, p. 88).

[135] SOUKARA ET AL. 2009, p. 496.

[136] FISHER 1995, p. 756-758.

[137] *Ibidem.*

In light of the above-mentioned professionalization of interview training, an evidence-based approach is often suggested. As Williamson puts it: 'sound, scientifically based training programmes are urgently needed to assist investigators to acquire the necessary interview skills to function at the higher professional standards that will be required in the twenty-first century'. Gudjonsson agrees that ever expanding scientific knowledge has led to improvements in police interview training.[138] Quality training in the PEACE model requires constructive collaboration between police interviewers and scientists. In his view, the fact that scientists are increasingly taking part in training of police officers should be viewed as a positive trend. In many countries, collaboration between scientists and police is a new development which is just beginning,[139] and such agreement on higher professionalism can only be encouraged. At the same time, some researchers have justly pointed out that in some countries there are a number of commercial initiatives in the field of training programmes where the content is often not grounded in scientific research.[140] These programmes are, for example, often found in the field of lie detection amongst others.

The importance of post-training follow-up is recognised in the UK as well in other countries.[141] In Belgium, there is no organised follow-up programme, but individual projects for coaching, peer review and supervision (including expert feedback) do exist.[142] Monitoring, by means of supervision, peer review and coaching, as well as refresher training is clearly crucial for maintaining newly acquired skills, as demonstrated by research pointing to the post-training skills loss that becomes apparent after a certain time lapse.[143]

4. SKILLS TRAINING IN CHINA

The project known as the 'Prevention of Torture in the PRC' comprised three components including one addressing police interview training. The aim was to have Chinese police officers become acquainted with current European interview techniques and to hint that similar techniques and didactics should be used in current Chinese training.

To reach this goal, the EU-Chinese interview training programme 'Skills for interviewing criminal suspects' was set up, based upon an extensive

---

[138] GUDJONSSON 2006, p. 162.
[139] SHAWYER, MILNE & BULL 2009, p. 34; CLÉMENT ET AL. 2009, p. 75-76.
[140] SNOOK ET AL. 2010, p. 218.
[141] ORD, SHAW & GREEN 2011, p. 137-140.
[142] The author was involved in local supervision and peer intervision projects.
[143] GRIFFITHS & MILNE 2006, p. 187.

exchange of knowledge concerning current legal procedures, practices and training in both the EU and China. Experts from the UK, Belgium, the Netherlands and China, scientific researchers as well as police officers, were gathered to build a three day training programme. This training was set up as basic training for recruits, and was also used for experienced police trainers. Besides the content, the didactics were also discussed, as a result of which this training could also serve as an opportunity to 'train the trainers'.[144] The first day addressed current issues in Chinese interview practice as well as important interview techniques and underlying psychological theories. The second and third day looked at similar topics in the EU.

The training programmes were delivered in two police academies, the first of which was at the Gansu Institute of Political Science and Law, in Lanzhou (Gansu) from 23rd to 26th May 2011, and the second was at the Sichuan Police Training College in Luzhou (Sichuan) from 4th to 7th November 2011. Prior to these, a scoping visit was organised at Shenyang Police College in October 2009 as well as a scoping visit, including a pilot programme, at PLOT (Police Academy Limburg, Belgium) in May 2010.

The final part of this chapter provides an outline of the two programmes and evaluates their strengths and weaknesses.

4.1.   PARTICIPANTS

Both training programmes targeted practitioners as well as police trainers. The Sichuan training programme was attended by 28 police officers from Universities in North West China (representing 10 western provinces including Chongqing, Gansu, Guizhou, Ningxia, Qinghai, Shaanxi, Sichuan, Tibet, Xi'an, and Xinjiang). In the second training programme, 30 police officers from 16 provinces across China (Fujian, Guangdong, Guangxi, Heilongjiang, Henan, Hubei, Hunan, Jiangxi, Shandong, Chongqing, Gansu, Guizhou, Jiangsu, Liaoning, Sichuan, Wuhan city, Yunnan, Zhejiang) participated. In sum, police officers from a total of 23 Chinese provinces were involved in the project.

In order to reach as many Chinese participants as possible, a large number of trainees was accepted. Role play is not a common practice in China, so it was decided to initiate this for a groups of more than 20 trainees, even though, ordinarily role-plays work better with smaller groups. Experienced practitioners (which only applies to some police trainers) and other trainers were invited to participate to achieve the right mix for effective role play.

---

[144]   This was possible by means of a minor didactical part since the majority of participants were experienced trainers.

Moreover, the heterogeneous composition of the trainee group was reflected in the pertinent questions asked. Finally, practitioners were able to reflect on the training from a practical perspective.

4.2. PROGRAMME

Content and didactics of the programme:

4.2.1. Content

On the second day of training, the Belgian interview model (derived from the PEACE model) was used to explain the information gathering approach which is currently favoured, and to a certain extent already implemented in most EU countries. The four components of the model were discussed: general premises, preparation, interview and evaluation. The major principles of each were addressed in-depth. Within the interview itself, the different steps (see 2.2.3.1 above) were explained and then the various skills required in each were reviewed, as follows:

1. Introduction: clarify interview process (legal notifications etc.), deal with resistance, establish communication pattern, make conversation, establish rapport, make agreements;
2. Free recall: invitation to free recall, active listening, note-taking, summarize and write official report (statement);
3. Questioning: maintain the thread, use of high-quality questions, evidence disclosure, positive confrontation;
4. Closure: create positive atmosphere.

The subject of suspects' right to legal advice was also on the agenda and in particular the right to confidential consultation with a lawyer before, and the presence of a lawyer during, the interview

The 'Green Dragon' case, a real-life murder case from Belgium was then presented as a model case. In this presentation, one of the EU experts participated as an expert interviewer and there was then an exchange of ideas between experienced practitioners and trainees.

The third day focused on specialised or advanced skills using two other real cases for demonstration purposes. The case scenarios were presented to the trainees and then used to discuss difficulties experienced in interview, particularly of difficult suspects. The first scenario with a non-cooperative suspect, involved the theory of balancing resistance with cooperation. The second, with an aggressive suspect, involved the subject of aggressive behaviour before and during the interview.

The final topic dealt with changing interview practices and the evaluation of interview. An evaluation of the training programme was then carried out, both orally and in writing.

4.2.2. Didactics

The skills training was given by three EU experts comprising two senior police officers who have expertise in suspect interview and are still actively involved in the field of criminal investigation. The third EU expert is a scientist who has conducted substantial research on the subject of interview, and is experienced in supporting the police with regard to interviews in complex investigations. The three trainers are experienced in teaching basic and advanced interview training in Belgium.

A variety of didactics was needed to cover the different parts of the training programme, which included an in-depth exploration of a 'new' information gathering approach as well as the underlying theoretical mechanisms, in addition to the active involvement of participants through practical skills training. Different didactics were adopted over the course of the two days. The second training day started with a theoretical introduction outlining the interview model and ended with some examples from police practice.[145] In addition, where appropriate, other exercises were conducted:

> Example: *In order to discuss the set up of the interview room, all trainees were invited to set up their own interview room. The different approaches were reviewed by the group.*

The 'Green Dragon Case' was then explained and discussed in the group so that it could be used as a model case throughout the training programme. The different steps of the interview were outlined with reference to the Green Dragon case, and illustrated by means of excerpts of DVD footage of real-time interview. These original fragments then served as material for group discussion at the end of the session. These exercises were conducted as follows:

---

[145] During the First training, there was an alternation between lectures, dvd fragments on the Green Dragon Case, exercises and group discussion. This routine was adjusted based on the evaluations received of the first training, stating that (1) Chinese training is more lecture-oriented and (2) trainees prefer to receive theory and cases as a whole. In order to concede to existing approved practices and not to deviate too much in terms of content as well as didactics, these adjustments were made.

1. Outline of the interview steps and explanation of the difficulties encountered;
2. Round table to suggest possible approaches; trainers tested out suggestions, where appropriate, with role play.
3. DVD excerpts and group discussion.

Active participation was gradually increased during the second day in order to give trainees time to get used to the idea of role play.

The third day focused on practising interview skills. The underlying theories were outlined and explained before presentation of the two scenarios, namely, the non-cooperative suspect and the aggressive suspect. The floor was then opened up to allow trainees to ask in-depth questions about each scenario and to suggest possible approaches. The most common suggestion was put into practice in a role play conducted by the EU experts. Excerpts of DVD footage of real-time interview of non-cooperative suspects were shown and discussed. This opportunity for in-depth analysis formed the basis for further role play by smaller groups of trainees, observed and critiqued by other trainees, before the roles were reversed. All trainees were provided with guidelines for giving feedback and then group results were discussed collectively. At this point, additional theoretical insights were added, if required.

The last part of interview, namely evaluation, was then discussed. Participants were asked to take part in a round-table discussion, as well as to produce a written evaluation of the training, as a part of this topic. They were invited to discuss the strengths and weaknesses of the three day programme. Almost all participants were willing to submit a written evaluation form, although this type of evaluation has not been customary in China.[146]

4.3. TRAINING MATERIALS

Various training materials were developed and bundled into a basic training manual, in an electronic form, with a view to implementing this training on a larger scale. It consists of:

1. a mini-manual: plan of action for trainers;
2. a reader: selection of relevant literature;
3. training materials: PowerPoint presentation, model case 'Green Dragon', role play scenarios and DVD role play of suspect interview in presence of lawyer.

---

[146] In total 48 (anonymous) evaluation forms were returned.

The mini-manual contains the programme overview and optimal timing of the different modules. The plan of action describes the working methodology regarding the training and explains the different educational activities and materials. A reader comprising relevant articles was developed providing background information on the training content. The training materials were those used for the 'train the trainers' session

> *Excerpt plan of action Guidelines 'giving feedback':*
> *Feedback can be negative or positive. To provide someone with constructive feedback is a difficult task and needs anchoring points. After all, people tend to compensate negative feedback with positive feedback, or try to disguise negative feedback, which minimises the opportunity for the receiver to really learn from it. Therefore, guidelines are given about what to give feedback about, and how to give it.*
>
> *About what?*
> - *about the behaviour and not the person (e.g.. "you don't say much about yourself" is stronger and clearer then "you are an introverted person")*
> - *about behaviour which can be changed, and not about things that can't e.g. appearance*
> - *concentrate on what is missing and could be improved instead of what is wrong (e.g. "some more informal speech could contribute to rapport" is better then "you act too formal to be able to create a rapport")*
>
> *How?*
> - *be honest and respectful*
> - *be positive: acknowledge the person*
> - *use 'I' messages (e.g. "I got the impression that you felt uncomfortable" instead of "you were uncomfortable")*
> - *perception/description versus interpretation: mention what you saw or heard without interpreting. e.g. "I saw you nodding at a certain point. Why did you do that?" instead of "you didn't agree at a certain point"*
> - *describing instead of judging (division between behaviour and own feelings). e.g. "You use the word 'lady'. For me it felt disrespectful" instead of "You were disrespectful"*
> - *provide direct feedback, don't disguise*
> - *be concrete (naming): every now and then, use examples*
> - *mirroring in stead of advising: give person who receives feedback the space and opportunity to decide about his behaviour. Don't go into conflict or try to convince*
>   *…*

The above-mentioned guidelines for feedback can be used by the trainers but can also be presented to the trainees in order to improve the quality of feedback in role play.

All participants received a cd-rom of the training manual so that they could implement parts of the training in their own police academy and interview techniques. The training materials such as the DVD role play and scenarios will need adjusting to make them better fit the Chinese context, for educational purposes.

4.4. TRAINING EVALUATION

In total, 48 feedback questionnaires were submitted by trainees who attended the three day event. The majority were satisfied from a content as well as a didactical perspective.

They mentioned, in particular, several interesting points regarding content which should be taken on board for future training. Firstly, the interview-gathering model was considered very helpful. Trainees in particular liked the five-steps interview approach and the division of speech (communication pattern) between interviewers and suspects within that, and stated that this does not correspond to current Chinese practice. Secondly, since Chinese interview training focuses heavily on psychological insights, the idea of understanding the psychology of suspects, in terms of building rapport to get co-operation was seen as very interesting but rather new. One of the trainees mentioned the added value of the human rights philosophy which aims to show respect to the suspect, in order to find the truth. Thirdly, the set-up of the interview room was considered an interesting approach. Trainees also appreciated the flexibility of working methods adopted by EU trainers for the specific purpose of enhancing interaction.

Overall the training was considered a good opportunity to better understand EU interview practices. Almost all of the trainees mentioned that the methodology, and the interview skills demonstrated during the programme, would be helpful to their future teaching and police work.

The experience did raise some questions however, which should be taken into account for future activities. Firstly, analysis is required to see how the EU interview model and skills can be adapted to the Chinese context and for that purpose an analysis of legal procedure as well as cultural differences was recommended. Secondly, the duration of the programme was too short to be able to look at theory and practice in sufficient depth although the attempt to do so was very much appreciated. In particular, more time is needed to build up the practical skills learned through role play. Ideally, sufficient time should be allocated to discuss scenarios, prepare and conduct interview, to discuss information gathered and the process. Thirdly, trainees proposed an elaboration on psychological insight and suggested inclusion of topics that cover such areas as lie detection (reading minds etc.).

Finally, both Chinese and European police trainers encouraged future collaboration between the Chinese and European experts. This will allow increased discussion on the new interview model and the required skills.

Furthermore through further communication, exchange and joint efforts, it may be possible to use this model and skills in the Chinese training context in the future.

5. CONCLUSION

To conclude, the importance of skills training in interview of suspects is emphasized by all parties involved. Through training and follow-up, interview skills can be acquired, improved upon and/or maintained. Not only is training important, but special attention needs to be paid to follow-up in order to maintain the skills acquired during training and to build up the necessary expertise. Moreover, scientific research is recommended so that strengths and weaknesses in interview practice can be identified and used to adjust and fine-tune future training based on actual need in the field of suspect interview. Audiovisual recording of interviews would not only contribute to the quality of interview as such, but also allow insight into the current practice which can serve scientific and training purposes as well. Therefore, an additional recommendation is to invest in audiovisual recording equipment which is indispensable if the police really want to improve interview quality.

In the context of the EU and China, a higher level of effort is required to successfully adopt an effective information gathering interview model in practice, particularly since research has shown that judges as well as mock juries, depend hugely on confession evidence. Unfortunately, it is currently the case that improper confessions lead to a significantly increased conviction rate in the absence of other evidence.[147] This undoubtedly motivates the police to aspire to the highest standards. Judges can only pass judgement of a high quality if provided with the required quality of information by the police. The avoidance of miscarriages of justice thus starts with the police and interview practice.

BIBLIOGRAPHY

VAN AMELSVOORT, RISPENS & GROLMAN 2010
AMELSVOORT, A., VAN, RISPENS, I. & GROLMAN, H., *Handleiding verhoor*, Amsterdam: Stapel & De Koning, 2010.

---

[147]   WALLACE & KASSIN 2011, p. 7-8.

BALDWIN 1993
BALDWIN, J., 'Police Interview Techniques. Establishing Truth or Proof?', *The British Journal of Criminology*, 1993, p. 325-351.

BLAIR 2005
BLAIR, J.P., 'A Test of the Unusual False Confession Perspective Using Cases of Proven False Confessions', *Criminal Law Bulletin*, 2005, p. 127-144.

BREAN 2011
BREAN, J., 'Police Interrogation Techniques under Scrutiny Due to False Confessions', *National Post*, 25 November 2011.

BULL & SOUKARA 2010
BULL, R. & SOUKARA, S., 'What Really Happens in Police Interviews', in: D.G. LASSITER & C.A. MEISSNER (eds.), *Police Interrogations and False Confessions. Current Research, Practice and Policy Recommendations*, Washington: American Psychological Association, 2010, p. 81-95.

CLÉMENT ET AL. 2009
CLÉMENT, S., PLAS, M., VAN DE, ESHOF, P., VAN DEN & NIEROP, N., 'Police interviewing in France, Belgium and the Netherlands: Something is Moving', in: T. WILLIAMSON, B. MILNE & S.P. SAVAGE (eds.), *International Developments in Investigative Interviewing*, Devon: Willan Publishing, 2009, p. 66-91.

COLLINS, LINCOLN & FRANK 2002
COLLINS, R., LINCOLN, R. & FRANK, M.G., 'The Effect of Rapport in Forensic Interviewing', *Psychiatry, Psychology and Law*, 2002, p. 69-78.

CROMBAG 2010
CROMBAG, H.F.M., 'Over tunnelvisie', in: P.J. VAN KOPPEN, H. MERCKELBACH, M. JELICIC & J.W. DE KEIJSER (eds.), *Reizen met mijn rechter. Psychologie van het recht*, Deventer: Kluwer, 2010, p. 387-399.

DANIELL 1999
DANIELL, *The Truth – The Whole Truth and Nothing but the Truth? An Analysis of Witness Interviews and Statements*, unpublished undergraduate dissertation, University of Plymouth, referred to in: C. CLARKE & B. MILNE, *National Evaluation of the PEACE Investigative Interviewing Course. Report no. PRAS/149*, London: The Home Office, 2001, p. 109 and p. 110.

DESLAURIERS-VARIN, LUSSIER & ST-YVES 2011
DESLAURIERS-VARIN, N., LUSSIER, P. & ST-YVES, M., 'Confessing their Crime: Factors Influencing the Offender's Decision to Confess to the Police', *Justice Quarterly*, 2011, p. 113-145.

DOMMICENT ET AL. 2008
DOMMICENT, J., VANDERHALLEN, M., WIEST, H., DE, BASTIAENS, M., PLAS, M., VAN DE & VERVAEKE, G., 'Interviewing Children in Belgium: An Evaluation of Practices', *The Police Journal*, 2008, p. 248-261.

FISHER & GEISELMAN 1992
FISHER, R.P. & GEISELMAN, R.E., *Memory-enhancing Techniques for Investigative Interviewing: The Cognitive Interview,* Springfield: Charles C. Thomas Publisher, 1992.

FISHER 1995
FISHER, R.P., 'Interviewing Victims and Witnesses of Crime', *Psychology, Public Policy and Law*, 1995, p. 756-758.

GELSO & CARTER 1985
GELSO, C.J. & CARTER, J.A., 'The Relationship in Counselling and Psychotherapy: Components, Consequences and Theoretical Antecedents', *The Counselling Psychologist,* 1985, p. 155-243.

GRANHAG, CLEMENS & STROMWALL 2009
GRANHAG, P.A., CLEMENS, F. & STROMWALL, L.A., 'The Usual and Unusual Suspects: The Level of Suspicion and Counter-interrogation Tactics', *Journal of Investigative Psychology and Offender Profiling*, 2009, p. 129-137.

GRANO 1986
GRANO, J.D., 'Selling the Idea to Tell the Truth: The Professional Interrogation and Modern Confession Law', *The Journal of Criminal Law and Criminology*, 1986, p. 1465-1498.

GRIFFITHS & MILNE 2006
GRIFFITHS, A. & MILNE, B., 'Will it All End in Tiers? Police Interviews with Suspects in Britain', in: T. WILLIAMSON (ed.), *Investigative Interviewing. Rights, Research, Regulation,* Devon: Willan Publishing, 2006, p. 167-189.

GRIFFITHS 2008
GRIFFITHS, A., *An Examination into the Efficacy of Police Advanced Investigative Interview Training?*, Unpublished PhD thesis, Portsmouth: University of Portsmouth.

GUDJONSSON 2003
GUDJONSSON, G.H., *The Psychology of Interrogations and Confessions. A Handbook*, Chichester: Wiley, 2003.

GUDJONSSON 2006
GUDJONSSON, G.H., 'The Psychology of Interrogations and Confessions', in: T. WILLIAMSON (ed.), *Investigative interviewing. Rights, research, regulation*, Devon: Willan Publishing, 2006, p. 123-146.

GUDJONSSON 2010
GUDJONSSON, G.H., 'Psychological Vulnerabilities During Police Interviews. Why are they Important?', *Legal and Criminological Psychology*, 2010, p. 161-175.

HARTWIG, GRANHAG & VRIJ 2005
HARTWIG, M., GRANHAG, P.A. & VRIJ, A., 'Police Interrogation from a Social Psychology Perspective', *Policing & Society*, 2005, p. 379-399.

HOLMBERG 2004
HOLMBERG, U., *Police Interviews with Victims and Suspects of Violent and Sexual Crimes. Interviewee's Experiences and Interview Outcomes*, Edsbruk: Akademitryck AB, 2004.

HOLMBERG 2009
HOLMBERG, U., 'Investigative Interviewing as a Therapeutic Jurisprudential Approach', in: T. WILLIAMSON, B. MILNE & S.P. SAVAGE (eds.), *International Developments in Investigative Interviewing*, Devon: Willan Publishing, 2009, p. 149-175.

INBAU, REID & BUCKLEY 1986
INBAU, F.E., REID, J.E. & BUCKLEY, J.P., *Criminal Interrogation and Confessions,* 3rd edn., Baltimore: Williams and Wilkins, 1986.

ISRAELS 2012
ISRAELS, H., 'Recensie Brandon L. Garrett, Convicting the Innocent: Where Criminal Prosecutions Go Wrong, Harvard University Press 2011', *Expertise en Recht,* 2012, p. 31-33.

KASSIN 2008
KASSIN, S.M., 'The Psychology of Confessions', *The Annual Review of Law and Social Science*, 2008, p. 193-217.

KASSIN, APPLEBY & PERILLO 2010
KASSIN, S.M., APPLEBY, S.C. & PERILLO, J.T., 'Interviewing Suspects: Practice, Science and Future Directions', *Legal and Criminological Psychology*, 2010, p. 39-55.

KASSIN ET AL. 2007
KASSIN, S.M., LEO, R.A., MEISSNER, C.A., RICHMAN, K.D., COLWELL, L.H., LEACH A-M. & LA FON, D., 'Police Interviewing and Interrogation: A Self-report Survey of Police Practices and Beliefs', *Law and Human Behaviour*, 2007, p. 381-400.

KASSIN, GOLDSTEIN & SAVITSKY 2003
KASSIN, S.M., GOLDSTEIN, C.C. & SAVITSKY, K., 'Behavioral Confirmation in the Interview Room: On the Dangers of Assuming Guilt', *Law and Human Behavior*, 2003, p. 187-203.

VAN KOPPEN 2011
KOPPEN, P.J., VAN, *Overtuigend bewijs. Indammen van rechterlijke dwalingen*, Amsterdam: Nieuw Amsterdam, 2011.

LEO 1996
LEO, R.A., 'Inside the Interrogation Room', *The Journal of Criminal Law and Criminology*, 1996, p. 266-303.

LEO & DRIZIN 2010
LEO, R.A. & DRIZIN, S.A., 'The Three Errors: Pathways to False Confessions and Wrongful Conviction', in: G.D. LASSITER & C.A. MEISSNER (eds.), *Police Interrogations and False Confessions. Current Research, Practice and Policy Recommendations*, Washington: American Psychological Association, 2010, p. 9-30.

MALSCH, HAKET & NIJBOER 2008
MALSCH, M., HAKET, V. & NIJBOER, H., 'De gevaren van het proces-verbaal', *Nederlands Juristenblad*, 2008, p. 2048-2020.

MALSCH ET AL. 2010
MALSCH, M., KEIJSER, J., DE, KRANENDONK, P.R. & GRUIJTER, M., DE, 'Het verhoren op schrift of op band? De gevolgen van het "verbaliseren" van verhoren voor het oordeel van de jurist', *Nederlands Juristenblad*, 2010, p. 2402-2407.

MEISSNER & LASSITER 2010
MEISSNER, C.A. & LASSITER, G.D., 'Conclusion: What have we Learned? Implications for Further Practice, Policy and Future Research', in: D.G. LASSITER & C.A. MEISSNER (eds.), *Police Interviews and False Confessions. Current Research, Practice and Policy Recommendations*, Washington: American Psychological Association, 2010, p. 225-237.

MEISSNER, RUSSANO & NARCHET 2010
MEISSNER, C.A., RUSSANO, M.B. & NARCHET, F.M., 'The Importance of a Laboratory Science for Improving the Diagnostic Value of Confession Evidence', in: D.G. LASSITER & C.A. MEISSNER (eds.), *Police Interrogations and False Confessions. Current Research, Practice and Policy Recommendations*, Washington: American Psychological Association, 2010, p. 111-126.

MILNE & BULL 1999
MILNE, R. & BULL, R., *Investigative Interviewing. Psychology and Practice*, Chichester: Wiley and Sons, 1999.

MOSTON & FISHER 2007
MOSTON, S. & FISHER, M., 'Perceptions of Coercion in the Questioning of Criminal Suspects', *Journal of Investigative Psychology and Offender Profiling*, 2007, p. 85-95.

NICKERSON 1998
NICKERSON, R.S., 'Confirmation Bias: A Ubiquitous Phenomenon in Many Guises', *Review of General Psychology*, 1998, p. 175-220.

ORD, SHAW & GREEN 2011
ORD, B., SHAW, G. & GREEN, T., *Investigative Interviewing Explained*, 3rd edn., Chatswood: Lexis Nexis, 2011.

VAN DE PLAS 2007
PLAS, M., VAN DE, *Handboek politieverhoor. Basistechnieken*, Brussel: Politeia, 2007.

POWELL, FISHER & WRIGHT 2005
POWELL, M.B., FISHER, R.P. & WRIGHT, R., 'Investigative Interviewing', in: N. BREWER & K. WILLIAMS (eds.), *Psychology and Law: An Empirical Perspective*, New York: The Guilford Press, 2005, p. 11-42.

REDLICH ET AL. 2004
REDLICH, A.D., SILVERMAN, M., CHEN, J. & STEINER, H., 'The Police Interrogation of Children and Adolescents', in: D.G. LASSITER (ed.), *Interviews, Confessions and Entrapment*, New York: Kluwer Academic/Plenum Publishers, 2004, p. 107-125.

SELLERS & KEBBELL 2009
SELLERS, S. & KEBBELL, M.R., 'When Should Evidence Be Disclosed in an Interview with a Suspect? An Experiment with Mock-suspects', *Journal of Investigative Psychology and Offender Profiling*, 2009, p. 151-160.

SHAWYER, MILNE & BULL 2009
SHAWYER, A., MILNE, B. & BULL, R., 'Investigative Interviewing in the UK', in: T. WILLIAMSON, B. MILNE & S.P. SAVAGE (eds.), *International Developments in Investigative Interviewing*, Devon: Willan Publishing, 2009, p. 24-38.

SNOOK ET AL. 2010
SNOOK, B., EASTWOOD, J., STINSON, M., TEDESCHINI, J. & HOUSE, J.C., 'Reforming Investigative Interviewing in Canada', *Canadian Journal of Criminology and Criminal Justice*, 2010, p. 203-217.

SOUKARA ET AL. 2009
SOUKARA, S., BULL, R., VRIJ, A., TURNER, M. & CHERRYMAN, J., 'What Really Happens in Police Interviews of Suspects? Tactics and Confessions', *Psychology, Crime and Law*, 2009, p. 493-506.

ST-YVES 2006
ST-YVES, M., 'The Psychology of Rapport: Five Basic Rules', in: T. WILLIAMSON (ed.), *Investigative Interviewing. Rights, Research, Regulation*, Devon: Willan Publishing, 2006, p. 87-106.

ST-YVES 2009
ST-YVES, M., 'Police Interrogation in Canada: From the Quest for Confession to a Search for the Truth', in: T. WILLIAMSON, B. MILNE & S.P. SAVAGE (eds.), *International Developments in Investigative Interviewing*, Devon: Willan Publishing, 2009, p. 92-110.

VANDERHALLEN 2010
VANDERHALLEN, M., *De werkalliantie in het politieverhoor*, Leuven: KULeuven, 2010.

VANDERHALLEN, MATKOSKI & VERVAEKE 2010
VANDERHALLEN, M., MATKOSKI, S. & VERVAEKE, G., 'De wijze waarop de verhoormethode kan bijdragen tot het verzamelen van waarheidsgetrouwe informatie', in: A. VRIJ & L. SMETS (eds.), *Het analyseren van de geloofwaardigheid van verhoren: het gebruik van leugendetectiemethoden*, Brussel: Politeia, 2008, p. 17-33.

VANDERHALLEN, VERVAEKE & HOLMBERG 2011
VANDERHALLEN, M., VERVAEKE, G. & HOLMBERG, U., 'Witness and Suspect Perceptions of Working Alliance and Interviewing Style', *Journal of Investigative Psychology and Offender Profiling*, 2011, p. 110-130.

VRIJ 2010
VRIJ, A., 'Het verhoren van verdachten', in: P.J. VAN KOPPEN, H. MERCKELBACH, M. JELICIC & J.W. DE KEIJSER (eds.), *Reizen met mijn rechter. Psychologie van het recht*, Deventer: Kluwer, 2010, p. 723-753.

WALLACE & KASSIN 2011
WALLACE, D.B. & KASSIN, S.M., 'Harmless Error Analysis: How Do Judges Respond to Confession Errors?', *Law and Human Behavior*, 2011, p. 1-11.

WALSCH & BULL 2004
WALSCH, D. & BULL, R., 'What Really is Effective in Interviews with Suspects? A Study Comparing Interviewing Skills Against Interviewing Outcomes', *Legal and Criminological Psychology*, 2004, p. 305-321.

WALSCH & BULL 2010
WALSCH, D. & BULL, R., 'What Really is Effective in Interviewing with Suspects? A Study Comparing Interviewing Skills Against Interviewing Outcomes', *Legal and Criminological Psychology*, 2010, p. 305-321.

WALSCH & BULL 2011
WALSCH, D. & BULL, R., 'How Do Interviewers Attempt to Overcome Suspects' Denials', *Psychiatry, Psychology and Law*, 2011, p. 1-18.

WILLIAMSON 2006
WILLIAMSON, T., 'Towards Greater Professionalism: Minimizing Miscarriages of Justice', in: T. WILLIAMSON (ed.), *Investigative Interviewing. Rights, Research, Regulation,* Devon: Willan Publishing, 2006, p. 147-166.

WRIGHTSMAN 2010
WRIGHTSMAN, L.S., 'The Supreme Court on Miranda Rights and Interrogations: The Past, the Present and the Future', in: D.G. LASSITER & C.A. MEISSNER (eds.), *Police Interrogations and False Confessions. Current Research, Practice and Policy Recommendations,* Washington: American Psychological Association, 2010, p. 161-177.

ZULAWSKI & WICKLANDER 2002
ZULAWSKI, D.E. & WICKLANDER, D.E., *Practical Aspects of Interview and Interrogation,* Boca Raton: CRC Press, 2002.

MAASTRICHT SERIES IN HUMAN RIGHTS

The *Maastricht Centre for Human Rights* supervises research in the field of human rights conducted at Maastricht University's Faculty of Law. This research is interdisciplinary, with a particular focus on public international law, criminal law and social sciences. The titles in the Series contribute to a better understanding of different aspects of human rights *sensu lato*.

Published titles within the Series:

1. Ineke Boerefijn, Fons Coomans, Jenny Goldschmidt, Rikki Holtmaat and Ria Wolleswinkel (eds.), *Temporary Special Measures. Accelerating de facto Equality of Women under Article 4(1) UN Convention on the Elimination of All Forms of Discrimination against Women* (2003)
   ISBN 90-5095-359-X
2. Fons Coomans and Menno T. Kamminga (eds.), *Extraterritorial Application of Human Rights Treaties* (2004)
   ISBN 90-5095-394-8
3. Koen De Feyter and Felipe Gómez Isa (eds.), *Privatisation and Human Rights in the Age of Globalisation* (2005)
   ISBN 90-5095-422-7
4. Ingrid Westendorp and Ria Wolleswinkel (eds.), *Violence in the domestic sphere* (2005)
   ISBN 90-5095-526-6
5. Fons Coomans (ed.), *Justiciability of Economic and Social Rights* (2006)
   ISBN 978-90-5095-582-9
6. Jan C.M. Willems (ed.), *Developmental and Autonomy Rights of Children: Empowering Children, Caregivers and Communities*, 2nd revised edition (2007)
   ISBN 978-90-5095-726-7
7. Alette Smeulers and Roelof Haveman (eds.), *Supranational Criminology: Towards a Criminology of International Crimes* (2008)
   ISBN 978-90-5095-791-5
8. Hans van Crombrugge, Wouter Vandenholte and Jan C.M. Willems (eds.), *Shared Pedagogical Responsibility* (2008)
   ISBN 978-90-5095-864-6
9. Hildegard Schneider and Peter Van den Bossche (eds.), *Protection of Cultural Diversity from a European and International Perspective* (2008)
   ISBN 978-90-5095-864-6
10. Fons Coomans, Fred Grünfeld and Menno T. Kamminga (eds.), *Methods of Human Rights Research* (2009)
    ISBN 978-90-5095-879-0

11. Jan C.M. Willems (ed.), *Children's Rights and Human Development. A Multidisciplinary Reader* (2010)
ISBN 978-94-000-0032-2

12. Martine Boersma and Hans Nelen (eds.), *Corruption & Human Rights: Interdisciplinary Perspectives* (2010)
ISBN 978-94-000-0085-8

13. Hans Nelen and Jacques Claessen (eds.), *Beyond the Death Penalty* (2012)
ISBN 978-1-78068-060-6

14. Fons Coomans and Rolf Künneman (eds.), *Cases and Concepts on Extraterritorial Obligations in the Area of Economic, Social and Cultural Rights* (2012)
ISBN 978-94-000-0046-9